To
Dick and Judy
Keep serving!
All the best
Ken Blanchard
1/1/19

# Contributors
## (in alphabetical order)

**Cheryl Bachelder**—former CEO of Popeyes® Louisiana Kitchen, speaker, and author of the bestselling book *Dare to Serve*

**Tony Baron**—professor at Azusa Pacific University, speaker, and author of *The Art of Servant Leadership* and *The Cross and the Towel*

**Colleen Barrett**—president emeritus of Southwest Airlines and coauthor of *Lead with LUV*

**Art Barter**—CEO/president of Datron World Communications, founder/CEO of the Servant Leadership Institute, and author of *Farmer Able* and *The Servant Leadership Journal*

**Richard Blackaby**—president of Blackaby Ministries International, minister, speaker, and author or coauthor of numerous books, including *Experiencing God* and *The Seasons of God*

**James H. Blanchard**—former CEO of Synovus Financial, the first company to be inducted into *Fortune*'s Best Companies to Work For Hall of Fame

**Ken Blanchard**—chief spiritual officer of The Ken Blanchard Companies®, cofounder of the Lead Like Jesus ministry, and coauthor of *The New One Minute Manager*® and more than sixty other books

**Margie Blanchard**—speaker, leadership consultant, coauthor of *The One Minute Manager Balances Work and Life*, and cofounder/former president of The Ken Blanchard Companies

**Robin Blanchard**—Colonel (retired), Washington Army National Guard, speaker, facilitator/trainer, strategy consultant, and CEO of Blanchard Consulting

**Renee Broadwell**—senior editor on numerous book projects for Ken Blanchard and editor of communications and social media for The Ken Blanchard Companies

**Brené Brown**—researcher/storyteller, author of the bestsellers *Braving the Wilderness*, *Rising Strong*, and *Daring Greatly*, and widely recognized for her TED Talk on "The Power of Vulnerability"

**John Hope Bryant**—author of *The Memo*, *How the Poor Can Save Capitalism*, and *Love Leadership*, and founder/chairman/CEO of Operation HOPE, Inc., and Bryant Group Ventures

**Shirley Bullard**—chief administrative officer of The Ken Blanchard Companies and human resources expert

**Michael C. Bush**—CEO of Great Place to Work®, speaker, professor of entrepreneurship, and author of *A Great Place to Work for All*

**Tamika Catchings**—four-time All-American for University of Tennessee women's basketball, ten-time WNBA All-Star and 2011 MVP, four-time Olympic gold medalist, owner of Tea's Me Café, and author of *Catch a Star*

**Henry Cloud**—psychologist, leadership coach/consultant, and bestselling author of more than twenty books, including *Boundaries* and *The Power of the Other*

**Stephen M. R. Covey**—author of *The Speed of Trust* and *Smart Trust* and cofounder of CoveyLink and the FranklinCovey Global Speed of Trust Practice

**Holly Culhane**—CEO/founder of Presence Point, Inc., a nonprofit organization focused on helping people live into their calling as shepherd leaders, and leadership coach/consultant

**Jim Dittmar**—president/CEO of 3Rivers Leadership Institute, leadership consultant, trainer, and coauthor of *A Leadership Carol*

**James Ferrell**—managing partner of Arbinger Institute and author or coauthor of its bestselling books *Leadership and Self Deception*, *The Anatomy of Peace*, and *The Outward Mindset*

**Mark A. Floyd**—speaker, entrepreneur, venture partner at TDF Ventures, and chairman at Ciber, Inc.

**Jeffrey W. Foley**—Brigadier General, U.S. Army (retired), president of Loral Mountain Solutions, LLC, speaker, leadership coach, consultant, and coauthor of *Rules and Tools for Leaders*

**Marshall Goldsmith**—the world's leading executive coach and bestselling author of *Triggers*, *What Got You Here Won't Get You There*, and *Mojo*

**Jon Gordon**—husband, father, speaker, leadership consultant, and bestselling author of more than fifteen books, including *The Energy Bus*, *The Carpenter*, and *The Power of Positive Leadership*

**Craig Groeschel**—founder/senior pastor of Life.Church and bestselling author of numerous books, including *#Struggles* and *Divine Direction*

**Phyllis Hennecy Hendry**—CEO of the Lead Like Jesus ministry, speaker, and coauthor of *Lead Like Jesus Revisited*

**Chris Hodges**—founder/senior pastor of Church of the Highlands, founder/chancellor of Highlands College, and bestselling author of *Fresh Air*, *Four Cups*, and *The Daniel Dilemma*

**Phil Hodges**—former Xerox executive, cofounder of the Lead Like Jesus ministry, and coauthor of *Lead Like Jesus Revisited*, *Lead Like Jesus for Churches*, and *The Servant Leader*

**Laurie Beth Jones**—business and life coach, speaker, and author of multiple bestselling books, including *Jesus CEO* and *The Path*

**James M. Kouzes**—coauthor of the bestselling book *The Leadership Challenge* and more than a dozen other books on leadership, and dean's executive fellow of leadership, Leavey School of Business, Santa Clara University

**Patrick Lencioni**—bestselling author of numerous books, including *The Five Dysfunctions of a Team*, *The Advantage*, and *The Ideal Team Player*, and founder/CEO of The Table Group

**Rico Maranto**—guardian of the culture and servant leadership evangelist at Waste Connections, Inc.

**John C. Maxwell (foreword)**—author of many bestselling books including *The 21 Irrefutable Laws of Leadership* and founder of EQUIP Leadership, Inc.

**Erwin Raphael McManus**—founder and lead pastor at Mosaic, speaker, and bestselling author of several books, including *The Barbarian Way*, *The Artisan Soul*, and *The Last Arrow*

**Miles McPherson**—founder and senior pastor of Rock Church, speaker, and author of *Do Something!* and *God in the Mirror*

**Mark Miller**—vice president of high performance leadership at Chick-fil-A, Inc., bestselling coauthor of *The Secret: What Great Leaders Know and Do*, and author of *Leaders Made Here* and many other books

**Tom Mullins**—founding pastor of Christ Fellowship Church, speaker, and author of *Passing the Leadership Baton* and *The Leadership Game*

**Neal Nybo**—ordained pastor, faith-based leadership consultant, coach, and author of *Move Forward, Shut Tight*, and *Discovering Your Organization's Next Step*

**Barry Z. Posner**—endowed professor of leadership and former dean at Santa Clara University, scholar, renowned workshop facilitator, and coauthor of the award-winning book *The Leadership Challenge* and many others

**Dave Ramsey**—popular radio personality, money management expert, and bestselling author of books that include *The Total Money Makeover* and *EntreLeadership*

**Garry Ridge**—CEO/president of WD-40 Company, speaker, and coauthor of bestselling book *Helping People Win at Work*

**Mark Sanborn**—leadership consultant, speaker, and author of *The Fred Factor, You Don't Need a Title to Be a Leader*, and *The Potential Principle*

**Simon Sinek**—optimist and *New York Times* bestselling author of *Start with Why, Leaders Eat Last, Together Is Better*, and *Find Your Why*

**Raj Sisodia**—global thought leader of the Conscious Capitalism movement, speaker, and coauthor of *Conscious Capitalism: Liberating the Heroic Spirit of Business*

**Larry C. Spears**—president of Larry C. Spears Center for Servant Leadership, author, editor, and premiere student and interpreter of the writings of Robert K. Greenleaf

# SERVANT
# LEADERSHIP
# *in* ACTION

# SERVANT
# LEADERSHIP
# *in* ACTION

## How You Can Achieve Great
## Relationships
## and Results

Edited by Ken Blanchard
& Renee Broadwell

Berrett–Koehler Publishers, Inc.
*a BK Business book*

**Berrett-Koehler Publishers, Inc.**
1333 Broadway, Suite 1000
Oakland, CA 94612-1921
Tel: (510) 817-2277
Fax: (510) 817-2278
www.bkconnection.com

ORDERING INFORMATION
**Quantity sales.** Special discounts are available on quantity purchases by corporations, associations, and others. For details, contact the "Special Sales Department" at the Berrett-Koehler address above.
**Individual sales.** Berrett-Koehler publications are available through most bookstores. They can also be ordered directly from Berrett-Koehler: Tel: (800) 929-2929; Fax: (802) 864-7626; www.bkconnection.com.
**Orders for college textbook / course adoption use.** Please contact Berrett-Koehler: Tel: (800) 929-2929; Fax: (802) 864-7626.

Distributed to the U.S. trade and internationally by Penguin Random House Publisher Services.

Berrett-Koehler and the BK logo are registered trademarks of Berrett-Koehler Publishers, Inc.

Printed in the United States of America

Berrett-Koehler books are printed on long-lasting acid-free paper. When it is available, we choose paper that has been manufactured by environmentally responsible processes. These may include using trees grown in sustainable forests, incorporating recycled paper, minimizing chlorine in bleaching, or recycling the energy produced at the paper mill.

Unless otherwise noted, Scripture quotations are taken from the Holy Bible, New International Version®, NIV®. Copyright © 1973, 1978, 1984, 2011 by Biblica, Inc.®. The "NIV" and "New International Version" are trademarks registered in the United States Patent and Trademark Office by Biblica, Inc.®. Scripture quotations marked MSG are from *The Message*. Copyright © by Eugene H. Peterson 1993, 1994, 1995, 1996, 2000, 2001, 2002.
Scripture quotations marked NKJV are from the New King James Version®. Copyright © 1982 by Thomas Nelson.

Library of Congress Cataloging-in-Publication Data

Names: Blanchard, Kenneth H., editor. | Broadwell, Renee, editor.
Title: Servant leadership in action : how you can achieve great relationships and results / edited by
    Ken Blanchard and Renee Broadwell.
Description: Oakland, Ca : Berrett-Koehler Publishers, [2018]
Identifiers: LCCN 2017038848 | ISBN 9781523093960 (hardcover)
Subjects: LCSH: Servant leadership.
Classification: LCC HM1261 .S4725 2018 | DDC 658.4/092—dc23
LC record available at https://lccn.loc.gov/2017038848

First Edition
30 29 28 27 26 25 24 23 22 21 20 19 18     10 9 8 7 6 5

Set in Adobe Garamond Pro by Westchester Publishing Services.
Cover design by Irene Morris
Interior design by R. Scott Rattray

This book is dedicated to all those who choose
to serve rather than to be served.
Keep up the good work!

All author royalties for *Servant Leadership in Action* will be donated to the Foundation for Servant Leadership, a nonprofit organization dedicated to spreading the message of servant leadership throughout the world. The board of directors for the Foundation for Servant Leadership includes James H. Blanchard, Ken Blanchard, Henry Cloud, Mark A. Floyd, and Erwin Raphael McManus—all contributors to this book and important encouragers throughout its development.

# Contents

Part Four

# Exemplars of Servant Leadership

Part Five

# Putting Servant Leadership to Work

Part Six

## Servant Leadership Turnarounds

# Foreword by John C. Maxwell

WHEN KEN BLANCHARD asked me to write the foreword for this wonderful collection of essays about servant leadership, I was thrilled for several reasons. First of all, Ken and I are soul mates. We both have been studying, teaching, and writing about leadership for years. In the process, we have come to the conclusion that the only way to create great relationships and results is through servant leadership. It's all about putting other people first.

I get a kick when I hear people say "It's lonely at the top." To me, if it's lonely at the top, it means nobody is following you. If that's true, you'd better get off the top and go where the people are—and then, in my terms, bring them to the top with you.

Ken and I have laughed about how immature people are who think about themselves first. It's a selfish way to lead. That's okay when you are a small child; however, it's not okay when you're 35, 45, or 55, and you haven't yet figured out that it's not about you. We keep on reiterating that when you become a leader, you give up your right to think of yourself first. Servant leadership is about always putting others first.

This is a long-winded way of saying I love this book.

Besides my admiration for Ken, another reason I'm excited has to do with the quality of contributors he has gathered here. I can't think of many people I admire in our field whom Ken hasn't talked into participating. While they all have different perspectives, the result is some common themes that truly highlight the tenets of servant leadership in action—not just the principles of what servant leadership is. I must admit that a number of the essays grabbed at my heart and didn't let go. I know you'll also find several that particularly resonate with you.

I think you'll appreciate the way the book is organized into six parts, starting with the fundamentals and elements of servant leadership and ending with first-person accounts of putting servant leadership to work and how it has dramatically changed organizations for the better. You'll also love Ken's personal introductions for each of the authors.

I'm so glad you have picked up this book. Read it, study it, read it again, and apply the wonderful lessons about the power of lifting others up—and, in the process, helping everyone win.

John C. Maxwell
Bestselling author and leadership expert
www.johnmaxwell.com

# SERVANT
# LEADERSHIP
# *in* ACTION

# Introduction
## *Serve First and Lead Second*

### KEN BLANCHARD AND
### RENEE BROADWELL

THE WORLD IS in desperate need of a different leadership role model. We all have seen the negative impact of self-serving leaders in every sector of our society. Why is that? Because these leaders have been conditioned to think of leadership only in terms of power and control. We think there is a better choice: to lead at a higher level. When people lead at a higher level, they make the world a better place because in addition to results and relationships, their goals are focused on the greater good. This requires a special kind of leader: a *servant leader.*

Our desire to develop servant leaders who are world changers has driven us to produce this book—a carefully curated collection of essays. Here to share their passion about servant leadership are some of Ken's very favorite people who are not only outstanding practitioners of servant leadership but also writers in the field. In addition to this introduction, throughout the book Ken will give short personal introductions to each of his colleagues' essays.

Robert K. Greenleaf coined the term *servant leadership* in his essay titled "The Servant as Leader."[1] He published widely on the concept for the next twenty years.[2] And yet it is an old concept. Two thousand years ago, servant leadership was central to the philosophy of Jesus, who exemplified the fully committed and effective servant leader. Mahatma Gandhi, Dr. Martin Luther King Jr., and Nelson Mandela are well-known modern examples of leaders who have exemplified this philosophy.

The book is organized into six parts. Part One, "Fundamentals of Servant Leadership," includes essays that describe basic aspects of servant leadership. Part Two, "Elements of Servant Leadership," highlights some of the different points of view of servant leaders. Part Three, "Lessons in Servant Leadership," focuses on what people have learned on a personal level from observing servant leadership in action. Part Four, "Exemplars of Servant Leadership," features people who have been identified as classic servant leaders. Part Five, "Putting Servant Leadership to Work," offers firsthand accounts of people who have made servant leadership come alive in their organizations. Part Six, "Servant Leadership Turnarounds," illustrates how servant leadership can dramatically impact both results and human satisfaction in organizations.

An important note: In the opening essay of Part Four, "Exemplars of Servant Leadership," Ken and Phil Hodges identify Jesus as the greatest servant leadership role model of all time, an identification they first wrote about in their book *Lead Like Jesus*.[3] A number of Ken's colleagues in their essays also refer to Jesus's servant leadership example and to the Bible as an important leadership reference book. Why? Because it's hard to deny Jesus's influence, as a servant leader, on the world. Rest assured that our intention is not to try to convert anyone. In fact, a major goal of this book is to prove that servant leadership has application in both secular *and* spiritual leadership in every kind of organization, including businesses, government agencies, educational institutions, and places of worship.

Although we organize this book around six parts describing various aspects of servant leadership, we don't want you to get discouraged or overwhelmed. Rather, we encourage you, as you read this book, to find four or five essays that really speak to your heart and motivate you to say "As a leader I want to serve rather than be served."

The audience for this book is wide. It's for anyone in a leadership position—from a frontline supervisor to the CEO of a company. In fact, every person who serves as a leader in a secular or nonsecular capacity could benefit from reading and practicing the leadership concepts from the essays in this book.

Our dream is that someday, everywhere, everyone will be impacted by someone who is a servant leader. Self-serving leaders will be a thing of the past. Leaders throughout the world will be people who, in Robert K. Greenleaf's terms, "serve first and lead second." We have created this book to help make that dream a reality. It's our hope and desire that reading *Servant Leadership in Action* will either confirm what you already are doing or be the beginning of a new and exciting chapter in your personal leadership journey.

We want this to be the book you refer to when you are interested in how to actually practice servant leadership in your life and work—how to get beyond the theory and philosophy to daily action. We believe you, too, can be a servant leader who makes a positive difference in the world.

Join us in our quest. We are counting on you.

> Ken Blanchard, coauthor of *The New One Minute Manager*, *Leading at a Higher Level*, and *Lead Like Jesus Revisited* and cofounder of The Ken Blanchard Companies and Lead Like Jesus
>
> Renee Broadwell, senior editor, The Ken Blanchard Companies

## Notes

1. Robert K. Greenleaf, "The Servant as Leader" (Atlanta: The Greenleaf Center for Servant Leadership, 1970).
2. A collection of Greenleaf's most mature writings on the subject can be found in *The Power of Servant Leadership* (San Francisco: Berrett-Koehler, 1998). The Greenleaf Center for Servant Leadership (www.greenleaf.org) is a resource for all of Greenleaf's work.
3. Ken Blanchard and Phil Hodges, *Lead Like Jesus: Lessons from the Greatest Leadership Role Model of All Time* (Nashville: Thomas Nelson, 2005).

## Part One

# Fundamentals of Servant Leadership

### Descriptions of Basic Aspects of Servant Leadership

- Ken Blanchard covers his leadership philosophy in "What Is Servant Leadership?" by emphasizing the two parts of servant leadership: the *leadership/strategic* aspect and the *servant/operational* aspect.

- Larry C. Spears, inspired by his mentor and pioneer in the field of servant leadership Robert K. Greenleaf, discusses "Characteristics of Servant Leaders."

- Raj Sisodia, cofounder of the Conscious Capitalism movement, shows in "Servant Leadership Is Conscious Leadership" how the qualities of *servant* leaders overlap considerably with those of *conscious* leaders.

- Stephen M. R. Covey, in "Servant Leadership at the Speed of Trust," reflects on how trust is inextricably linked to the practice of servant leadership.

- Mark Miller, in "Great Leaders SERVE," relates how the SERVE acronym developed at Chick-fil-A can help you become a servant leader.

- Mark A. Floyd offers advice to new servant leaders in his essay "Servant Leadership: What Does It Really Mean?"

- Michael C. Bush, CEO of Great Places to Work For All, shows that the most extraordinary organizations are led by servant leaders in "Servant Leaders Create a Great Place to Work for All."

- Holly Culhane, in "The Leader as Shepherd," presents a compelling argument that the shepherd is one of the best examples of a servant leader.

- Simon Sinek, in "The Evolution of Servant Leadership," shares his thoughts about the roots of servant leadership—and why it matters.

# Chapter 1

# What Is Servant Leadership?

## KEN BLANCHARD

*Okay, let's get started. As Julie Andrews sang in* The Sound of
Music, *"Let's start at the very beginning. . . ." What is servant
leadership all about? In this essay, I'll give you my thoughts. —KB*

WHEN PEOPLE HEAR the phrase *servant leadership*, they are often confused.
Their assumption is that it means managers should be working for their people,
who would decide what to do, when to do it, where to do it, and how to do
it. If that's what servant leadership is all about, it doesn't sound like leadership to them at all. It sounds more like the inmates running the prison, or
trying to please everyone.

The problem is that these folks don't understand leadership—much less
servant leadership.[1] They think you can't lead and serve at the same time. Yet
you can, if you understand that there are two parts to servant leadership:

- a visionary/direction, or strategic, role—the *leadership* aspect of servant
  leadership; and
- an implementation, or operational, role—the *servant* aspect of servant
  leadership.

Some people say that leadership is really the visionary/direction role—
doing the right thing—and management is the implementation role—doing
things right. Rather than getting caught in the leadership vs. management
debate, let's think of these *both* as leadership roles.

In this book, we focus on leadership as an influence process in which you
try to help people accomplish goals. All good leadership starts with a visionary role, as Jesse Stoner and I explain in our book *Full Steam Ahead!*[2] This
involves not only goal setting, but also establishing a compelling vision that

tells you who you are (your purpose), where you're going (your picture of the future), and what will guide your journey (your values). In other words, leadership starts with a sense of direction.

I love the saying "a river without banks is a large puddle."[3] The banks permit the river to flow; they give direction to the river. Leadership is about going somewhere; it's not about wandering around aimlessly. If people don't have a compelling vision to serve, the only thing they have to serve is their own self-interest.

Walt Disney started his theme parks with a clear purpose. He said, "We're in the happiness business." That is very different from being in the theme park business. Being in the happiness business helps cast members (employees) understand their primary role in the company.

When it comes to a purpose statement, too many organizations, if they have one, make it too complicated. I'll never forget talking to all of the key managers of a major bank. Prior to my speech, I asked them to send me their purpose statement if they had one, which they did. When I got up in front of the group, I told them how much I appreciated their sending me their purpose statement. "Ever since I got it, I've slept so much better. Why? Because I put it next to my bed and if I couldn't sleep at night I would read it." The purpose statement droned on and on. I said, "If I were working with you, I would hope you would say 'We are in the financial peace of mind business—if people give us money, we will protect it and even grow it.'" Everyone laughed because they knew that would be something that all their people could easily share and follow.

Once you have a clear purpose that tells you who you are, you need to develop a picture of the future so that everyone knows where you are going. Walt Disney's picture of the future was expressed in the charge he gave every cast member: "Keep the same smile on people's faces when they leave the park as when they entered." Disney didn't care whether a guest was in the park two hours or ten hours. He just wanted to keep them smiling. After all, they were in the happiness business. Your picture of the future should focus on the end results.

The final aspect of a compelling vision involves your values, which are there to guide your journey. Values provide guidelines for how you should proceed as you pursue your purpose and picture of the future. They answer the questions "What do I want to live by?" and "How?" They need to be clearly described so that you know exactly what behaviors demonstrate those values as being lived.

The Disney theme parks have four rank-ordered values: safety, courtesy, the show, and efficiency. Why is safety the highest ranked value? Walt Disney knew that if a guest were to be carried out of one of his parks on a stretcher, that person would not have the same smile on their face leaving the park that they had when they entered.

The second-ranked value, courtesy, is all about the friendly attitude you expect at a Disney theme park. Why is it important to know that it's the number-two value? Suppose one of the Disney cast members is answering a guest question in a friendly, courteous manner, and he hears a scream that's not coming from a roller coaster. If that cast member wants to act according to the park's rank-ordered values, he will excuse himself as quickly and politely as possible and race toward the scream. Why? Because the number-one value just called. If the values were not rank-ordered and the cast member was enjoying the interaction with the guest, he might say, "They're always yelling at the park," and not move in the direction of the scream. Later, somebody could come to that cast member and say, "You were the closest to the scream. Why didn't you move?" The response could be, "I was dealing with our courtesy value."

Life is a series of value conflicts. There will be times when you can't act on two values at the same time. I have a hunch that's why Walt Disney put efficiency—running a profitable business—as the fourth-ranked value. He wanted to make clear they would do nothing to save money that would put people in danger, nor do a major downsizing in the park that impacted in a negative way their courtesy value.

Once an organization has a compelling vision, they can set goals and define strategic initiatives that suggest what people should be focusing on right now. With a compelling vision, these goals and strategic initiatives take on more meaning and therefore are not seen as a threat, but as part of the bigger picture.

The traditional hierarchical pyramid (see Figure 1.1) is effective for the *leadership* aspect of servant leadership. Kids look to their parents, players look to their coaches, and people look to their organizational leaders for vision and direction. While these leaders should involve experienced people in shaping direction, the ultimate responsibility remains with the leaders themselves and cannot be delegated to others.

Once people are clear on where they are going, the leader's role shifts to a service mindset for the task of implementation—the second aspect of servant leadership. The question now is: How do we live according to the vision

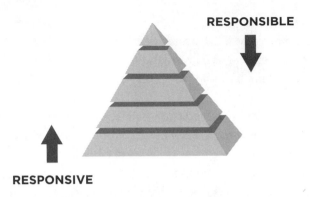

**Figure 1.1** Visionary/leadership role

and accomplish the established goals? Implementation is where the *servant* aspect of servant leadership comes into play.

Most organizations and leaders get into trouble in the implementation phase of the leadership process. With self-serving leaders at the helm, the traditional hierarchical pyramid is kept alive and well. When that happens, who do people think they work for? The people above them. The minute you think you work for the person above you for implementation, you are assuming that person—your boss—is *responsible* and your job is being *responsive* to that boss and to his or her whims or wishes. Now "boss watching" becomes a popular sport and people get promoted on their upward-influencing skills. As a result, all the energy of the organization is moving up the hierarchy, away from customers and the frontline folks who are closest to the action. What you get is a duck pond. When there is a conflict between what the customers want and what the boss wants, the boss wins. You have people quacking like ducks: "It's our policy." "I just work here." "Would you like me to get my supervisor?" Servant leaders know how to correct this situation by philosophically turning the traditional hierarchical pyramid upside down when it comes to implementation (see Figure 1.2).

When that happens, who is at the top of the organization? The customer contact people. Who is *really* at the top of the organization? The customers. Who is at the bottom now? The "top" management. As a result, who works for whom when it comes to implementation? You, the leader, work for your people. This one change, although it seems minor, makes a major difference. The difference is between who is *responsible* and who is *responsive*.

When you turn the organizational pyramid upside down, rather than your people being responsive to you, they become responsible—able to

**RESPONSIBLE**

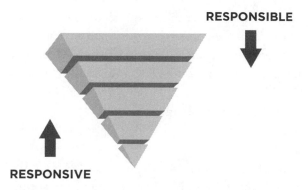

**RESPONSIVE**

**Figure 1.2**   Implementation/servant role

respond—and your job as the leader/manager is to be responsive to your people. This creates a very different environment for implementation. If you work for your people as servant leaders do, what is the purpose of being a manager? To help your people become eagles rather than ducks and soar above the crowd—accomplishing goals, solving problems, and living according to the vision.[4]

As a customer, you can always tell an organization that is run by a self-serving leader. Why? Because if you have a problem and go to a frontline customer contact person to solve it, you are talking to a duck. They say, "It's our policy," quack quack; "I didn't make the rules," quack quack; "Do you want to talk to my supervisor?" quack quack.

Several years ago, a friend of mine had an experience in a department store that illustrates this point well. While shopping, he realized he needed to talk to his wife but he had left his cell phone at home. He asked a salesperson in the men's department if he could use the telephone.

"No," the salesperson said.

My friend replied, "You have to be kidding me. I can always use the phone at Nordstrom."

The salesperson said, "Look, buddy, they don't let *me* use the phone here. Why should I let *you*?"

That certainly isn't what servant leadership is all about. Who do you think that salesperson worked for—a duck or an eagle? Obviously, a supervisory duck. Who does that duck work for? Another duck, who works for another duck. And who sits at the top of the organization? The head mallard—a great big duck. If the salesperson had worked for an eagle, both he and the customer would have been able to use the phone!

Now contrast that with the eagle experience one of my colleagues had when he went to Nordstrom one day to get some perfume for his wife. The woman behind the counter said, "I'm sorry; we don't sell that perfume in our store. But I know where I can get it in the mall. How long will you be in our store?"

"About 30 minutes," my colleague said.

"Fine. I'll go get it, bring it back, gift wrap it, and have it ready for you when you leave."

This woman left Nordstrom, went to another store, got the perfume my colleague wanted, came back to Nordstrom, and gift wrapped it. You know what she charged him? The same price she had paid at the other store. So Nordstrom didn't make any money on the deal, but what did they make? A raving fan customer.

To me, servant leadership is the only way to guarantee great relationships and results. That became even clearer to me when I realized that the two leadership approaches I am best known for around the world—The One Minute Manager® and Situational Leadership® II (SLII®)—are both examples of servant leadership in action.

After all, what's the First Secret of The One Minute Manager? One Minute Goals. All good performance starts with clear goals—which is clearly part of the *leadership* aspect of servant leadership. Once people are clear on goals, an effective One Minute Manager wanders around and tries to catch people doing something right so that they can deliver a One Minute Praising—the Second Secret. If the person is doing something wrong or not performing as well as agreed upon, a One Minute Re-Direct is appropriate—the Third Secret. When effective One Minute Managers deliver praisings and re-directs, they are engaging in the *servant* aspect of servant leadership—they are working for their people to help them win—accomplish their goals.[5]

Situational Leadership® II[6] also has three aspects that generate both great relationships and results: goal setting, diagnosis, and matching. Once clear goals are set, an effective SLII leader works with their direct report to diagnose the direct report's development level—competence and commitment—on each specific goal. Together they then determine the appropriate leadership style—the amount of directive and supportive behavior—that will match the person's development level on each goal so that the manager can help them accomplish their goals. The key here, in the *servant* aspect of servant leadership, is for managers to remember they must use different strokes for different folks and also different strokes for the same folks, depending on the goal and the person's development level.

Why are the concepts of The One Minute Manager and SLII so widely used around the world? I think it's because they are clear examples of servant leadership in action. Both concepts recognize that vision and direction—the *leadership* aspect of servant leadership—is the responsibility of the traditional hierarchy. The *servant* aspect of servant leadership is all about turning the hierarchy upside down and helping everyone throughout the organization develop great relationships, get great results, and, eventually, delight their customers. That's what servant leadership is all about.

## Notes

1. Ken Blanchard et al., *Leading at a Higher Level* (Upper Saddle River, NJ: FT Press, 2006, 2010). See chapter 14 for a more extensive discussion of what servant leadership is all about.
2. See Ken Blanchard and Jesse Stoner, *Full Steam Ahead: Unleash the Power of Vision in Your Company and Your Life* (San Francisco: Berrett-Koehler, 2003, 2011) for more about the visionary role of leadership.
3. This expression was coined by Alan Randolph. See Ken Blanchard, John Carlos, and Alan Randolph, *Empowerment Takes More Than a Minute* (San Francisco: Berrett-Koehler, 1996).
4. Ken first heard this distinction between ducks and eagles from author and legendary personal growth guru Wayne Dyer.
5. Ken Blanchard and Spencer Johnson, *The One Minute Manager* (New York: William Morrow, 1982, 2003). See also their *The New One Minute Manager* (New York: William Morrow, 2015).
6. Ken Blanchard first developed Situational Leadership® with Paul Hersey in the late 1960s. It was in the early 1980s that Ken and founding associates of The Ken Blanchard Companies—Margie Blanchard, Don Carew, Eunice Parisi-Carew, Fred Finch, Laurie Hawkins, Drea Zigarmi, and Patricia Zigarmi—created Situational Leadership® II. The best description of this thinking can be found in Ken Blanchard, Patricia Zigarmi, and Drea Zigarmi, *Leadership and the One Minute Manager* (New York: William Morrow, 1985, 2013).

# Chapter 2

# Characteristics of Servant Leaders

## LARRY C. SPEARS

*In the late 1960s, I had the privilege of spending the weekend with Robert K. Greenleaf shortly after he retired from AT&T and began writing about servant leadership. I was on the faculty of Ohio University in Athens, Ohio, at the time. Several years later I got to know Larry Spears, who, during his time as director of the Robert K. Greenleaf Center for Servant Leadership, became the premier student of Greenleaf's writings. When you read Larry's essay about the ten characteristics of a servant leader, you will see why his participation in this book was a must. —KB*

THE WORDS *SERVANT* and *leader* are usually thought of as being opposites. In deliberately bringing those words together in a meaningful way in 1970, Robert K. Greenleaf, a retired AT&T executive, gave birth to the paradoxical term *servant leadership*. In doing so, he launched a quiet revolution in the way in which we view and practice leadership. In the decades since then, many of today's most effective managers and top thought leaders are writing and speaking about servant leadership, as exemplified in this book.

What is servant leadership? Let's take a look at Greenleaf's big picture definition:

> The servant leader is servant first. It begins with the natural feeling that one wants to serve. Then conscious choice brings one to aspire to lead. The best test is: do those served grow as persons: do they, while being served, become healthier, wiser, freer, more autonomous, more likely themselves to become servants? And, what is the effect

on the least privileged in society; will they benefit, or, at least, not be further deprived?[1]

## Ten Characteristics of a Servant Leader

Back in 1992, I extracted from Robert K. Greenleaf's writings a set of ten characteristics of the servant leader, which I view as being of critical importance and central to the development of servant leaders. In the decades since that time, part of my own work in servant leadership has focused on encouraging a deepening understanding of the following characteristics and how they contribute to the meaningful practices of servant leaders. These ten characteristics are:

1. *Listening.* Leaders traditionally have been valued for their communication and decision-making skills. Although these are also important skills for the servant leader, they need to be reinforced by a deep commitment to listening intently to others. The servant leader seeks to identify the will of a group and helps to clarify that will. He or she listens receptively to what is being said and not said. Listening also encompasses hearing one's own inner voice. Listening, coupled with periods of reflection, is essential to the growth and well-being of the servant leader.

2. *Empathy.* The servant leader strives to understand and empathize with others. People deserve to be accepted and recognized for their special and unique spirits. One assumes the good intentions of coworkers and colleagues and does not reject them as people, even when one may be forced to refuse to accept certain behaviors or performance. The most successful servant leaders are those who have become skilled empathetic listeners.

3. *Healing.* The healing of relationships is a powerful force for transformation and integration. One of the great strengths of servant leadership is the potential for healing one's self and one's relationship to others. Many people have broken spirits and have suffered from a variety of emotional hurts. Although this is a part of being human, servant leaders recognize that they have an opportunity *to help make whole* those with whom they come in contact. In his essay "The Servant as Leader," Greenleaf writes, "There is something subtle communicated to one who is being served and led if, implicit

in the compact between servant leader and led, is the understanding that the search for wholeness is something they share."[2]

4. *Awareness.* General awareness, and especially self-awareness, strengthens the servant leader. Awareness helps one in understanding issues involving ethics, power, and values. It lends itself to being able to view most situations from a more integrated, holistic position. As Greenleaf observes, "Awareness is not a giver of solace—it is just the opposite. It is a disturber and an awakener. Able leaders are usually sharply awake and reasonably disturbed. They are not seekers after solace. They have their own inner serenity."[3]

5. *Persuasion.* Another characteristic of servant leaders is reliance on persuasion, rather than on one's positional authority, in making decisions within an organization. The servant leader seeks to convince others, rather than coerce compliance. This particular element offers one of the clearest distinctions between the traditional authoritarian model and that of servant leadership. The servant leader is effective at building consensus within groups. This emphasis on persuasion over coercion finds its roots in the beliefs of the Religious Society of Friends (Quakers)—the denominational body to which Robert K. Greenleaf belonged.

6. *Conceptualization.* Servant leaders seek to nurture their abilities to *dream great dreams.* The ability to look at a problem or an organization from a conceptualizing perspective means that one must think beyond day-to-day realities. For many leaders, this is a characteristic that requires discipline and practice. The traditional leader is consumed by the need to achieve short-term operational goals. The leader who wishes also to be a servant leader must stretch his or her thinking to encompass broader-based conceptual thinking. Within organizations, conceptualization is, by its very nature, a key role of boards of trustees or directors. Unfortunately, boards can sometimes become involved in the day-to-day operations—something that should always be discouraged—and thus fail to provide the visionary concept for an institution. Trustees need to be mostly conceptual in their orientation; staffs need to be mostly operational in their perspective; and the most effective executive leaders probably need to develop both perspectives within themselves. Servant leaders are called to seek a delicate balance between conceptual thinking and a day-to-day operational approach.

7. *Foresight.* Closely related to conceptualization, the ability to foresee the likely outcome of a situation is hard to define but easier to identify. One knows foresight when one experiences it. Foresight is a characteristic that enables the servant leader to understand the lessons from the past, the realities of the present, and the likely consequence of a decision for the future. It is also deeply rooted within the intuitive mind. Foresight remains a largely unexplored area in leadership studies, but it is one most deserving of careful attention.

8. *Stewardship.* Peter Block, author of *Stewardship* and *The Empowered Manager,*[4] defines stewardship as "holding something in trust for another." Robert K. Greenleaf's view of all institutions was one in which CEOs, staffs, and trustees all played significant roles in holding their institutions in trust for the greater good of society. Servant leadership, like stewardship, assumes a commitment to serving the needs of others. It also emphasizes the use of openness and persuasion rather than control.

9. *Commitment to the growth of people.* Servant leaders believe that people have an intrinsic value beyond their tangible contributions as workers. As such, the servant leader is deeply committed to the growth of each individual within his or her organization. The servant leader recognizes the tremendous responsibility to do everything in his or her power to nurture the personal and professional growth of employees and colleagues. In practice, this can include concrete actions such as making funds available for personal and professional development, taking a personal interest in the ideas and suggestions from everyone, encouraging worker involvement in decision making, and actively assisting laid-off employees to find other positions.

10. *Building community.* The servant leader senses that much has been lost in recent human history as a result of the shift from local communities to large institutions as the primary shaper of human lives. This awareness causes the servant leader to seek to identify some means for building community among those who work within a given institution. Servant leadership suggests that true community can be created among those who work in businesses and other institutions. Greenleaf said, "All that is needed to rebuild community as a viable life form for large numbers of people is for enough servant leaders to show the way, not by mass movements, but by each servant leader demonstrating his or her unlimited liability for a quite specific community-related group."[5]

These ten characteristics of servant leadership are by no means exhaustive. However, they do serve to communicate the power and promise that this concept offers to those who are open to its invitation and challenge.

We are experiencing a rapid shift in many businesses and not-for-profit organizations—away from the more traditional autocratic and hierarchical models of leadership and toward servant leadership as a way of being in relationship with others. Interest in the meaning and practice of servant leadership continues to grow. Many books, articles, and papers on the subject have now been published. Workshops, courses, and degrees in servant leadership are now available. Many of the companies named to *Fortune* magazine's annual listing of "The 100 Best Companies to Work For" espouse servant leadership and have integrated it into their corporate cultures. My own work in servant leadership over the past quarter century has brought me into direct or indirect contact with millions of people who embrace servant leadership, and who are now working to create servant-led organizations of all kinds.

Servant leadership characteristics often occur naturally within many individuals and, like many natural tendencies, they can be enhanced through learning and practice. Servant leadership offers great hope for the future in creating better, more caring, institutions.

*Larry C. Spears, a noted author and speaker on servant leadership, is president and CEO of the Spears Center for Servant Leadership (www.spearscenter.org) and also serves as servant leadership scholar at Gonzaga University. From 1990 to 2007, Larry was president and CEO of the Robert K. Greenleaf Center for Servant Leadership. He is the editor and contributing author of more than a dozen books on servant leadership including* Insights on Leadership, *as well as editor of five books of Greenleaf's writings.*

## Notes

1. Robert K. Greenleaf, *Servant Leadership: A Journey into the Nature of Legitimate Power and Greatness* (Mahwah, NJ: Paulist Press, 1977).
2. Robert K. Greenleaf, "The Servant as Leader" (Atlanta: The Greenleaf Center for Servant Leadership, 1970).
3. Ibid.
4. Peter Block, *The Empowered Manager: Positive Political Skills at Work* (San Francisco: Jossey-Bass, 1987), and *Stewardship: Choosing Service over Self Interest* (San Francisco: Jossey-Bass, 1993).
5. Greenleaf, "The Servant as Leader."

# Chapter 3

# Servant Leadership Is Conscious Leadership

## Raj Sisodia

*When I shared the platform a few years ago with Raj Sisodia, I was amazed how complementary his thinking about Conscious Capitalism was with my beliefs about servant leadership—in essence, that profit is the applause you get for creating a motivating environment for your people so that they will take care of your customers. Read this essay and see how well Conscious Capitalism fits in with the beliefs on servant leadership that Larry Spears and I have shared. —KB*

THE INSTITUTION OF business, as practiced in a system of free market capitalism, has been the prime driver in elevating human prosperity and flourishing to unprecedented heights for more than two hundred years. These huge gains in material prosperity have come at a cost, however. People are experiencing extremely high levels of stress, depression, and chronic diseases.

How is this state of affairs acceptable? We are more intelligent, more educated, better informed, more connected, more caring, less violent, and more conscious than ever before. Yet our work continues to be a source of deep suffering for most of us. In large measure, we can place the blame on poor leadership.

Leaders are products of the systems that give rise to them. The existing system has elevated people into positions of leadership who lack the qualities needed to lead in today's world. These people do whatever it takes to deliver the numbers without regard to human cost or long-term consequences for organizational health.

The consciousness with which a business operates is a direct function of the consciousness of its leader. A leader whose consciousness is rooted in fear, scarcity, and survival will create an organization that is all about those qualities.

But there is a new way of doing business that is radically different. Actually, it is not new at all—companies have been operating this way for over a century. These *conscious capitalist* organizations have four defining characteristics:

1. They operate with a purpose other than profit maximization as their reason for being.
2. They seek to create value for all their stakeholders, not just shareholders.
3. Their leaders are motivated by service to the company's purpose and its people, not by power or personal enrichment.
4. They strive to build cultures infused with trust, openness, and caring instead of fear and stress.

In the long run, our research shows that such companies generate far more financial wealth than do traditional profit-centered firms—outperforming the S&P 500 index by 14 to 1 and the companies featured in Jim Collins's *Good to Great* by 6 to 1 over a 15-year period.[1] Conscious businesses know that it is possible to do business with a spectrum of positive effects. And if it is possible, why would we choose not to?

You cannot have a conscious business without a conscious leader, and you cannot be a conscious leader without being a conscious human being. The qualities of *servant leaders* overlap considerably with those of *conscious leaders*. For the purposes of this essay, please consider the two terms interchangeable as we explore the characteristics of servant leaders/conscious leaders and how they can be cultivated.

## Conscious Leaders are SELFLESS

*Only three things happen naturally in organizations: friction, confusion, and underperformance. Everything else takes leadership.* —Peter Drucker

The essential elements of what it means to be a conscious leader can be captured in this single word, which also serves as an acronym: SELFLESS—

defined as placing the interests of others before your own. True leaders transcend the self. A leader who operates with a primary emphasis on self-interest naturally views other people as a means to that end. You cannot be a true leader if you operate at that level of consciousness.

Selfless does not mean eradicating the ego; that is nearly impossible. It is about harnessing the ego in healthy ways. As the Dalai Lama has said, "We cannot and need not eradicate our ego; rather, we must make sure it is a *serving* ego and not a *deserving* ego."

As an acronym, SELFLESS refers to the qualities of conscious leaders: Strength, Enthusiasm, Love, Flexibility, Long-Term Orientation, Emotional Intelligence, Systems Intelligence, and Spiritual Intelligence. The servant leader is a whole person, not a fragmented being. SELFLESS reflects a harmonious blend of mature masculine and mature feminine qualities. Too many leaders today manifest only immature hypermasculine qualities such as domination, aggression, hypercompetitiveness, winning at all costs, etc. They view every leadership challenge through the lens of war—a mindset that is at best win-lose, and usually lose-lose. Let's take a closer look at what each letter of the SELFLESS acronym stands for.

### Strength

We start with strength because conscious leaders are strong, resolute, and resilient. They have to have moral fiber, self-confidence, and the courage of their convictions. They are unshakable in standing up to doubters or obstructionists with self-serving agendas. They are confident without being arrogant. The key is that their strength is deployed in the service of noble ends: the flourishing of all the lives they lead and touch. This strength is sourced from within as well as from outside.

Conscious leaders draw on the strength of their teams without depleting the power of those teams. They tap into the moral power of the universe—which is available to anyone engaged in genuinely "right" action. Dr. Martin Luther King Jr. famously said, "The arc of the moral universe is long, but it bends toward justice." Leaders who try to bend that arc in other directions will find their efforts ultimately stymied, while those who engage in right actions and pursue noble goals can access unlimited righteous power. It is power *with*, not power *over*, those they seek to lead. For leaders to be powerful, followers don't have to be rendered powerless. Collectively, they have access to all the power they need by being connected to the source of infinite power.

### Enthusiasm

Conscious leaders are connected to an infinite source of power because of their commitment to a higher purpose and a righteous path. This power gives them great energy and enthusiasm. This doesn't mean that they have to be gregarious extroverts. Introverts make exceptional leaders, as many studies have found. But when you're aligned with your purpose, you can't help but be enthusiastic. That is hard to fake if you don't have it.

### Love

A fundamental leadership quality is the ability to operate from love and care. Throughout human history, the great leaders who transformed society for the better—Emperor Ashoka, Lincoln, Gandhi, Mandela, and King—all possessed tremendous strength along with a powerful capacity for caring. They were able to expand their circle of caring to encompass more and more of humanity—often including their own so-called enemies. They truly, deeply cared about human beings and had a clear sense of right and wrong. Truly great leaders are those who take the world to a better place. They manifest love that is rooted in a foundation of caring. When a leader comes from a place of genuine caring and possesses great strength, they become a peaceful warrior, able to battle steep odds for a just and righteous cause.

The opposite of love is fear. An organization suffused with fear is inherently incapable of genuine creativity and innovation. Its people are condemned to daily lives of intense stress, unhappiness, ill health, and dysfunctional families. Conscious leaders seek to drive fear out of their organizations. As Simon Sinek, author of *Start with Why* and *Leaders Eat Last*,[2] says, they create a "circle of safety" within which everyone in the organizational family can grow and thrive.

### Flexibility

Flexibility is the capacity to switch modes seamlessly and to bend without breaking as the situation or the context requires. Conscious leaders are like golfers with a full set of clubs; they know how to select and implement the right approach for each situation. These leaders are able to bend but not break, adapting to circumstances in a principled way without sacrificing their core values.

A phrase that captures the idea of flexibility states that conscious leaders are "wise fools of tough love." They simultaneously embody wisdom and playfulness, strength and tenderness. They cultivate a sensitive sonar that enables them to gauge the approach needed in each leadership moment.

### Long-Term Orientation

Conscious leaders operate on a time horizon that goes beyond not only their tenure as leaders but also their own lifetimes. The Founding Fathers of the United States led with an eye toward eternity, seeking to put in place ideas and principles that would endure for centuries if not millennia. Organizations have the potential to be immortal. Whether they endure depends on the actions of their leaders.

The success of a leader is best gauged by what happens after they are gone. Does the organization continue to operate with high principles and moral clarity? Jim Collins and Jerry Porras, in their book *Built to Last*,[3] wrote about leaders who are "clock builders" vs. those who are "time tellers." Clock builders create organizations that will endure when they are gone, because no one is reliant on them to tell the time. Conscious leaders ensure that the essential elements of what makes the business special become part of the DNA of the organization. They often accomplish this by creating documents akin to the U.S. Declaration of Independence—who we are and what we stand for; and the Constitution—how we do things.

### Emotional Intelligence

For leaders, a high level of analytical intelligence (IQ) is a given. In the past, most companies only valued that. Today, other forms of intelligence are even more important—in particular, emotional intelligence, spiritual intelligence, and systems intelligence. The great news is that while our analytical intelligence is fixed at birth and can only decline, other kinds of intelligence can be cultivated and enhanced.

Emotional intelligence (EQ) combines self-awareness (understanding oneself) and empathy (the ability to feel and understand what others are feeling). High EQ is increasingly being recognized as important in organizations because of the growing complexity of society and the variety of stakeholders that must be communicated with effectively. Unfortunately, research shows that the higher the position in the organization, the lower the level of EQ, with the CEO typically having the lowest level.[4]

Growing our self-awareness is a continuous process that lasts a lifetime—an entire universe is within us, waiting to be discovered. We learn about ourselves by becoming aware of our emotions and understanding why we're experiencing them. Each emotion is a window into who we are and what we care about, often at a subconscious level. As Carl Jung said, "Until you make the unconscious conscious, it will direct your life and you will call it fate."

### Systems Intelligence

Systems intelligence (SYQ) is an intelligence many societies don't yet recognize, understand, or cultivate. Yet in the twenty-first century, as organizations become more complex and the world becomes increasingly interdependent, it's hard to overstate how valuable this type of intelligence is.

Systems thinking focuses on the way that a system's constituent parts interrelate and how systems work over time and within the context of larger systems. Systems thinking contrasts sharply with symptomatic thinking, which causes us to constantly react to surface-level symptoms rather than understand the underlying processes that are giving rise to those symptoms.

Conscious leaders work to become natural systems thinkers. They understand the roots of problems and how the problems relate to organizational design and culture, and they devise fundamental solutions instead of applying symptomatic quick fixes. As Winston Churchill said, "We shape our buildings, and then our buildings shape us." The same can be said of systems.

### Spiritual Intelligence

According to Danah Zohar and Ian Marshall, "Spiritual intelligence (SQ) is the intelligence with which we access our deepest meanings, values, purposes, and higher motivations. It is . . . our moral intelligence, giving us an innate ability to distinguish right from wrong. It is the intelligence with which we exercise goodness, truth, beauty, and compassion in our lives."[5] SQ helps us to discover our higher purpose in our work and our lives. Leaders with high SQ have a remarkable ability to align their organizations with a higher purpose. They also have uncanny discernment to sense when things are beginning to go off track.

Servant leadership matters now more than ever. The human seed has never been more potent, powerful, or filled with promise. But even the best seed, in order to flourish, needs the right soil: conditions that enable us to realize our extraordinary, almost divine, potential. In the organizational context, that means having the right kind of leadership that gives rise to a culture in which people can flourish. But if met with toxic leadership that seeks only to use and exploit precious human lives, that same seed can wither away, or worse, mutate into a malignant force and spread further pain and suffering in the world. Our great collective calling in the world today is to enhance joy. That takes leaders with great hearts and great courage who seek only to serve, to imagine a better future, and to devise ways in which we can realize it together.

*A global thought leader of the Conscious Capitalism movement, Raj Sisodia (www. rajsisodia.com) is the Franklin Olin Distinguished Professor of Global Business and Whole Foods Market Research Scholar in Conscious Capitalism at Babson College. He is also cofounder and cochairman of Conscious Capitalism, Inc. Raj has an MBA from the Bajaj Institute of Management Studies in Bombay and a PhD in marketing from Columbia University. He is coauthor of the bestselling book* Conscious Capitalism: Liberating the Heroic Spirit of Business.

## Notes

1. Jim Collins, *Good to Great: Why Some Companies Make the Leap and Others Don't* (New York: HarperBusiness, 2001).
2. Simon Sinek, *Start with Why: How Great Leaders Inspire Everyone to Take Action* (New York: Penguin, 2009). See also his *Leaders Eat Last: Why Some Teams Pull Together and Others Don't* (New York: Penguin, 2014).
3. Jim Collins and Jerry I. Porras, *Built to Last: Successful Habits of Visionary Companies* (New York: HarperBusiness, 1994).
4. Travis Bradberry and Jeanne Greaves, "Heartless Bosses?," *Harvard Business Review* (December 2005).
5. Danah Zohar and Ian Marshall, *Spiritual Capital: Wealth We Can Live By* (San Francisco: Berrett-Koehler, 2004).

## Chapter 4

# Servant Leadership at the Speed of Trust

### STEPHEN M. R. COVEY

*I met Stephen R. Covey in 1976. Over time, we spoke at many of the same sessions and became great supporters of each other's work. When Steve passed away a few years ago, I was sad our field had lost such an important voice. Little did I know then that his son, Stephen M. R. Covey, with whom I have shared the platform many times since, would take up the banner and even go beyond where his father had journeyed. You'll understand what I'm saying after you read this wonderful essay about the role of trust in being an effective servant leader. —KB*

THERE IS AN intuition that I've had for a long time now. As a student of Robert K. Greenleaf's principles of servant leadership, I felt that intuition grow as I developed my original manuscript for *The Speed of Trust*,[1] and grow ever stronger as Greg Link and I followed it with *Smart Trust*.[2] I became increasingly convinced that the practices of servant leadership and trust are inextricably linked. Today I find it difficult to talk about serving without also talking about trust—and vice versa.

Consider this contrast: both servant leadership and trust-based leadership stand in opposition to traditional positional leadership, which is steeped in the language of control: "You have to do what I say because I'm the boss."

On the other hand, servant leaders and trust-based leaders alike draw from a deeper well of meaning. They serve first and they extend trust first. Leadership is the by-product and positional authority is, at best, an afterthought.

Given the link between servant leadership and trust, which comes first? Is one driven by the other? For the leader who seeks to lead their organization into the stratosphere of success, how should these two disciplines be balanced? Here are five key insights that have become clear to me.

1.  The defining outcome for the servant leader is trust.

    How do you know if you are a servant leader? The answer is trust. Trust is the litmus test. Trust is to servant leadership what profit is to a business. It's the outcome. It's the core measure. The scoreboard.

    It's a simple assessment you can conduct right now. Pause for a moment to think about the people you lead. *What is the level—and quality—of trust?* If you are an authentic servant leader, you have enormous trust. But if you are surrounded by low or damaged trust, then you may safely conclude that your servant orientation is in some way compromised or diluted.

    If you lead as a servant, you'll know it—because you will be surrounded by high-trust relationships and a high-trust team. And your company will reap the dividends of a high-trust organization. It's that simple.

2.  The clear intent of the servant leader is to serve others.

    Trust and servant leadership share another similarity in that both are built on intent. Intent—your motive, your agenda—may be intangible and invisible. But don't think for a moment that it is hidden. People sense your intent in everything you say and do.

    Think about positional leaders. What is the intent of leaders who drive change purely through the force of their position in the organizational hierarchy? To generate business outcomes first. If they can do so while also creating a win for other people, that's certainly a nice bonus. But when tempted with a forced choice, they will go straight for the results even if it means that people get bruised in the process. I've worked with plenty of those leaders. At the end of the day, positional leaders are self-serving.

    Servant leaders are different. Their intent is purely and simply to serve others—coworkers, customers, partners, communities. Servant leaders are motivated by caring and the agenda they seek is mutual benefit: "I want to win—but it is even more important to me that *you* win." I have worked with plenty of those leaders as well. When their intent was pure, I knew it. I never needed to second-guess their agenda or motive. And, significantly, I wanted to give them my best in terms of quality work and personal loyalty. They truly inspired me to perform better and they absolutely brought out the best in me.

But why wait for people to infer your intent? You can accelerate trust by *declaring* your intent. John Mackey, the beloved CEO of Whole Foods Market, did this in dramatic fashion eight years ago when he wrote a letter to all employees of the organization. Here is an excerpt from that remarkable—and now legendary—company communication:

> The tremendous success of Whole Foods Market has provided me with far more money than I ever dreamed I'd have and far more than is necessary for either my financial security or personal happiness. . . . I am now 53 years old and I have reached a place in my life where I no longer want to work for money, but simply for the joy of the work itself and to better answer the call to service that I feel so clearly in my own heart. Beginning on January 1, 2007, my salary will be reduced to $1, and I will no longer take any other cash compensation. . . . The intention of the board of directors is for Whole Foods Market to donate all of the future stock options I would be eligible to receive to our two company foundations.

> What do you imagine was the cultural impact of that statement? If you were an employee at Whole Foods Market, do you think this might have reawakened your own aspirations and commitment to the mission? And might it have increased Mackey's credibility as he led this fast-growing organization? It did both of those things, in abundance.

There are more tangible outcomes as well. Over time, a servant leader's authentic intent will eventually materialize in behavioral norms, and then ultimately in systems and structures. Today, Mackey's intent is manifest in Whole Foods' servant leadership culture. Intent shapes the organization. And it becomes real.

3. The deliberate behavior of the servant leader is authentic, trust-building behavior.

Behavior is ground zero for the servant leader. It is the place where conviction becomes real; where intent becomes a potent force for value-creating change; and where the leader can make intentional moves for the purpose of establishing a servant leadership culture.

For the servant leader, behavior isn't just *what* gets done but *how* it gets done. This principle shows up in the norms of many servant leader cultures. The former chairman and CEO of Procter & Gamble, Bob McDonald, put it this way: "How we achieve growth is as important as the results themselves." Similarly, at Marriott they say, "How we do business is as important as the business we do." Expressed another way: for the servant leader, the means preexist in the ends.

This stands in contrast to the positional leader, for whom the results take precedence over process; the *what* supersedes the *how*; and the end justifies the means. In dramatic cases this may show up as visibly unethical or illegal behavior. But most positional leaders I know are not overtly nefarious. Indeed, their behaviors may appear on the surface to build trust. But when they lack the servant leader intent, closer examination reveals a subtly counterfeit quality to the behaviors.

In *The Speed of Trust*, I identify behaviors that powerfully build trust. Each of those behaviors has an accompanying *opposite* and, perhaps more significantly, an accompanying *counterfeit*, which reflect how a positional leader more typically behaves. For example, one of the behaviors is to demonstrate respect. A positional leader may practice the counterfeit of demonstrating respect only to some—such as those who can do something for him; and not to others—those who can't.

Similarly, another trust-building behavior is to talk straight. The counterfeit would be to appear to deliver straight talk while in reality withholding or spinning some parts of the message.

You can see the subtle temptations that make these counterfeit behaviors appealing. I find that without self-reflection, many leaders actually believe their counterfeit behaviors come from a place of integrity. But they don't stand up to scrutiny. These behaviors may generate results for a while, but they're not sustainable—and worse, they diminish trust. Sooner or later, people always infer your real intent.

4. The strong bias of the servant leader is to extend trust to others.

   Extending trust to others doesn't have to be an exercise in blind gullibility. It is an intentional action I call Smart Trust. It begins with a willingness to trust others—what I refer to as a person's *propensity to trust*. It is balanced with an analysis of the stakes and risks of extending that trust, which includes an assessment of the credibility of those being trusted. But the clear and decided bias is to start with trust. That starting point is what opens up boundless possibilities.

   The positional leader seeks to control. The servant leader seeks to unleash talent and creativity by extending trust to others. Why? Because the servant leader fundamentally believes deeply in others—and in their potential.

   I truly do empathize with the positional leader! It is a risk to extend trust to others. Many leaders I know have advanced in their careers by minimizing risk. They say, "I want it done right, so I do it myself." Some are even celebrated for this approach. But this orientation is exhausting, unsustainable, and incapable of delivering the endless innovation, energy, and engagement of an organization that has been electrified by trust.

   Muhammed Yunus extended Smart Trust to the masses, and it won him the Nobel Peace Prize. Yunus was a university professor in Bangladesh who was grieved by the vicious cycle of poverty he saw around him. He believed his community would have the capacity to lift itself out of poverty through entrepreneurship if it only had access to capital. A person wouldn't need a lot of money—just $25, for example, to purchase inventory for a vending cart. Out of this need, and ultimately out of millions of extensions of trust, Yunus founded the global microcredit movement.

   Early in the process of making these small loans available to individual people, Yunus encountered a challenge. "The people said they couldn't provide collateral," Yunus reflected. "I said I will provide the collateral for them." And Grameen Bank was born.

   Listen to Yunus's declaration of intent in describing the microcredit movement: "We are going to make a difference and draw people out of poverty. We are going to extend trust and people will thrive in it." Yunus understood a basic yet powerful principle of trust, which is that *people want to be trusted*. It's the most compelling form of human motivation. Grameen Bank has the results to prove this principle: the microcredit movement has helped to lift literally tens of millions of people out of poverty. And the more than 98 percent rate of payback on loans demonstrates the world-changing results that can be achieved when a servant leader extends trust. Compare that to the 88 percent payback rate of traditional small business loans!

5. The purpose of the servant leader is *contribution*—to make a difference; to give back.

The positional leader serves the bottom line, or the self. The servant leader serves something greater, inspiring trust not only in the leader, but potentially in all of society as well.

Pedro Medina was a businessperson in the Republic of Colombia who helped to establish McDonald's restaurants there in 1999. He was painfully aware of the volatility of the neighborhoods where he lived and did business. His country was plagued with social instability. Kidnappings and terrorist acts dominated the daily headlines.

While teaching at a local university, he asked his students how many of the talented young people he was investing in intended to leave Colombia after graduation. Most of them raised their hands.

This pained him. "Why do you want to leave?" he asked. They told him, "We have lost hope. Can you tell us why we should stay?"

The question haunted him. So he founded an organization called Yo Creo en Colombia (I Believe in Colombia). A grassroots initiative, the organization's primary purpose was—and still is—to increase trust and confidence in Colombia, first at home and then abroad. It reaches out to Colombians to advocate for the achievements, potential, and resources of the country, and to leverage them "in order to build a fair, competitive, and inclusive nation." Since its inception, the foundation has touched hundreds of thousands of Colombians in 157 cities and 26 countries.

Medina created a powerful social movement and did it without positional authority. His efforts have not only taken root at the grassroots level, but also spawned institutional and structural changes at the national level. Three years after Medina began this initiative, a man named Alvaro Uribe, motivated by the impact of Yo Creo en Colombia and the numerous like-minded initiatives it inspired, was elected president on the very platform of *restaurando la confianza* ("restoring trust") that Medina had identified. Not only was Uribe able to succeed, he was the first Colombian to be reelected president in over a century. Today there is still great work to do, but the country has made massive strides in restoring trust in security, investment, and social cohesion.

Medina was just an ordinary businessperson with the heart of a servant leader, a vision and purpose bigger than himself, and the courage to take action. That was enough to change his entire country.

Though closely related, trust and servant leadership are not synonymous. But they do share some important commonalities. Both find their genesis in choice. And both are born in the intent of the leader. They are simple disciplines, but they are not easy. In fact, they are hard. Both trust and servant leadership require the full engagement of the leader as well as the courage to set aside self-serving pursuits in the service of other people and higher outcomes.

In fact, you can choose to accelerate your practice of trusting servant leadership right now, at this very moment. It begins with a self-audit and a commitment. Ask yourself:

- What is the level of trust I share with my relationships, my team, my stakeholders?
- What is my real intent? Is it truly to serve others, or is it to serve myself?
- What are some opportunities for declaring my real intent to others?
- What are some ways in which I can deliberately demonstrate my intent to serve through my behaviors?

Yes, there are risks involved when you set aside your own self-interests and extend trust to those around you. But I believe the greater risk is to withhold trust.

By both inspiring and extending trust, you enable yourself to create a mighty culture of servant leadership that speaks to the highest aspirations of the people you lead. I am confident that within just a few hours of reading this chapter, you will encounter an opportunity to demonstrate your servant leadership intent through trust-building behaviors.

Are you ready to seize that moment?

*Stephen M. R. Covey (www.speedoftrust.com) is cofounder of CoveyLink and the FranklinCovey Global Speed of Trust Practice. He is bestselling author of* The

Speed of Trust, *coauthor of* Smart Trust, *and a sought-after keynote speaker and adviser on trust, leadership, ethics, sales, and high performance. You can follow Covey on Twitter @StephenMRCovey.*

## Notes

1. Stephen M. R. Covey, *The Speed of Trust: The One Thing That Changes Everything* (New York: Free Press, 2006).
2. Stephen M. R. Covey and Greg Link, *Smart Trust: Creating Prosperity, Energy, and Joy in a Low-Trust World* (New York: Simon and Schuster, 2011).

# Chapter 5

# Great Leaders SERVE

## MARK MILLER

*I met Mark Miller several years ago when I went to Atlanta to speak to all the Chick-fil-A managers. I was instantly blown away by his creative thinking about servant leadership. As a result, he became one of my favorite coauthors, on both* The Secret *and* Great Leaders Grow. *When you read this essay, you'll see what I mean.*
*—KB*

ALMOST TWENTY YEARS ago, our team at Chick-fil-A, Inc., began work on a project to accelerate leadership development across the organization. Our first conclusion: we needed a common definition of leadership. Any attempts to scale the process of helping leaders grow would be frustrating, if not futile, without a clear picture of success.

After a lot of research, discussion, and debate, we thought we might have an idea worth pursuing. However, we had what I would call a crisis of confidence as we looked at a simple outline representing our point of view. I clearly remember one of the group members saying, "What if this isn't right?"

Although collectively we had read a couple of hundred books on leadership, we knew a lot more about chicken than we did creating a leadership culture. We knew the stakes were high: we were about to declare our very definition of leadership. Such a simple and definitive statement would drive countless hours of development, tens of millions of dollars of investment, and, perhaps most important, this definition would shape the caliber of our leaders for decades to come.

Then someone said, "I have an idea . . . What if we seek some outside perspective?" Well, you can chalk it up to coincidence or divine intervention, but I was scheduled to be with Ken Blanchard the next day! I offered to share our outline with him, and the team was in full agreement.

I'll never forget that encounter with Ken. I handed him a single sheet of paper and quickly explained how we were trying to accelerate leadership development. And then I said, "Do you think our model is true? Have we missed anything? Will it stand the test of time?"

Ken's response was strong and immediate: "This has got to be a book!"

As you may or may not know, that conversation led to my first book with Ken, *The Secret: What Great Leaders Know and Do.*[1] He and I took a simple outline and transformed it into a parable that today is being shared around the world in more than twenty-five languages.

Why has the book been so successful? Besides Ken's powerful global brand, I think the book has struck a chord in the hearts and minds of leaders around the planet because of the truth contained within its pages. The secret is out!

Here's a quick overview of five strategic ways great leaders SERVE:

*See and shape the future.* Leadership always begins with a picture of the future. Leaders who cannot paint a compelling picture of a preferred future are in jeopardy of forfeiting their leadership. People want to know: Where are we going? What are we trying to accomplish? What are we trying to become? And why does it matter? We encourage leaders not to give away their influence by failing to answer these critical questions. If you don't know the answers, start figuring them out. Clarity will often come in the midst of activity. If you are stuck, get moving. Who wants to follow a leader who doesn't know where they are trying to go? When the vision is clear and compelling, it will create life, energy, and momentum.

*Engage and develop others.* Ken and I were writing about engagement before it was cool—but make no mistake, it has always been critical. Engagement is about creating the context for people to thrive. The annual engagement survey of American workers, year after year, paints a grim picture of staggeringly low engagement. This is not an indictment of the workers; it is the leaders who need to make a change. The reason development is called out is because of its critical importance. Yes, it could be considered a strategy for raising engagement levels. However, it could also be missed. We believe leaders who are not proactively developing others are missing a vital aspect of their role.

*Reinvent continuously.* This fundamental of great leaders is a big idea. Most leaders have heard the expression "If you do what you've always done, you'll get what you always got." To make progress, to move forward, to accomplish bigger and better, something has to change! To help leaders break it down into manageable pieces we talk about three arenas, each having its own diagnostic questions. *Self:* How are you reinventing yourself? *Systems:* Which work processes need to change to generate better results? *Structure:* What structural changes could you make to better enable the accomplishment of your goals? There are many more questions, but these will usually start a productive conversation.

*Value results and relationships.* This is the tenet that generates the most angst for many leaders. Having taught this content around the globe for almost twenty years, there is no doubt in my mind this is the most challenging element of our model. Would you agree? I bet you would. The reason: virtually every leader has a natural bias. Our wiring pulls us toward one or the other. This is not necessarily bad—but if we aren't careful, it can severely limit our effectiveness. Having a default setting won't destroy your leadership if you can successfully compensate for your bias. The best leaders value both! There is a principle at play here: the tremendous power in the tension. Our challenge as leaders is to manage the tension. Only then can we productively channel its power.

*Embody the values.* People always watch the leader—whether we want them to or not! They are generally looking for clues regarding what's important to the leader. They are also trying to determine if the leader is trustworthy. So what's the link between embodying the values and trustworthiness? If a leader says something is important, people expect that person to live like it's important. The gap between what we say and do as leaders can be lethal. People generally don't follow a leader they don't trust. Worse yet, if someone doesn't trust the leader but stays on the payroll, you don't have an advocate for your organization and your culture, you have an adversary. Leaders must do everything humanly possible to walk the talk!

Are you ready to become a serving leader? I hope so!

I have one closing thought for you. If you are looking for the latest techniques in coercing people to do your bidding, you can continue your search.

Servant leadership is not for you. It's not a strategy or shortcut to success. However, if you are willing to begin the long journey of adding value to others, putting their interests ahead of your own, helping them win, and mastering the five fundamentals we just reviewed, you will enjoy new levels of success, satisfaction, and impact.

Great leaders SERVE!

*In more than thirty years with Chick-fil-A, Mark Miller has served in numerous leadership capacities including restaurant operations, quality and customer satisfaction, and corporate communications. He travels extensively, teaching on a variety of topics including teams, servant leadership, and training. He is the author of* Chess Not Checkers, The Secret of Teams, The Heart of Leadership, *and his latest,* Leaders Made Here: Building a Leadership Culture. *He is also coauthor with Ken Blanchard of* Great Leaders Grow *and the international bestseller* The Secret: What Great Leaders Know and Do. *Follow Mark Miller on Twitter: @LeadersServe.*

## Note

1. Ken Blanchard and Mark Miller, *The Secret: What Great Leaders Know and Do* (San Francisco: Berrett-Koehler, 2009, 2014).

# Chapter 6

# Servant Leadership

## *What Does It Really Mean?*

### MARK A. FLOYD

*I've come to admire Mark Floyd from our work together at conferences designed to spread the word about servant leadership. He's not only a successful entrepreneur, but also an extraordinary thinker about what it takes to be a servant leader. Mark and I both believe that everyone is a potential servant leader. Regardless of whether we have an organizational position, we are all potential servant leaders as we interact with others on a day-to-day basis, as Mark emphasizes in this essay. —KB*

SERVANT LEADERSHIP IS about helping people succeed both professionally and individually. It's all about serving those you are responsible *for* and those you are responsible *to*.

Who was the greatest servant leader of all time? There is no doubt in my mind it was Jesus. He demonstrated it in His time and continues to demonstrate it today. It's in His nature. We mortals think we have to work at being servant leaders, but it's not impossible. In fact, it's amazing—for me, the harder I tried to be a servant leader, the tougher it was. But the more I prayed about it and let it just enter me, the easier and better it was.

Who are potential servant leaders? We all are. Whether you're a CEO, a self-employed professional, a stock room clerk, a receptionist, a stay-at-home parent, or a good friend to someone—whatever you do, at times you are a leader. What you do every day—what people see you do—is a reflection on yourself, your faith, your life, and everything else. So what I'm talking about in this essay is *you* as a leader. I hope my thoughts will help.

## Don't Let Other People Set Your Leadership Style for You

I remember my first job out of college when I went to work for a *Fortune* 500 company. I had great respect for the CEO and for the company. It had a great culture that had been developed by the founder. My first couple of weeks there, I listened to tapes that helped me define the company and its style and values. Shortly afterward, though, a new CEO came on board with a different leadership style—one I didn't particularly care for. I was a young, naïve guy, but I noticed that the whole organization was changing. People were changing their leadership styles to adapt to this person—the new CEO. He was very terse, demeaning, and demanding. From my vantage point he wasn't a very good leader—he was the antithesis of what servant leadership is all about. As time went on, I found that most of the organization was moving in his direction. I told myself I couldn't go there—it wasn't my leadership style. The CEO eventually left the company and a new leader came in and turned things back around. Today it is a very successful company. So hold true to your leadership style. Don't let influences change you. *You* change the influences.

## Servant Leadership Works in Any Type of Organization

A business should be functional. If you ever see an organizational chart for your company, pick out your name. If you have at least one name below you that has a line to you, you're considered a manager.

Now notice all the people at the bottom of the chart: the sales people, clerks, accounting people, receptionists, and others who don't have anyone reporting to them. *Those* are the people who talk to the customers. I believe that to reflect reality you need to take the chart and turn it upside down. That way, the CEO and the management teams serve the employees who serve the customers. Ken Blanchard said it right: "How can you serve your customers with excellence when your people are serving the CEO?"

In Mark 9:35, after the disciples have talked among themselves about which of them was the greatest, Jesus says, "Anyone who wants to be first must be the very last, and the servant of all." That's what servant leadership is about.

## The Importance of Your Organizational Culture

Some companies are known for great products, great designs, and the way they take care of their people. Southwest Airlines, for example, is an amazing organization. Southwest's founder and former president, Herb Kelleher, once had a dispute with a gentleman in North Carolina about the use of a name. Lawsuits were being threatened and they needed to figure out a way to settle the dispute. Finally, Herb said, "Look, I'm just going to fly out to where you are and I'll arm wrestle you for it." He actually did this—and he lost. So he relinquished the name. I think that was pretty classy.

My wife likes Nordstrom. It is my understanding that they have a shoe department that is five times bigger than most department stores. Anyway, they do great things. She tells me if you buy something and don't like it, you can take it back—they just refund your money. If you go down a list of these or other great companies such as Apple, Google, and Whole Foods Market, you'll find the organizational culture—what they value and live by—is defined and understood by everyone from the management team all the way through the employee base. Your culture can't help but manifest itself in the position you have in the industry. I'll guarantee you: it's not the product that makes the difference. It's the people involved who sell it, service it, manage it, talk to customers, help them find what they need, and do all the little extra things. That's why customers come back.

Let me tell you about the opposite of a great company. One night I came home from work, flipped on my television, and got a blank screen. Nothing was happening. So I called the cable company and talked to about five different machines before I got a person. We talked for several minutes and finally she decided she needed to send a service rep out. Four days later, a guy came to my door and fixed the cable. When I asked what had happened, he said, "We were installing a service next door to you and our own guy cut your cable by mistake."

When I received my bill, I naïvely thought those four days without service would be deducted from the bill. But they weren't. I thought *It wasn't that much money, don't worry about it.* But then I decided that these people need to learn that they can't let something like this happen. So I called them and after a few recordings, I reached a live person who couldn't help me. I thought about contacting their CEO—but I looked at the stock market listings and found that this company's stock was at the bottom of its industry. So I figured that this CEO probably had more important things on his plate and didn't need to hear about the four extra days on my bill. So I left it alone.

## Leadership Teams Are Important

When you put together a team, two different dynamics are working: the *vertical* and the *horizontal*. The vertical is your position. I had a VP of sales, a VP of marketing, a VP of human resources, a VP of engineering, and a CEO. That's the management team. The horizontal is the company goals, mission, and vision statement. This is what we're doing—what we're all about.

What happens in a lot of companies is that the vertical starts taking over the horizontal. Too many people start forgetting about the big picture—the reason for existence—and start worrying about their vertical position. The VP of engineering is too worried about his department to help out. The VP of finance is worried about her budgets getting in on time. Each department has its problems and responsibilities and no one other than the sales person is focused on the customer. But the whole idea of the enterprise is to grow the employees and take care of your customers—so what is the answer?

I went to a staff meeting in my organization and issued everybody on my team new business cards. Except for the person's name, they were all the same—including the title. The title under each person's name was "Vice President." It didn't say of engineering, sales, manufacturing, or any other department. It just said "Vice President." The point is that when you are a servant leader, whatever you do has to support the mission you are trying to accomplish. The more you communicate with and serve your employees, the more naturally this happens. But if you have your organization set up where you are dictating down, I guarantee that your people will get into their vertical mode and forget about the horizontal. That's why a lot of companies don't do well.

One day, a young leader—whom I thought of highly and had mentored—came to me and said, "Mark, I have a very important issue I really want to talk to you about." He was on his own, running his own little department. He said, "I really need a vice president title."

I said, "Really? Vice president of what?"

"You know, vice president of my department. I can't get things done because people disregard me sometimes. If I had that title, I would have the power to be the leader everyone wants. I would be respected. I could get things done."

I told him, "You're only a leader if you turn around and people are following you. Titles don't mean anything."

## Servant Leaders Are Self-Aware

I think one of the hardest things for people to do is to be self-aware. I'm not good at it. Everyone has strengths and weaknesses. I recently had a meeting where someone asked me what my strengths and weaknesses are. I started thinking—my strengths? I couldn't think of anything. Weaknesses? Also nothing. I later took time to reflect on my leadership and came to the conclusion that there's only one person who has ever walked this earth who was perfect, and I'm certainly not in that category. But it made me realize I have to be more self-aware as a leader because it is a valuable part of servant leadership. We all have blind spots. When you figure out your blind spots, you can serve people much better.

## Do the Right Thing

I was once asked to talk to a board of directors and chairman of a company who wanted to replace their CEO. The chairman said to me, "Mark, I want a take-charge executive with a take-no-prisoners attitude." I thought that sounded pretty interesting. I knew what he thought he wanted, and I clearly understood what he said, but I didn't think he had a clue what he was asking for—and neither did the board. When an organization goes sideways, sometimes boards and management want to swing the pendulum all the way to the other side. If a company has a leader who is ineffective for building teams or closing big deals, the board wants to go get a high-powered sales manager to come in and stay with the company to close big deals. But the person they would choose may not have the interpersonal skills to run inside the organization—because they want a gunslinger.

I decided to translate what I thought he was looking for. I said, "Here's what I think you want. You want a strong leader who is capable of leading your organization toward positive change. What you really need is a servant leader."

He looked at me kind of funny and said, "No, no, no. I need someone who is going to take charge and right this ship."

People hear the phrase *servant leader* and think it means someone who is always congenial and nice, and handles everything with kid gloves. But look at Jesus. He threw out the money lenders in the temple with tough love. Servant leadership means you do the right thing. Every CEO knows what decisions need to be made and what the right answer is. They might not know all the details but I think they know the right direction to go.

So I told the board, "You need a servant leader to come in here and take care of the two largest constituencies you have in this enterprise: your customers and your employees. How well they do that will directly affect how well or how poorly the company will perform."

Their response was, "We've got to think about profitability."

But companies that focus on running their company only for the numbers get in trouble. I can list many, many companies that got into trouble because they quit focusing on their customers and employees and just focused on the numbers. The important thing is how well you run your business—not the numbers themselves.

I'm telling you, business is really not that difficult. Just do the right thing. Whether you run a dry cleaning business or a multimillion-dollar company—you know the right thing to do. Just do it.

Servant leaders are not always perfect, but they stay true to their leadership style. They stay humble by turning the organizational chart upside down and serving others. They communicate to their teams the goals and values that form their culture so that everyone stays in focus. They are aware of their own strengths and weaknesses—through feedback and by following the greatest servant leader of all time. And they continually strive to do the right thing.

God Bless!

*Mark A. Floyd is a venture partner at TDF Ventures and chairman of the board at Ciber, Inc. He was the recipient of the 2001 Ernst & Young Entrepreneur of the Year award for the Southwest region. He holds a BBA in finance from the University of Texas at Austin and an honorary doctorate of science in business from Southeastern University.*

# Chapter 7

# Servant Leaders Create a Great Place to Work for All

## MICHAEL C. BUSH

*I'm a great believer in catching people doing things right. The first time I heard Michael Bush speak at a conference, I knew he was a great believer in catching organizations doing things right. As a result, he took the helm at Great Place to Work and has been traveling around the country looking for organizations that have a servant leadership culture. I think you'll be fascinated by the common characteristics these great companies have when you read Michael's essay. —KB*

MY ORGANIZATION, CONSULTING and research firm Great Place to Work, has spent more than two decades studying and celebrating the best workplaces around the world. Since 1998 we have produced the annual *Fortune* 100 Best Companies to Work For list as well as other best workplaces lists. We operate in more than 50 countries and each year our Trust Index© survey captures the views of roughly 10 million employees globally. We, along with other scholars, have documented the way the 100 Best have outperformed peers in terms of profitability, revenue growth, stock performance, and other key business measures.

But we also see a shift to a new era—a new frontier in business. This largely uncharted territory is about developing every ounce of human potential so that businesses can reach *their* full potential. To do those things, the best workplaces know they have to create an outstanding culture for everyone, no matter who they are or what they do for the organization. The best workplaces have to build what we call a Great Place to Work For All. These companies have employees across the board who consistently trust their leaders, take pride in their work, and enjoy their colleagues—the three core elements of a great workplace.

These emerging organizations develop and support leaders toward a servant mindset and approach—that is, they cultivate servant leaders who create cultures where all people feel trusted, empowered, supported, and treated fairly.

In these companies, leaders relinquish the autocratic, command-and-control ways that dominated business cultures in the twentieth century. Thanks to a shift to servant leadership, lower-ranked employees experience more passion about work, collaborate more, and engage in innovation behaviors that propel the business. These leaders also reject what's been common management practice for decades: claiming people are your greatest asset but really valuing only about 10 percent or so of the souls in the upper echelons of the company. That elitist approach to business leaves human potential on the table, ultimately letting down individuals who work there as well as the business itself.

By contrast, the leaders of companies identified as Great Places to Work For All appreciate and develop the talents of everyone at every level of the organization—from the basement boiler room to the penthouse C-suite.

What does servant leadership look like at a company identified as a Great Place to Work For All? Five features stand out:

- *Trust at the top.* Leaders at Great Places to Work For All establish trusting relationships on their executive team. They know servant leadership is only effective and sustainable when the executive can fully trust the people they work with. If a high level of trust is not present, the leader cannot humbly serve and selflessly support people. The trusting mindset servant leaders need to maintain is possible only when the leader is surrounded by people they see as highly credible, consistently respectful, and fair to everyone they meet. The leader, of course, must be seen in an identical way. Trust at the top is the first step in becoming a servant leader. We find the hard work related to this step often is avoided due to the "but that person is an outstanding individual performer" excuse. But when this first step is avoided, it leads to a servant leader being a servant leader to some but not all.
- *A generous trust mindset.* Leaders at Great Places to Work For All trust people in general. They see others in the organization as glasses half full rather than half empty. They extend trust widely to a large number of

people, including those on the front lines and those who may look different from them. And they extend trust deeply, giving each person the benefit of the doubt. That's not to say these leaders are naïve—they will not tolerate the same mistakes endlessly. But their default position when a teammate fails is curiosity rather than condemnation. They have an abiding faith that people can grow and that they generally want to do the right thing. It's a mindset summed up by Jim Goodnight, CEO of software firm SAS Institute, a longtime *Fortune* 100 Best company: "If you treat your employees like they make a difference, they will."

- *Decentralized power.* Leaders at Great Places to Work For All free people to work autonomously and include others in decision making. They know people need significant control over their jobs to reach their full potential. There's no room for micromanagement. Beyond providing employees with autonomy in their day-to-day tasks, leaders at these companies actively seek their people's input and feedback on matters ranging from team projects to organizational strategy. Leaders in these settings do not abdicate their power. In fact, the respect they show to employees—their vulnerability in sharing authority—increases their own influence even as others have a voice. Construction firm TDIndustries, a *Fortune* 100 Best mainstay, captures the wisdom of employee empowerment with its principles around communication: "No rank in the room," "Everyone participates—no one dominates," and "Listen as an ally."

- *Caring support.* Leaders at companies identified as a Great Place to Work For All care for their people. They support them as holistic human beings, encouraging their well-being both in and out of work. This starts with getting to know employees as people, extends to training and development opportunities, and includes benefits such as health insurance. While servant leaders in the past may have been motivated by a sense of duty, today a raft of science justifies a big heart. Google, for example, has found that *psychological safety* is the key factor in its most effective teams. Our own research, meanwhile, has found that a caring community is one of the strongest drivers of revenue growth at small and medium workplaces with high-trust cultures. We have also discovered that a key disparity at work between whites and ethnic minorities is whether employees perceive a caring climate.

- *Intentional fairness.* Leaders at Great Places to Work For All work deliberately to treat all people fairly. They know that fairness is at the heart of the employee experience. It is central to trusting relationships, serves as a foundation for empowering employees to make decisions, and is crucial to people feeling genuinely cared for. Fairness is a simple concept. But it is not easy for leaders to achieve—especially in large, complex organizations. Fair treatment in pay and other matters isn't necessarily equal treatment, given different job levels and responsibilities. Persistence, courage, and creativity are required to change a socioeconomic system that historically has been unfair. But the Best Workplaces have made significant progress over the past twenty years, according to results from our Trust Index Employee Survey. Employee ratings of fairness have improved 22 percent at the 100 Best from 1998 to 2017, outpacing the other four workplace dimensions we measure (respect, credibility, pride, and camaraderie).

## Serving People, Serving Business

Leaders at Great Places to Work For All who establish high-trust executive teams, who trust people, share power, care for employees, and strive for fairness serve their people well. They also serve their business. Our research into the 100 Best shows that companies identified as Great Places to Work For All grow faster than their less inclusive competitors. In studying the 100 Best alongside the nonwinning contender companies for 2017, we discovered that the more consistent an organization is regarding key factors related to innovation, leadership effectiveness, and trust in the workplace, the more likely it will outperform peers when it comes to revenue growth.

The Great Place to Work For All Score (see Figure 7.1) is a composite measure of how consistently employees rate their workplace on metrics related to innovation, leadership effectiveness, and trust, regardless of who they are and what they do within their organization. Companies in the top quartile on these metrics enjoy *three times* the revenue growth of companies in the bottom quartile.

To see how servant leadership focused on fairness pays off for all parties, consider the $3 million investment that Salesforce.com CEO Marc Benioff and his team made to address gender pay inequities in 2015. Along with a host of other equality efforts at the software firm to make all employees feel fully valued and included, this move has reaped results:

- *Better for business.* Salesforce is becoming a beacon for talented women in technology and is enjoying the fruits of a more fully engaged workforce. The percentage of women employees who say they want to

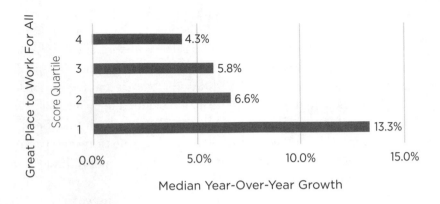

**Figure 7.1** Great Places to Work For All race ahead

work at Salesforce for a long time rose from 85 percent in 2014 to 93 percent in 2016. Also, 92 percent of female employees in 2016 said people look forward to work at Salesforce, up from 85 percent in 2014. Not surprisingly, the company has been growing faster than its rivals.

- *Better for people.* In the wake of the pay equity push, women at Salesforce have a better work experience and all staffers feel more pride about their employer. In 2014, 84 percent of women at Salesforce felt pay was fair at the company, compared to 91 percent of men. By 2016, the share of women perceiving their pay as fair had climbed to 90 percent. The focus on leveling up women didn't make men feel overlooked—91 percent of men continued to believe people get paid fairly. And for both sexes, levels of pride climbed such that in 2016, a whopping 97 percent of both men and women reported feeling proud when telling others they work at Salesforce.

- *Better for the world.* Happy Salesforce employees go home to be better parents, friends, and neighbors, even as the company—like many other best workplaces—gives generously to the community. Against the backdrop of the pay equity initiative and a major focus on mindfulness as a way to prevent stress, the share of employees who rate Salesforce a "psychologically and emotionally healthy place to work" rose from 83 percent in 2014 to 89 percent in 2016. Also, Salesforce operates a 1-1-1 integrated philanthropy model, through which it contributes 1 percent of its equity, product, and employee time back into the community. As part of that giving back effort, the company has donated more than $137 million in grants since it was founded in 1999.

## Work as Church

Salesforce, as well as most of the organizations we work with, is secular by nature. But the leaders of companies building Great Places to Work For All act in keeping with the great faith traditions, regardless of personal religion or spiritual beliefs. They demonstrate humility, elevate the least powerful, and treat all people with dignity. In fact, these leaders turn work into a kind of church. Great Places to Work For All bring out the best in people as individuals and as members of the human community. We have documented, for example, how employees at the 100 Best have felt increasing levels of solidarity and connection with colleagues over the past two decades.

The world desperately needs more of these companies—companies that can help heal the economic, social, and political divides that have emerged in recent decades. Great Places to Work For All can act as servant institutions, as conceived by author Robert K. Greenleaf: "If a better society is to be built, one that is more just and more loving, one that provides greater creative opportunity for its people, then the most open course is to raise both the capacity to serve and the very performance as servant of existing major institutions by new regenerative forces operating within them."[1]

At Great Place to Work, we have a vision similar to Greenleaf's. Our mission is "to build a better world by helping organizations become Great Places to Work For All." Servant leaders are needed in these organizations. Given that Great Places to Work For All are the way forward for business, we are hopeful that more and more leaders will see themselves as servants first; that these leaders will establish the trust on their teams that is the crucial first step; and that these leaders will put themselves in service of a better future.

*Michael C. Bush is CEO of the SaaS-enabled research and consulting firm Great Place to Work (www.greatplacetowork.com). Michael is a founding board member of Fund Good Jobs, a private equity seed fund, and was a member of President Barack Obama's White House Business Council. He is the author of* A Great Place to Work For All: Better for Business, Better for People, Better for the World.

## Note

1. Robert K. Greenleaf, "The Institution as Servant" (Westfield, IN: The Greenleaf Center for Servant Leadership, 1972).

# Chapter 8

# The Leader as Shepherd

## HOLLY CULHANE

*I met Holly Culhane seventeen years ago when she became an independent consultant for The Ken Blanchard Companies to help us spread the word about our training programs. We became better acquainted a few years later through our Lead Like Jesus ministry, where she is one of our certified trainers. What I love most about Holly is that she continually challenges her own thinking and explores new ideas. I think you'll admire that aspect of her, too, when you read her essay. —KB*

A WHILE BACK, in reference to a self-serving leadership scandal I had experienced, a wise and dear friend remarked, "A shepherd is supposed to lay down his life for his sheep." The analogy hit me hard. The self-serving leaders involved hadn't considered the needs of their followers a priority—but were first only concerned about their own well-being.

I had heard the term *shepherding* in a leadership context from time to time in speeches, books, and the media. Earnest leaders spend much time discussing the values of servant leadership. But was there a skill or tool or philosophy of shepherds that would bring even more depth and meaning to those lessons of leadership?

What did the word "shepherd" mean beyond Webster's definitions: "a person who herds, tends or guards sheep" and "a person who protects, guides, or watches over a person or group of people"?

Fascinated by this concept, I did internet searches, read books about shepherding, and conducted interviews with modern-day shepherds. I learned about methodologies and medical techniques, philosophies and opinions, processes and procedures. It became clear that the term *shepherd* needed consideration from a servant leadership perspective.[1]

After researching multiple interviews, articles, and even readings of ancient prophets, a premise emerged: shepherding is a universal—and I would say godly—leadership principle. It applies to supervising and managing at work in for-profit and nonprofit organizations and the government sector, parenting and partnering at home, and friendships and work relationships across cultures, socioeconomic levels, ethnicities, and generations. Everyone who is interested in becoming a servant leader can connect with the message of shepherding. After all, a shepherd is the ultimate example of a servant leader, often laying down their life for the sheep.

It became clear that it was time for me to develop this remarkably simple yet uniquely profound concept.

## True Shepherding

The responsibilities of a shepherd are to ensure that the sheep are in good health on a consistent basis, well fed, and shielded from predators. The needs of sheep are remarkably similar to the needs of people. Sheep need:

- a calming presence to rest;
- discipline to stay on task with the flock;
- a leader who knows their condition and responds accordingly; and
- special attention when they are young, new to a flock, or struggling.

Sheep have no desire for change. In fact, it takes some time for them to produce wool again after their lifestyle has been altered in any way. They can be the most beneficial of all livestock when well managed—and they can be destructive, causing ruin almost beyond remedy, when mismanaged.

Sound familiar? If you're a parent, a pastor, a coach, or a supervisor, you'll immediately see the analogy for what people and sheep need to perform well.

## The Leader's Shield: Provision, Protection, and Presence

The skills that make up the job description of a responsible shepherd are the same as those of an effective servant leader. Every responsibility of a shepherd and, ultimately, of a servant leader, can be captured in three words: *provision, protection,* and *presence.* Effective shepherding is grounded in these three pivotal elements of leadership. It's only when provision, protection, and presence are intertwined that shepherds can truly fulfill their calling as leaders.

Good shepherds care for sheep, providing nourishment and ensuring the availability of clean water. Similarly, effective servant leaders care for team members or family, providing a suitable space for them to work or live and resources to sustain them. Pastors and priests provide nourishment through their teaching for those under their care.

Good shepherds delight in the flock, shelter them from storms, protect them from enemies, and keep them healthy. Effective servant leaders take pleasure in the successes of their team or family, protect them from danger, and as much as possible ensure their physical and emotional health.

Good shepherds ensure their sheep are free from stress and conflict with other sheep. They bring a calming presence and make sure those that stray are quickly brought back to the flock. Effective servant leaders address problems between employees or family members when they arise and strive to assist those who are struggling, while offering a reassuring and comforting presence.

Good shepherds guide, train, and discipline the sheep when necessary. Effective servant leaders praise employees, congregants, or family members when things are going well, redirect when behavior dictates, and provide training, development, coaching, and opportunities for growth.

Effective shepherds and servant leaders provide, protect, and are present at a variety of levels. We use these definitions for the three terms:

*Provision*: To take care of or to furnish or supply the need of another.

*Protection*: The act of safeguarding, shielding from harm, or guarding against danger.

*Presence*: At hand—physically and/or emotionally available and engaged.

These three pivotal elements form the Leader's Shield—not to protect the leader *from* those they lead but, in fact, to act as a shield *for* those they lead.

What would employee engagement statistics look like if leaders at work cared for their people at a level that encompassed provision, protection, and presence? What would the future of the world's children be if parents and caregivers shepherded them with an emphasis on all three elements? Would prison overcrowding become a concern of the past? Would the turnover rate of volunteers drop if nonprofits, churches, synagogues, and mosques truly shepherded those who gave of their time, talents, and treasure to further the mission of their organizations?

## Provision, Protection, and Presence in Action

There's no formulaic equation to determine how the three responsibilities in the Leader's Shield are demonstrated. Every work, home, and volunteer environment, as well as different cultures of countries or organizations, will dictate how leaders live out provision, protection, and presence.

The shepherd's rod has always provided discipline to help sheep make the right choices. The shepherd's staff represents protection and is on hand to pull the sheep to safety or to help them avoid slipping into a ravine or crevice. The shepherd's presence allows both of these tools to be available when needed and provides a trust and peace the sheep need to live well and produce effectively.

For an entrepreneur, supervisor, or manager in a first world country, provision may be a necessary piece of equipment or a fair wage. Protection may be ergonomically designed chairs and desks or a facilitated conflict resolution meeting when a team is struggling. Presence may be responding to emails in a timely manner or electronic face-to-face chats when the leader isn't personally available. In a third world environment, provision may be paying transportation fees for employees. Protection may include ensuring that employees leave their work environment in time to arrive at home before dark, or assisting them in techniques of how to address potential bribery by vendors. Presence may look similar in many settings. It may include the leader being available for conversations, seeking people's input with problem solving, and helping address concerns with coworkers.

In the case of a parent, provision may include providing basic food and shelter for a child or assisting with funding a college education. Protection may be an emotionally safe environment where family members can learn and thrive as they share life together. Presence may take the form of electronics-free family time, date nights between partners, attending children's important events, or listening attentively to a teenager's angst over friendships or high school.

Leaders of volunteers may demonstrate provision by assuring that people know how their tasks are to be performed. They may demonstrate protection by assuring that conflict among volunteers is addressed, and presence by candid, face-to-face communication, holding meetings on a consistent basis, or seeking volunteers' feedback in their areas of expertise.

It's important to add two additional points of interest with regard to these responsibilities. First, whether a behavior is defined as provision, protection, or presence is not imperative. What is imperative is for the leader to be conscientious in carrying out these responsibilities. Second, presence is not about simply attending an event or an online conference call—it is about focused attention. People want their leaders to be engaged in what they do. Engaged presence is a significant behavior that separates a shepherd from every other kind of leader.

## The Reality

We humans are complicated beings—difficult to understand, at times a struggle to lead, and imperfect in our actions and responses. It's often easier to love the child who challenges and stretches our leadership than the coworker, team member, or volunteer who pushes our limits. But remember: we don't have the option of discriminating between those we shepherd well and those we leave in need.

As I studied biblical writings describing the shepherd, it was clear the responsibilities within this leadership concept are to be applied for the benefit of everyone servant leaders work to influence—even in lateral relationships such as peers and friends. Servant leaders are called to shepherd well when they take on any influence or leadership role. And the Leader's Shield is a tool to be implemented at all times—not just in comfortable circumstances. The reality is that our responsibility as servant leaders is to shepherd well *all* of those in our care.

## Intention and Informed Purpose

A number of organizations are seeing remarkable results in how their teams work together and perform when servant leaders ramp up their attention to provision, protection, and presence. The same is true of families who focus on all three areas of responsibility.

It is crucial that every person who wants to be a servant leader is intentional in the provision, protection, and presence provided to people in their life. As shepherds we must be purposefully informed and able to answer the question of why we do what we do. Intention and informed purpose must support each action, decision, and step we take as a shepherd on the servant leadership journey. The people in our lives are too important for us to offer them less.

*Holly Culhane is CEO and founder of Presence Point, Inc. (www.presencepoint. com), a nonprofit organization focused on helping people live into their calling as shepherd leaders. She is also consultant emeritus with P•A•S Associates, an HR consulting firm she founded in 1987. She is a leadership coach and consultant who facilitates leadership development workshops with The Ken Blanchard Companies and Lead Like Jesus. She also serves a variety of nonprofit organizations through board involvement.*

## Note

1. Dr. Owen Phelps, in *The Catholic Vision for Leading like Jesus* (Huntington, IN: Our Sunday Visitor Publishing, 2009), captures this concept when he boldly states that an effective leader is a combination of servant, steward, and shepherd.

# Chapter 9

# The Evolution of Servant Leadership

## Simon Sinek

*Simon Sinek and I met at a conference where I first heard him talk about his "Start with Why" philosophy. The clarity of his thinking really impressed me. Then when I read his book* Leaders Eat Last, *I knew we were soul mates. I am elated that he agreed to participate in this book. I knew whatever he chose to write would be creative and would stimulate new thinking. This essay did that for me, and I'm sure it will do the same for you. —KB*

LEADERSHIP IS HARD. So why should an aspiring leader add the extra burden of service to their role? A strong argument can be made that the additional work is worth it based on the results servant leadership can achieve. The problem is, any authority who eschews the *servant* part of the leadership role can line up case studies to prove their point of view that they can achieve strong results without it. The real answer to why we should make an effort to practice servant leadership requires an understanding of where servant leadership comes from and why it matters. The reason servant leadership matters is, in fact, firmly grounded in our anthropology.

Homo sapiens have roamed this planet for about fifty thousand years. During the Paleolithic era, the world was full of uncertainty and great danger. Whether it was lack of food or resources, extreme weather, or wild animals, around every corner were unpredictable and often violent forces that could—and often did—kill us. As we were neither the strongest nor the fastest animals on the planet, there was only one way we were going to survive and thrive: together.

It wasn't just our big brains that gave us an edge in those dangerous times; it was also our ability to cooperate. And trust was the name of the game. The more we trusted those with whom we lived and worked, the more likely we were to coordinate our efforts, align around common interests, and work together to take care of the tribe. If someone fell asleep at night, for example, they could trust that other members of the tribe would wake them and alert them to danger. That's a good system for survival of individuals and the group as a whole. If they hadn't been able to trust each other, no one would ever have gone to sleep at night. That's a bad system for survival.

Nothing has changed in our modern world. Though the dangers are different, our brain chemistry and how we work together remain the same. A lack of food and wild animals, for example, may have been replaced by the uncertainty of the stock market or the unpredictability of economies and world events, but our ability to survive and thrive in our modern world is still based on how well we cooperate. And that depends on how much we trust those in our tribe.

But there is a problem. Trust isn't an instruction. We can't just tell people to trust us. Leaders can't simply order their employees to trust them. It doesn't work that way. Trust is a feeling. And that feeling is a biological reaction to the environments in which we live and work. That's why we have leaders in the first place: leaders shape the environment.

As social animals, we respond to the environments we are in. If we take a good person and put them in a bad environment, the odds increase that that person will do bad things. If we take a person who is considered untrustworthy, who may even have performed bad acts, and put them in a good environment, they are capable of turning their lives around and becoming a valuable and trusted member of the group. When a leader gets the environment right, the normal human response is trust and cooperation. When they get it wrong, cynicism, paranoia, mistrust, and self-interest prevail.

In a toxic work environment, trust is replaced by fear or anxiety. When we fear making mistakes or fear losing our jobs if we miss our numbers, for example, the natural human reaction is to put ourselves before anyone or anything else—including ethics and sometimes the law. This is what happened at United Airlines on April 9, 2017. The airline had oversold the flight, a common practice. After they boarded all their ticketed passengers, the crew asked for volunteers to give up their seats for four United employees who needed to travel to work other flights. No passengers volunteered, so the crew did what the rule book said to do: they randomly selected passengers and demanded that they leave the aircraft. One of those passengers was Dr. David Dao, who was flying home to Louisville, Kentucky. A paying customer, Dr. Dao refused to leave his seat. And again the crew did what the rule book stated: they called security guards to forcibly remove him. In the ensuing melee, Dr. Dao lost two teeth, suffered a significant concussion, and got a broken nose at the hands of four security personnel. Other passengers captured the incident on video, which went viral online, forcing United Airlines to admit their failure and change their policies.

Policies, however, were only part of the problem. Other airlines have similar policies but don't end up assaulting paying customers in the course of following those policies. The bigger problem at United Airlines was the culture. It was a fear-based environment in which employees were more afraid to break a rule than to do the right thing. I can almost guarantee that no crew members on that flight thought what they were doing was a good idea or even fair practice. But given the culture in which they worked, I expect many defended their actions with "I was just following the rules" or "I was doing what the company told me to do."

Only when people feel trusted by and are able to trust their leadership; only when people feel they can make mistakes without fear of dismissal; and only when people feel they can break a rule because it's the right thing to do without fear of humiliation or retribution will a company ever inspire their people to work at their natural best—our most productive, innovative and co-operative selves. In a strong leadership environment, leaders don't trust their people to follow the rules—they trust them to know when to break the rules. Rules are there for when things run normally. But sometimes, when things go wrong, following the rules to the letter can actually make things worse.

In weak leadership environments, all the decision-making power is focused at the top. Leaders in these environments expect information to be pushed up to those in authority positions. Servant leaders do the opposite. They push authority down to those with the information. And in that kind of environment, people feel accountable for and trusted to do the job for which they've been trained without leaders putting undue pressure or stress on them or using fear to drive them.

If giving people authority makes an organization run better, then why not get rid of the leaders altogether? It seems like a logical conclusion. But leaders exist for a reason. For 40,000 of the 50,000 years our species has inhabited this planet, we lived in populations of about 150 people. And given the times in which we were living, there were some obvious challenges. If hunters and gatherers brought food back to the tribe, for example, who would get to eat first? I mean, if you were built like a professional wrestler, you could shove your way to the front of the line. However, if you were the "artist" of the family, you were one of those who got shoved to the side. But odds are, if you elbowed someone in the face that afternoon, they probably wouldn't wake you and alert you to danger that night. That's a bad system if we are stronger as a cooperative group than we are as individuals.

To avoid this reality and better equip us for cooperation, we evolved into hierarchical animals. We constantly assessed and judged those around us to figure out who was more dominant or senior. We tried to figure out who was alpha. Instead of fighting to be the first to eat, we would defer to the hierarchy. If we assessed that others were more senior in the social hierarchy, we would voluntarily step back and allow our alphas to eat first. And though we may not have had first choice of meat, we would have been guaranteed food and we wouldn't get an elbow in the face. This is a much better system to promote cooperation in the tribe.

Though the standards may be different in our modern day and age, we are still constantly assessing and judging each other, trying to figure out where we sit on the social hierarchy. Sometimes the standards are informal. Among scientists, for example, greater respect may be shown to the scientist who has been published more, won more awards, or made a more notable discovery than their peers. Among movie stars, the alpha treatment may be given to the actor with more awards or greater box office success. In most organizations, however, that hierarchy is more formal. We have titles—and even when we don't, there is still a hierarchy based on experience or levels of responsibility. For example, we all know a vice president is more senior than an intern.

This is why few people turn down promotions. Rising through the hierarchy often comes with perks—more money, a bigger office, or a better parking space. We show deference for the most senior people in organizations. Often, we are willing to do basic tasks for them simply because of their high status. If you're senior and you leave your coat in the other room, for example, someone will probably volunteer to get it for you. If you're junior and you leave your coat in the other room . . . you get your own coat. As Mel Brooks aptly pointed out in his film *History of the World, Part I*, "It's good to be the king."

However, these perks do not come for free. A deep-seated social contract is hardwired into all human beings. There is an expectation that when danger threatens, the alpha—the person who is often smarter, stronger, or more confident—will rush toward the danger to protect the tribe. It is this anthropological requirement that defines the essence of servant leadership. Leadership, it turns out, is not about being in charge. Leadership is about taking care of those in your charge. The closest thing I can equate to servant leadership is the responsibility of a parent. We all know Mom and Dad are in charge.

We all know they have all the authority. They set rules and enforce them. However, parents also have a responsibility to their children. Any decent parent would gladly sacrifice for them. Money, time, the kind of car they buy, the kind of vacation they take—the list goes on—are all elements of sacrifice: putting one's interests aside to benefit the life of another human being.

Just as we are morally offended by a parent who would put themselves before their child—leaving the child in a car while the parent goes gambling, for example—so, too, are we morally offended when people in leadership positions are willing to sacrifice the lives of their people to advance their personal interests. Trust cannot exist in a culture in which people fear—or know—that their leaders would sooner announce a round of layoffs to protect the numbers than sacrifice the numbers to protect the people. This is the reason why so many people are viscerally offended by some banking CEOs. It is not their huge bonuses or salaries that upset us—we are okay with our alphas getting paid more than we do. It's the knowledge that they would sacrifice their people to protect their salaries and bonuses that is so inconsistent with the anthropological requirements of leadership. Few if any of us would be offended if we heard Nelson Mandela was given a $50 million bonus. Few if any of us would be offended to learn that Mother Teresa was given a $100 million bonus. It's not the money that matters. It's the knowledge that our leader would, and does, sacrifice to protect us.

Our species started farming around 10,000 to 12,000 years ago. Only then could we sustain populations that were larger than about 150. Living and working at this scale, a scale for which we were not designed, produced a whole new set of leadership challenges that we continue to face today. These challenges make servant leadership not just more important but also the only viable, long-term solution.

All good leaders practice servant leadership. It is a teachable, learnable, and practicable skill. And the more the servant leader practices that skill—the more they create an environment in which people can feel vulnerable at work—the more trust, loyalty, and cooperation thrive. Where weak leaders demand trust be given to them, servant leaders inspire it.

Creating a space in which people can feel vulnerable means a person can walk into their boss's office to admit a mistake without fear of losing their job. It means someone can raise their hand and ask for help, admit they have been given a responsibility they don't feel prepared or knowledgeable enough to complete, or admit they are scared without any fear of humiliation or retribution. We trust that the servant leader will come running to our aid. This is what happens inside great organizations. In contrast, in a work environment that lacks good servant leaders, people will go out of their way to follow the rules at all costs, cover up mistakes, and deny accountability. Remember United Airlines?

The daily practice of servant leadership is less grand than people tend to think. It is based not on a series of transactions, but on the promise of being there when someone needs you most. Individuals don't fall in love because one is rich and the other stands to benefit. The same is true in an organization. A leader who offers money or the potential for future riches is not earning loyalty. They are setting up a transactional relationship that is likely to promote self-interest. Individuals don't fall in love simply because someone remembered their birthday or bought them flowers on Valentine's Day. The same is true in an organization. A few scattered, well-intentioned actions by a leader can't hurt, but they won't breed loyalty. They won't be enough to earn trust. Just like any relationship in which trust is the basis, it is the accumulation of a lot of little things that makes all the difference.

Servant leaders practice putting their interests aside in order to enhance the lives of those around them. For example, if you're standing in an elevator, running slightly late for a meeting, and just as the doors start closing you see someone running toward the elevator, what do you do? The act of holding the doors for someone even if you're running late is an act of servant leadership. If you pour yourself the last cup of coffee at work and instead of putting the empty pot back you spend a few minutes making another pot of coffee, that is an act of servant leadership. If one of your people has missed their numbers three quarters in a row and instead of walking into their office and saying, "You have to make your fourth quarter numbers otherwise I don't know what's going to happen," you walk into their office and say, "Are you okay? You missed your numbers again. I'm worried about you," that level of empathy—concern for the person before the numbers—is an act of servant leadership.

As I said before, servant leadership is not a rank or an event. It is a practice, and the servant leader will remain a student for their entire life. They will always want to learn more about the practice, talk about it, read about it, and hear what others have to say about it. They will constantly be on the hunt for new tactics, new perspectives, new ways to hone their skills. Every parent, partner, spouse, and servant leader knows that the act of caring for another is very hard work, the results of which are impossible to predict according to a timeline. The impact of servant leadership isn't conveniently parsed into quarters. It is a human experience.

Like going to the gym or eating healthily, servant leadership is a lifestyle. We can get into shape if we go to the gym regularly and improve our diets.

And we can turn an unhealthy culture into a thriving one, filled with trust and cooperation. But we have to commit to the lifestyle. Once we achieve our goals, to stay fit we have to keep working out and eating smart. And to maintain a servant leadership culture we must keep caring, serving, trusting, and earning trust.

Though someone may choose servant leadership for the results, the reason we continue to practice the discipline is for the joy of the journey.

*Simon Sinek (www.startwithwhy.com) is an unshakable optimist and the author of three bestselling books:* Start with Why, Leaders Eat Last, Together Is Better, *and his most recent,* Find Your Why. *A trained ethnographer, Simon has a bold goal to help build a world in which the vast majority of people go home every day feeling fulfilled by their work. His first TED Talk in 2009 is the third most watched talk of all time on TED.com.*

Part Two

# Elements of
# Servant Leadership

## Different Points of View about Servant Leadership

- In Marshall Goldsmith's essay, "One Question Every Servant Leader Should Ask," he emphasizes that great leaders are willing servants of people, organizations, and causes. To help these leaders stay focused on making a positive difference, he has developed a simple formulation to help them avoid the pervasive triggers that would pull them off course.

- Brené Brown, in "In the Service of Others: When Leaders Dare to Rehumanize Work," introduces the concept that servant leadership cannot exist in a culture of shame—of blaming, gossiping, bullying, humiliation—primarily because shame breeds fear and the foundation of servant leadership is courage.

- Tom Mullins, in "Servant Leaders Celebrate Others," shows why accentuating the positive and celebrating success is a key factor in servant leadership.

- James Ferrell, in "The Servant Leader's Focus," stresses that for servant leaders service should not be the true focus. Every act of service is a behavioral extension of the real root of servant leadership: a caring, outward mindset.

- In Chris Hodges's essay, "What You See Determines How You Serve," he illustrates how servant leaders serve people differently because they see people differently. People are here not to be judged, but to be loved.

- Craig Groeschel, in "Compassion: The Heart of Servant Leadership," emphasizes that compassion is not a feeling; it is an action. And a simple act of compassion from one human being to another can change a life.

- Patrick Lencioni tells us "Why Ideal Team Players Make Great Servant Leaders"—it's because the three primary values of an ideal team player are three of the most essential qualities of an effective servant leader.

- Laurie Beth Jones, in "The Servant Leader's Identity," points out the importance of understanding yourself and others so that you can get clear about your leadership style and how to relate to the people around you.

- Henry Cloud, in "The Four Corners of the Leader's Universe," helps you answer the question "Where are my people today—inside their hearts, minds, and souls?" so that you can better serve them and help them succeed.

# Chapter 10

# One Question Every Servant Leader Should Ask

## MARSHALL GOLDSMITH

*When Marshall Goldsmith was in his early twenties and finishing his doctoral degree at UCLA, he was asked to teach a course at California American University, where I was teaching with founder Paul Hersey. Marshall and I immediately became soul mates and I have admired his teaching and writing skills ever since. I think you'll see why I'm a big fan of his after reading his essay.* —KB

A DECISION MAKER, a game changer, a force to reckon with, a wielder of power: this is a leader in the popular imagination. As an executive coach who has been helping successful leaders achieve positive, lasting change in behavior for more than thirty-five years, I have worked with many influential people who fit this description. The best of them understand that, for a servant leader, power is beside the point.

For example, one of the most inspiring servant leaders I have ever met is Frances Hesselbein, president and CEO of the Frances Hesselbein Leadership Institute and former CEO of the Girl Scouts of the USA. Her motto is *To serve is to live.* This kind of humility may seem at odds with the image of the heroic, powerful leader. But as my friend Frances has pointed out, great leaders are willing servants of people, organizations, and causes. Instead of worrying about how powerful they are or what position they hold, these leaders focus on what others need. Without the distractions of ego, they can see the clearest path to positive outcomes. (For more on Frances Hesselbein, see the essay by Jim Dittmar in Part Four of this book.)

Maintaining this clarity is a challenge, as any tested leader knows. In competitive situations or organizations, staying committed to a servant leadership mentality is a monumental challenge that requires daily, if not hourly, attention. To keep my coaching clients on track, I developed a simple formulation—one that helps them focus on making a positive difference instead of demonstrating their own superiority. It can help you, too. Follow it and you will dramatically shrink your daily volume of stress, unpleasant debate, and wasted time, while getting closer to the results you want.

The next time you run into a conflict, ask yourself this question:

AM I WILLING
AT THIS TIME
TO MAKE THE INVESTMENT REQUIRED
TO MAKE A POSITIVE DIFFERENCE
ON THIS TOPIC?

It pops into my head so often each day that I've turned the first five words into an acronym: AIWATT (it rhymes with "say what"). Like the physician's principle "First, do no harm," it doesn't require you to do anything other than merely avoid doing something foolish.

Perhaps you're thinking *I don't need to repeat a simple question to remember to make a positive difference.* But I believe all of us need exactly this kind of help. In *Triggers: Becoming the Person You Want to Be,*[1] I make the case that relying on structure—even something as simple as the AIWATT question—is key to changing our leadership behavior. In every waking hour we are bombarded by *triggers*—people, events, and circumstances that have the potential to change us. We often fail to appreciate just how much these triggers affect us, and how difficult it is to fend them off without some kind of support.

AIWATT is just one of the tactics I suggest. Of course, it isn't a universal panacea for all our interpersonal problems, but it has a specific utility. It's a reminder that our environment tempts us many times a day to engage in pointless arguments and prove ourselves the winner. We can do something about this unfortunate tendency—by doing nothing. In our Western, action-focused culture, that sounds like laziness or failure. But it can be a surprisingly powerful position to take. I'll explain using two complementary insights: a Buddhist parable and an observation from Peter Drucker, one of my heroes and the father of modern management theory.

## The Parable of the Empty Boat

A young farmer laboriously paddled his boat up the river to deliver his produce to the village. It was a hot day, and he wanted to make his delivery and get home before dark. As he looked ahead, he spied another vessel, heading rapidly downstream toward his boat. He rowed furiously to get out of the way, but it didn't seem to help.

He shouted, "Change direction! You are going to hit me!" to no avail—the vessel hit his boat with a violent thud. He cried out, "You idiot! How could you manage to hit my boat in the middle of this wide river?"

As he glared into the boat, seeking out the individual responsible for the accident, he realized no one was there. He had been screaming at an empty boat that had broken free of its moorings and was floating downstream with the current.

We behave one way when we believe there is another person at the helm. We can blame that stupid, uncaring person for our misfortune. This blaming permits us to get angry, act out, assign blame, and play the victim. We behave more calmly when we learn that it's an empty boat. With no available scapegoat, we can't get upset. We make peace with the fact that our misfortune was the result of fate or bad luck. We may even laugh at the absurdity of a random unmanned boat finding a way to collide with us in a vast body of water.

The moral: There's *never* anyone in the other boat. We are always screaming at an empty vessel. An empty boat isn't targeting us. And neither are all the people creating the sour notes in the soundtrack of our day.

I like to make this point in leadership classes with a simple exercise. I'll ask a random audience member to think of one person who makes them feel bad, angry, or crazy. "Can you envision that person?" I ask.

A nod, a disgusted face, and then, "Yes."

"How much sleep is that person losing over you tonight?" I ask.

"None."

"Who is being punished here? Who is doing the punishing?" I ask.

The answer inevitably is, "Me and me."

I end the exercise with a simple reminder that getting mad at people for being who they are makes as much sense as getting mad at a chair for being a chair. The chair cannot help but be a chair, and people cannot help but be themselves. If there's a person who drives you crazy, you don't have to like, agree with, or respect them; just accept them for being who they are.

## False Positives

The empty boat parable is a useful metaphor for understanding how others affect us. To grasp how we affect others, I turn to Drucker, who has been an enormous influence on my life and work. "Our mission in life should be to make a positive difference," he said, "not to prove how smart or right we are." It sounds so obvious—given the choice, who wouldn't opt to make a positive difference?

But Drucker is highlighting two notions that we have trouble holding in our heads simultaneously. When we have the opportunity to demonstrate our brainpower, we're rarely thinking about a positive result for the other people in the room. We're actually issuing what I like to call *false positives*—making statements to upgrade ourselves, often at the expense of others. They appear in many forms:

- *Pedantry*: A subordinate makes a grammatical error in a presentation—using *who* instead of *whom*—and you correct him. Smart, perhaps, if the objective is punctilious grammar—but hardly a contribution that improves the room's vibe.
- *Saying "I told you so"*: You tell your wife the two of you need to leave the house at least sixty minutes in advance to make an eight o'clock Broadway show. She delays, and you arrive late. You proceed to ruin her night in proportion to how much she ruined yours.
- *Moral superiority*: You tell a friend or loved one that she shouldn't smoke, that he doesn't need another beer, or that you would have taken a faster route home. How often do these efforts elicit a genuine thank you, or anything but an eye roll?
- *Complaining*: The average American worker spends fifteen hours a month complaining about upper management, making it one of the more popular workplace activities. When you complain, you're disagreeing with what someone else decided, planned, or did. By definition, you're being disagreeable and adding the implication that you would have done better. It's rarely a positive contribution, especially if you do it behind people's backs rather than to their faces.

From wake-up to bedtime, when we're in contact with another human being, we face the option of being helpful, hurtful, or neutral. If we're not paying attention, it's easy to choose hurtful—especially if in the process we prove we're smarter, better, or more right than the other guy. Often we're not aware that we're being counterproductive. Nor is it our intention to be cruel, as if we have chosen to speak our minds and damn the consequences. Consequences don't enter the picture. We're only thinking about elevating ourselves. We're trying to prove how smart we are to an empty boat!

This is where AIWATT is useful, if only to create a split-second delay in our potentially prideful, cynical, judgmental, argumentative, and selfish responses to our environment. The delay gives us time to consider a more positive response. AIWATT helps us after a trigger creates an impulse and before we exhibit behavior we may later regret. The nineteen-word text deserves close analysis. Each part is something aspiring servant leaders should know:

- *Am I willing* implies that we are exercising volition—taking responsibility—rather than surfing along the waves of inertia that otherwise rule our day. We are asking "Do I really want to do this?"
- *At this time* reminds us that we're operating in the present. Circumstances will differ later on, demanding a different response. The only issue is what we're facing now.
- *To make the investment required* reminds us that responding to others is work—an expenditure of time, energy, and opportunity. And like any investment, our resources are finite. We are asking "Is this really the best use of my time?"
- *To make a positive difference* places the emphasis on the kinder, gentler side of our nature. It's a reminder that we can help create either a better us or a better world. If we're not accomplishing one or the other, why are we getting involved?
- *On this topic* focuses us on the matter at hand. We can't solve every problem. The time we spend on topics where we can't make a positive difference is stolen from topics where we can.

Like closing our office door so people hesitate before they knock, asking ourselves "Am I willing, at this time, to make the investment required to make a positive difference on this topic?" gives us a thin barrier of breathing room—time enough to inhale, exhale, and reflect on whether the outcome we seek is a true positive that is intended for the benefit of others, or a false positive that is intended to polish our own image. For servant leaders who want to make serving others their primary mission, that's a vital distinction.

*Marshall Goldsmith (www.marshallgoldsmith.com) has been recognized by Thinkers50, Global Gurus, Fast Company, and Inc. as the world's leading executive coach. He is the author of the New York Times bestsellers Triggers,*

*What Got You Here Won't Get You There, Mojo, and several other books. He received his PhD from UCLA Anderson School of Management. His client list is a who's who of the world's CEOs.*

## Note

1. Marshall Goldsmith and Mark Reiter, *Triggers: Becoming the Person You Want to Be* (New York: Crown, 2015).

# Chapter 11

# In the Service of Others

## *When Leaders Dare to Rehumanize Work*

### B R E N É   B R O W N

*I first got acquainted with Brené Brown when people told me about her TED Talk on "The Power of Vulnerability." As I watched it, I immediately made the connection between the importance of vulnerability and effective servant leadership. Brené and I agree that having a servant heart is definitely an inside-out job. In this essay she details how, when heart-led leadership prevails in an organization, shame will not be a factor. —KB*

GIVEN WHAT I'VE learned from research and what I've observed over the past decade as I've worked with leaders from companies of all sizes and types, I believe we have to completely reexamine the idea of engagement. To reignite creativity, innovation, and learning, leaders must dare to rehumanize education and work. This means understanding how scarcity is affecting the way we lead and work, learning how to engage with vulnerability, and recognizing and combating shame.

Make no mistake: honest conversations about vulnerability and shame are disruptive. The reason we're not having these conversations in our organizations is that they shine light in dark corners. Once there is language, awareness, and understanding, turning back is almost impossible and carries with it severe consequences. We all want to dare greatly. If you give us a glimpse into that possibility, we'll hold on to it as our vision. It can't be taken away.

Sir Ken Robinson speaks to the power of making this shift in his appeal to leaders to replace the outdated idea that human organizations should work like machines with a metaphor that captures the realities of humanity. In his book *Out of Our Minds: Learning to Be Creative,*[1] Robinson writes: "However seductive the machine metaphor may be for industrial production, human organizations are not actually mechanisms and people are not components in them. People have values and feelings, perceptions, opinions, motivations, and biographies, whereas cogs and sprockets do not. An organization is not the physical facilities within which it operates; it is the networks of people in it."

## Recognizing and Combating Shame

Servant leadership and shame culture cannot coexist for a simple reason: the foundation of servant leadership is courage and shame breeds fear. Shame crushes our tolerance for vulnerability, thereby killing engagement, innovation, creativity, productivity, and trust. And worst of all, if we don't know what we're looking for, shame can ravage our organizations before we see one outward sign of a problem. Shame works like termites in a house. It's hidden in the dark behind the walls and constantly eating away at our infrastructure, until one day the stairs suddenly crumble. Only then do we realize that it's only a matter of time before the walls come tumbling down.

In the same way that a casual walk around our house won't reveal a termite problem, a stroll through an office or a school won't necessarily reveal a shame problem. Or at least we hope it's not that obvious. If it is—if we see a manager berating an employee or a teacher shaming a student—the problem is already acute and more than likely has been happening for a long time. In most cases, though, we have to know what we're looking for when we assess an organization for signs that shame may be an issue.

## Signs That Shame Has Permeated a Culture

Blaming, gossiping, favoritism, name-calling, and harassment are all behavior cues that shame has permeated a culture. A more obvious sign is when shame becomes an outright management tool. Is there evidence of people in leadership roles bullying others, criticizing subordinates in front of colleagues, delivering public reprimands, or setting up reward systems that intentionally belittle, shame, or humiliate people?

I've never been to a shame-free organization. I'm not saying it doesn't exist, but I doubt it. In fact, once I've explained how shame works, I normally have several leaders approach me and explain that they use shame on a daily basis. Most ask how to change that practice—but a few proudly say, "It works." The best case scenario is that it's a limited or contained problem rather than a cultural norm. This is also true in schools. Approximately 85 percent of the men and women we interviewed for our shame research could recall a school incident from their childhood that was so shaming it changed how they thought of themselves as learners. What makes this even more haunting is that approximately half of those recollections were what I refer to as *creativity scars*. The research participants could point to a specific incident where they were told or shown that they weren't good writers, artists, musicians, dancers, or something creative. This helps explain why the gremlins are so powerful when it comes to creativity and innovation at work. We're afraid to reopen wounds by sharing new ideas and taking creative risks.

When we see shame being used as a management tool in the workplace (again, that means bullying, criticism in front of colleagues, public reprimands, or reward systems that intentionally belittle people), we need to take direct action because it means that we've got an infestation on our hands. And we need to remember that this doesn't just happen overnight. Equally important to keep in mind is that shame rolls downhill. If employees are constantly having to navigate shame, you can bet they're passing it on to their customers, colleagues, and even families.

So, if it's happening and it can be isolated to a specific unit, work team, or person, it has to be addressed immediately *and without shame*. We learn shame in our families of origin, and many people grow up believing that it's an effective and efficient way to manage people, run a classroom, and parent. For that reason, shaming someone who's using shame is not helpful. But doing nothing is equally dangerous, not only for the people who are targets of the shaming but also for the entire organization. Shame begets shame.

Several years ago a man came up to me after an event and said, "Interview me! Please! I'm a financial adviser and you wouldn't believe what happens in my office." When I met Don for the interview, he told me that in his organization you choose your office each quarter based on your quarterly results: the person with the best results chooses first and sends the person in the desired office packing.

He shook his head, and his voice cracked a bit when he said, "Given that I've had the best numbers for the past six quarters, you'd think I'd like that. But I don't. I absolutely hate it. It's a miserable environment." He then told me how after the previous quarterly results were in, his boss walked into his office, closed the door, and told him that he had to move offices.

"At first I thought my numbers had dropped. Then he told me that he didn't care if I had the best numbers or if I liked my office; the point was to terrorize the other guys. He said, 'Busting their balls in public builds character. It's motivating.'"

Before the end of our interview, he told me he was job hunting. "I'm good at my job and even enjoy it, but I didn't sign up to terrorize people. I never knew why it felt so lousy, but after hearing you talk, now I do. It's shame. It's worse than high school. I'll find a better place to work, and you can be darn sure I'm taking my clients with me."

In *I Thought It Was Just Me*,[2] I tell the following story about Sylvia, an event planner in her thirties who jumped right into our interview by saying, "I wish you could have interviewed me six months ago. I was a different person. I was so stuck in shame." When I asked her what she meant, she explained she had heard about my research from a friend and volunteered to be interviewed because she felt her life had been changed by shame. She had recently had an important breakthrough when she found herself on the "losers list" at work.

Apparently, after two years of what her employer called "outstanding winner's work," she had made her first big mistake. The mistake cost her agency a major client. Her boss's response was to put her on the losers list. She said, "In one minute I went from being on the winners board to being at the top of the losers list." I guess I must have winced when Sylvia referred to the losers list because, without my remarking at all, she said, "I know, it's terrible. My boss has these two big dry erase boards outside of his office. One is the winners list, and one is for the losers." She said for weeks she could barely function. She lost her confidence and started missing work. Shame, anxiety, and fear took over. After a difficult three-week period, she quit her job and went to work for another agency.

Shame can only rise so far in any system before people disengage to protect themselves. When we're disengaged we don't show up, we don't contribute, and we stop caring. On the far end of the spectrum, disengagement allows people to rationalize all kinds of unethical behavior including lying, stealing, and cheating. In the cases of Don and Sylvia, they didn't just disengage; they quit—and took their talent to competitors.

## The Blame Game

Here's the best way to think about the relationship between shame and blame: if blame is driving, shame is riding shotgun. In organizations, schools, and families, blaming and finger-pointing are often symptoms of shame. Shame researchers June Tangney and Ronda Dearing explain that in shame-bound relationships, people "measure carefully, weigh, and assign blame." They write,

"In the face of any negative outcome, large or small, *someone* or *something* must be found responsible and held accountable. There's no notion of water under the bridge." They go on to say, "After all, if *someone* must be to blame and it's not me, it must be you! From blame comes shame. And then hurt, denial, anger, and retaliation."[3]

Blame is simply the discharging of pain and discomfort. We blame when we're uncomfortable and experience pain—when we're vulnerable, angry, hurt, in shame, grieving. There's nothing productive about blame, and it often involves shaming someone or just being mean. If blame is a pattern in your culture, then shame needs to be addressed as an issue.

## Cover-Up Culture

Related to blame is the issue of cover-ups. Just like blame is a sign of shame-based organizations, cover-up cultures depend on shame to keep folks quiet. When the culture of an organization mandates that it is more important to protect the reputation of a system and those in power than it is to protect the basic human dignity of individuals or communities, you can be certain that shame is systemic, money drives ethics, and accountability is dead. This is true in all systems, from corporations, nonprofits, universities, and governments, to churches, schools, families, and sports programs. If you think back on any major incidents fueled by cover-ups, you'll see this pattern.

In an organizational culture of servant leadership where respect and the dignity of individuals are held as the highest values, shame and blame don't work as management styles. There is no leading by fear. Empathy is a valued asset, accountability is an expectation rather than an exception, and the primal human need for belonging is not used as leverage and social control. We can't control the behavior of individuals; however, we can cultivate organizational cultures where bad behaviors are not tolerated and people are held accountable for protecting what matters most: human beings.

The four best strategies for building shame-resilient organizations are:

1. Encourage servant leaders to courageously facilitate honest conversations about shame and cultivate shame-resilient cultures.
2. Make a conscientious effort to see where shame might be functioning in the organization and how it might even be creeping into the way we engage with our coworkers and students.
3. A critical shame resilience strategy is normalizing. Leaders and managers can cultivate engagement by helping people know what

to expect. What are common struggles? How have other people dealt with them? What have your experiences been?
4. Train all employees on the profound dangers of shame culture and teach them how to give and receive feedback in a way that fosters growth and engagement.

We won't solve the complex issues we're facing today without creativity, innovation, and engaged learning. As servant leaders, we can't afford to let our discomfort with the topic of shame get in the way of recognizing and combating it in our schools and workplaces.

*Brené Brown is a research professor at the University of Houston where she holds the Huffington Foundation-Brené Brown Endowed Chair at the Graduate College of Social Work. She has spent the past sixteen years studying courage, vulnerability, shame, and empathy and is the author of three #1* New York Times *bestsellers:* The Gifts of Imperfection, Daring Greatly, *and* Rising Strong. *Her latest book is* Braving the Wilderness: The Quest for True Belonging and the Courage to Stand Alone.

## Notes

1. Ken Robinson, *Out of Our Minds: Learning to Be Creative* (London: John Wiley and Sons, 2001).
2. Brené Brown, *I Thought It Was Just Me (but It Isn't)* (New York: Gotham, 2007).
3. June Price Tangney and Ronda L. Dearing, *Shame and Guilt* (New York: Guildford, 2002).

# Chapter 12

# Servant Leaders
# Celebrate Others

## TOM MULLINS

*I met Tom Mullins when we were speakers at a servant leadership conference. He is such a positive, energetic person that I was drawn to him right away. When I heard his feelings about celebration, I was even more of a fan. Why? Because of all the things that I've ever taught over the years, the one concept I would never give up is my feeling that the key to developing people and creating great organizations is to catch people doing things right. In this essay, Tom shows why accenting the positive and celebrating success is a key element of servant leadership. —KB*

ONE OF THE most important things I've learned from being both a football coach and a pastor is that you cannot celebrate your team's victories often enough. People thrive when they are recognized and affirmed for their contributions to your organization's success. As a matter of fact, your team members' longevity and continued engagement in the execution of your vision is directly influenced by your ability to celebrate them in meaningful ways.

Accordingly, servant leaders understand the impact celebration has on the health of their organization. They make celebration a high priority in their leadership and are always looking for new ways to acknowledge their team's success. They understand that when the team experiences a win, they must pause to celebrate that win before they can expect the team to move on to the next goal.

For my book *The Leadership Game*,[1] I had the privilege of interviewing Coach Gene Stallings, the former national championship coach at the University of Alabama. He told me a story about overhearing one of his assistant coaches ripping into the team after they had *won* a game. Coach Stallings ended up letting the assistant coach go because his philosophy and behavior didn't represent the Alabama organization's emphasis on celebration. Sadly, the assistant coach was more interested in highlighting what could have gone better rather than celebrating what went well.

That's a valuable lesson for all of us in leadership. When you celebrate your team's wins, big or small, you are affirming the effort made to reach team goals. Winning calls for celebration!

I have found there are five benefits of celebration: it demonstrates that you value your team, it reinforces core organizational values, it builds team morale, it increases retention and productivity, and it is a great recruiting tool. Let's investigate each of these benefits.

## Celebration Demonstrates You Value Your Team

Celebrating your people demonstrates that you value them and you acknowledge their part in making the victory possible. Simply put, your people need to feel valued and affirmed by their leader.

In a world where so many people focus on the negative and beat others down for their imperfections, servant leaders need to look for any way possible to show care and gratitude. It's been said that for every critical comment we receive, it takes nine affirming comments to balance the negative effect of that one criticism. A servant leader is invested in nurturing the positive qualities and contributions of their team members by recognizing and celebrating the diversity of their particular strengths.

When the affirmation of others becomes a habit in your leadership style, it quickly becomes part of the culture among all of your team members. When they see your example of looking for opportunities to celebrate others, they will soon find themselves doing the same for their teammates. This is a win-win for everyone!

## Celebration Reinforces Core Organizational Values

Celebration also has the benefit of reinforcing your organization's core values, which in turn helps shape its culture and environment. The things you celebrate as a leader send a clear message to your team about what you deem to be important qualities of a successful team player. For example, when you acknowledge the hard work and productivity of an individual team member, your team will know that hard work and productivity are important to you.

Servant leaders are always mindful that they must live out these core values first. You cannot expect your team to share your stated values if your actions do not reflect these values. If you say you value integrity, you must show your team members, through your daily choices, that you have this value. Once you've adopted the principle of integrity in your own life, look for this quality in your team members and celebrate it publicly when you see it.

At Christ Fellowship, the church I cofounded with my wife, Donna, we use our weekly staff meeting to affirm the outstanding job our team members do in ministering to others through the lens of our core values. We always look for ways to praise one another and then tie that praise directly back to what we value. This reminds our team of the importance of modeling our core values for our congregation so they, too, can live a life fully immersed in the key principles and precepts of God's Word.

My friend Jerry Anderson instituted a program called Virtual High Five where his employees try to catch each other living out the values of their organization. They post on a virtual bulletin board the actions they witness, and these praisings are celebrated at department as well as all-company meetings. Jerry's program clearly articulates the qualities of a successful team player and the virtues his company stands on. When he acknowledges these qualities and virtues through celebration, it naturally reinforces them with his people.

## Celebration Builds Team Morale

Celebration increases team members' morale when they get to enjoy victories together. Celebration is a high motivator because everyone enjoys the thrill of victory and wants to experience it as often as possible!

I have found that one of the most motivating things I can do to serve and celebrate my team members is to take time to learn how each person is uniquely motivated. It is the leader's responsibility to learn what each team member values and how that person prefers to celebrate.

Some people respond best to public acknowledgment, some to a handwritten note of gratitude. Others value face time with me, so I make sure to pop in on them, praise their efforts, and point out how their particular assistance made the difference in a recent win. Still others respond best to gifts like a day off or a fun corporate social event like a special lunch together. Many are motivated by pay increases—so when the budget permits, that's a good way to send a message that their hard work has not gone unnoticed and that they are a valuable asset to our team.

A servant leader also tries to regularly celebrate the contributions of the unsung heroes on the team. It takes an entire team—each person functioning within their own skill set and giving their best at every level—to create a win. Accordingly, it's important that you acknowledge everyone's position and participation, not just the people on the front lines.

As you can imagine, one department that rarely gets public accolades in the church is the accounting department. Because of this, Donna and I try to be intentional about celebrating that team's hard work and behind-the-scenes ministry. We once took everyone in the department to lunch at a nice restaurant at a local mall, where we talked with them and listened to them share about their lives. Then we gave each person $100 and told them they had to spend every penny on themselves, right then and there. When they returned, it was fun to watch their faces light up as they shared how they spent the money. I believe it increased morale in their department for months to come. In fact, many of our accounting staff still talk about how special that was for them. It was a small gesture but it spoke highly of our love for them and gratitude for their contribution.

Find out what motivates your people and clearly demonstrates your gratitude, and then do it regularly!

## Celebration Increases Retention and Productivity

When you are deliberate about celebrating all of your team members, you will find that retention and productivity naturally increase. The U.S. Department of Labor recently reported that 46 percent of employees who leave their jobs do it because they feel unappreciated. I believe one of the ways this statistic can be easily reversed is by leaders encouraging their people by celebrating their roles on the team.

In addition, people are more productive in positive surroundings. Celebration creates an environment where people want to work to meet the organization's goals. Simply stated, what gets celebrated gets done! The more you affirm your team, the more productive they are. A servant leader who is intentional about celebrating will have a happy, hardworking team.

## Celebration Is a Great Recruiting Tool

Celebration also serves as a great recruiting tool for your organization. I've found that when a recruit witnesses the ways we celebrate wins together as a team, they are eager to be a part of what's happening here. Celebration is attractive partly due to its rarity in many organizations. In contrast, servant leaders always prioritize celebration.

Being intentional about seeking out the contributions of your team members and then elevating them publicly requires humility on the part of the leader. I firmly believe it is the duty of a servant leader to create wins for their people and then to celebrate those wins together. You have to forgo your own praise and set your people up for success. And if your focus as a servant leader is to position your people for victory, it will mean more to you in the long run if you celebrate their participation and effort.

Do whatever it takes to provide clear vision, direction, training, and oversight so that your people can accomplish attainable goals—and when they do, be the first person in line to celebrate their win. Your staff will be all the more engaged when they see that you care enough to invest in them and acknowledge that their contributions have contributed to the organization's success.

*Tom Mullins is founding pastor of Christ Fellowship Church, a multisite church of more than forty thousand people meeting on nine campuses in South Florida and online. Previously, he was a successful football coach at both the high school and collegiate levels. He and Donna, his wife of more than fifty years, are cofounders of Place of Hope and Place of Hope International, which serve the needs of abused and neglected children. Tom has written four books including* Passing the Leadership Baton *and* The Leadership Game.

## Note

1.  Tom Mullins, *The Leadership Game* (Nashville: Thomas Nelson, 2005).

# Chapter 13

# The Servant Leader's Focus

## JAMES FERRELL

*I've never met James Ferrell, but I've admired Arbinger Institute from a distance—and their books up close. I think when you read James's essay, you'll realize why I was excited to have him participate in this book—and why I'm thinking of giving a copy of the book to my garbage man! —KB*

I DISLIKE THE word "service."

There, I said it. And I believe it needs to be said in a book about servant leadership. As odd as it might sound, I believe that a focus on service is incompatible with servant leadership. True servant leaders don't focus on service; they focus on something else entirely. In this chapter, I will explore the kind of nonservice focus that forms the foundation of servant leadership.

## Two Tones or Mindsets

Years ago, I recorded a podcast for Arbinger Institute in which I drew an analogy between tonal spoken languages, such as Chinese, and life itself.

When speaking Chinese, the speaker's intonation determines the meaning of every word and phrase. In Cantonese, for example, there are nine different tonal variations. Two of these are too subtle for Westerners, so foreigners usually learn just seven intonations. These intonations begin with three variations—low, mid, and high—in the initial pitch the speaker uses when uttering a word. There are additional variations within each pitch level: the low pitch can stay steady, rise, or fall; the mid-level pitch can stay steady or rise; and the high-level pitch can stay steady or fall. The meaning of every Chinese utterance depends on these tones. For example, consider the following Cantonese sentence: "Go go go go go go go go go go." Its meaning, when uttered with different tones, is "That tall man over there is taller than his older brother." No joke. The speaker's tone determines the meaning of everything.

Without realizing it, we too are living in the middle of a tonal language—a tonal system that determines the meaning of everything we do and say. One of the insights contained within Arbinger's work is that we can see others either as people who matter like we matter (we call this an *outward mindset*), or as objects (an *inward mindset*).

## Mindset and Impact

These different mindsets operate the way the different tones operate in Chinese—they change the meaning of everything we say. For example, I may tell a colleague, "I appreciate the effort you put into your presentation." If I am seeing that colleague as a person when I say this, she will likely interpret my comment as a kind compliment regarding her effort. However, she may experience the comment differently—and attach entirely different meaning to it—if she senses I have an inward mindset and am seeing her as an object. In that case, she may interpret the meaning as "It's about time you put effort into something around here!" Although I utter the same words, my underlying mindset—my tone—can change the meaning of what I have said.

This brings me to what I think is troubling about the word "service." What is true about the meaning and impact of our words is equally true of the meaning and impact of our actions—even our acts of service. We can perform almost any action with an inward or an outward mindset. When our mindsets are outward, we are serving *others*. When our mindsets are inward, on the other hand, we are serving *ourselves*. This inward orientation corrupts everything—our self-understanding, our views of others, our intentions, and even our service. This means that the foundation of servant leadership can never be a focus on mere actions—even on actions that may seem, on their face, to be for the benefit of others. True servant leaders focus on something else.

## The Servant Leader's Focus

What does a servant leader focus on? I'll answer that question by returning to the story of the podcast. In that presentation, I invited people not to speak *about* Arbinger with others, but rather to put more effort into simply living in the right tone, which I called *speaking Arbinger*. My invitation was to focus less on talking about Arbinger concepts and more on living the tonal language of seeing people as people.

After the podcast, a robust discussion broke out about it on social media channels. People generally were complimentary of the ideas I shared, but then one gentleman completely shattered my whole argument.

The man said that after listening to the podcast, he resolved to apply what he had learned in his interactions with his wife. Instead of speaking *about* Arbinger concepts with her, he resolved to focus on simply *speaking Arbinger* with her—that is, on simply seeing her as a person. However, he said that this new approach wasn't yielding any better results than before. Then he shared an epiphany—an insight that completely changed the nature of his interactions and relationship with his wife. He said, "I realized that instead of focusing on *speaking Arbinger*, I needed to focus instead on *speaking Becky*."

If you think about those in your life whom you would call servant leaders, you will see the truth in this gentleman's insight. What distinguishes true servant leaders and makes them so precious to us is not that they *do* things for us—although they do. No, we are grateful to them because we know that they *see and value* us. We are, as it were, Becky, and the servant leaders in our lives have cared enough about us to learn to speak our language.

## The Example of My Garbage Man

Let me share an example of one such person in my life: the man who collects the trash in our neighborhood every week—the inspiring servant leader who is my garbage man.

Our trash is collected on Friday mornings. I am the one in our home primarily responsible for making sure that our trash bins get out to the street in time. However, one Friday morning, as I heard the garbage truck pull into our cul-de-sac, I realized that I had forgotten to take the bins out. Panicked, I hurriedly threw on some clothes and hustled down the stairs. However, before I reached the front door, I heard the truck pull away. *A week with no room in our garbage bins!* I grimaced, feeling frustrated. I glanced out the front window as the truck rolled down our street. There in front of our house were our two bins—empty! My frustration washed away in an instant. I was overwhelmed with a feeling of gratitude for our amazing neighbors.

A few weeks later, I was talking with two of those neighbors—David, whose home is directly across from ours in the cul-de-sac, and Randy, who lives around the corner. David was telling a story.

"About a month ago on a Friday morning, I noticed the garbage truck parked in front of my house. The driver was walking around and picking up trash that was all over the street. I remembered that I had overpacked my bins the night before and I guess maybe there was a wind storm, or some kind of animal got in the bin and made a mess. Either way, here was the truck driver picking up a mess that I had caused. When he was finished, he climbed back into his truck, emptied the bins, and drove away," David said.

"As I watched the garbage truck go, I realized I had never even acknowledged the man—not even just then—and I felt ashamed. I decided that the next week I'd go out and thank him and give him a gift.

"So the next Friday, the truck got here earlier than I had expected. I ran to put on some shoes and rushed out the front door but I was too late—the truck was already rounding the corner. I grabbed my coat and ran out into the snow to catch the truck. Rounding the corner, I saw the truck parked in front of Randy's house. Then I saw the driver wheeling Randy's two garbage bins down from the side of his house!"

"Wait!" Randy interjected. "The garbage man did that? I remember that morning. I thought the neighbors had helped us out."

Of course, listening to the story, I had the same reaction. The driver must have helped me with *my* bins as well. Our neighbors are great, but it was the garbage man who had helped me.

Now, you might think that David, Randy, and I, and the others in our neighborhood had it made at this point. After all, we wouldn't even have to take our trash out to the street anymore; the garbage man would do it for us! But that isn't at all how we responded. On the contrary—suddenly I felt very motivated to make our driver's life as easy as possible. I *never* wanted to forget to take my bins to the street again—not just because I didn't want to have to go another week without room for our trash, but also because I didn't want to make things harder for our driver. Until that moment, for example, I had never cared a lick about making sure to leave ample room— five feet or so—between bins, which I had heard we were to do. But from the moment David shared his story, I began pacing off space between my bins every Thursday evening so that our driver wouldn't have any trouble emptying them.

In a way, our garbage man trained an entire neighborhood to make his life easier. How did he do this? *By making our lives easier*—which is the essence of what servant leaders do. And they don't tire of doing it, as they would if they just focused on all the tasks they must perform for others. What a drag it is to do things for those we view as mere objects! And yet how invigorating it is to do the same things for those we see and value as people.

## Counterfeit Service vs. the Real Thing

At times, we might be tempted to congratulate ourselves for all the good we do for others—for all the service we render. Perhaps, like me, you have too often been this counterfeit kind of servant leader—the person who wants to be noticed, seen, appreciated, and thanked. This is why it is almost an over-powering experience to be in the presence of someone who is devoid of such self-concern, and whose efforts truly are for the good of others. What a blessing it is to know them, and to be known by them.

My mother was this kind of person. She passed away from brain cancer fourteen years ago. A few years before she passed, when life was good and there was yet no hint of the trial she would face, she sat down at the piano in our home. Earlier she had spoken with one of our young children, Jacob, about his favorite children's songs. He named twenty-four of them. My mother sat down at the piano to record herself playing and singing all twenty-four of her grandson's favorite numbers. She recorded those songs on side A of the cassette tape she was using. When she had finished, she turned the tape over and recorded the same twenty-four songs on side B—just so that Jacob wouldn't have to rewind the tape in order to listen to the songs again.

I still have that tape. It is a reminder of what true service looks like. And what does it look like? It looks like the face of a child who motivates you to action, or the needs of a partner that you finally try to see, or the invitation of a full trash bin still sitting at the side of a customer's house.

For a servant leader, their service is not the point. Their actions are merely the behavioral extensions of their caring. They have learned to speak Becky and Jacob and David and Randy—*and* to speak those languages with an out-ward mindset.

It is worth asking: If we would serve, whose languages do we still need to learn?

*James Ferrell is managing partner of Arbinger Institute (www.arbinger.com), and author or coauthor of multiple bestselling books, including Arbinger's international bestsellers* Leadership and Self-Deception, The Anatomy of Peace, *and* The Outward Mindset.

# Chapter 14

# What You See Determines How You Serve

## CHRIS HODGES

*I was blown away when I heard Chris Hodges speak at a leadership conference a few years ago. To me, he made the Bible come alive. I would venture to say that's one of the reasons he has built one of the biggest megachurch communities in the United States— Church of the Highlands. One of my favorite Bible imperatives is Luke 6:37—"Do not judge, and you will not be judged." Chris brings this message to life in his essay. —KB*

YEARS AGO, I served as a youth pastor at a great church in Colorado Springs, Colorado. We had one of the largest and fastest-growing youth groups in the country, with a vibrant service called TAG every Wednesday night. This wasn't one of those services students attended because their parents wanted them to. Instead of talking, texting, or passing notes, each week hundreds of students actually engaged in worship and took notes on the teaching because they were so eager to connect with God.

One week, a young kid showed up dressed all in black, his dark hair in a severe style and a sneer on his face—clearly a "goth." Now, working in youth ministry, I had learned quickly not to judge anyone based on appearances. But this guy clearly had an edge to him. And he immediately let us all know it.

He sat in the back row, made obnoxious comments, and laughed throughout my message. I tried to correct him nicely, but when he persisted I decided that I had had enough. I told one of our youth workers to get him in my office after the service to settle things between us.

When I walked in the office and glanced at him, I noticed he had a little smirk on his face, which only irritated me more. I sat down across from him with a sigh of frustration and we just glared at each other in silence. Finally, I leaned in toward him and said, "Bro—what's your deal?"

Before I could launch into my rant, he stood up, turned around, and pulled up his shirt. Angry red scars—some fresher than others—ran across his pale back, where someone (his father, I would later find out) had been beating him. "This is my deal," he said in a quiet voice. I was undone. In one second my anger dissolved into compassion and we immediately began the process of working with him and his family.

I learned a lot that day. How you see people determines how you serve people. And most of us tend toward the extremes: we see people as either a problem to be avoided or a person to be loved.

This is the lesson Jesus taught in the famous parable of the Good Samaritan:

> Approaching Jesus was a man who was trying to figure out who he was supposed to serve. "Who is my neighbor?" he asked Jesus. And in classic style, Jesus responded to the man's question with a story.
>
> "There was once a man traveling from Jerusalem to Jericho. On the way he was attacked by robbers. They took his clothes, beat him up, and went off, leaving him half dead. Luckily, a priest was on his way down the same road, but when he saw him, he angled across to the other side. Then a Levite religious man showed up; he also avoided the injured man. A Samaritan traveling the road came on him. When he saw the man's condition, his heart went out to him. He gave him first aid, disinfecting and bandaging his wounds. Then he lifted him onto his donkey, led him to an inn, and made him comfortable. In the morning he took out two silver coins and gave them to the innkeeper, saying, 'Take good care of him. If it costs any more, put it on my bill—I'll pay you on my way back.'"
>
> Then Jesus asked, "What do you think? Which of the three became a neighbor to the man attacked by robbers?"
>
> "The one who treated him kindly," the religion scholar responded.
> Jesus said, "Go and do the same." (Luke 10:30–37, MSG)

## The Robbers

Our traveler in this story encountered three different types of people. First, of course, are the robbers. They beat him, robbed him, and completely exploited him. While most of us would never even consider doing anything like this, sometimes we're still tempted to see people as commodities, resources, or obstacles rather than flesh-and-blood human beings. We want to manipulate them, avoid them, or take from them. They become our adversaries instead of individuals God has called us to love and to serve.

This affliction hits home with me when I'm driving in traffic. It's so easy for me to get irritated with people when they cut me off or get in my way. When we see people as a problem—the person taking forever in the express lane at the grocery store or the teenager working the fast food drive-through who gets our order wrong—we tend to mistreat them right back.

## The Priests

In Jesus's story, the second group our victim encountered was the priests. These religious leaders didn't rob the man, beat him, or exploit him. They simply avoided him altogether. They were too busy doing what they saw as more important spiritual work to stop and help someone in need. Before you think that you would never ignore someone bleeding on the side of the road, think again. From time to time, we all think the best way to handle a situation is to avoid it altogether. The priests in this story didn't think they were responsible—after all, they were busy, important people. So they didn't serve the man; they went around him.

Maybe we think someone else will do it. Maybe we think someone else *is* doing it. Either way, we are not seeing the situation the way God wants us to see it. The Bible says, "When He (Jesus) looked out over the crowds, His heart broke. So confused and aimless they were, like sheep with no shepherd" (Matt. 9:36, MSG). This explains why Jesus was so effective. He saw people in the condition they were in, and their need motivated Him to do something about it.

## The Good Samaritan

The last person this poor victim encountered, the Good Samaritan, was the only one who saw him through the eyes of a servant leader. He didn't see a victim to exploit or a problem to avoid. He saw a person to be loved. And that's why he served.

## Choose to Serve Anyway

So how can we see people through the lens of a servant? Simple—it's a choice. Every day we have to choose to see people the way God does. Too many of us wait for our feelings to lead, and then if we feel compassion, sympathy, or obligation toward someone, our action will follow. Too often we view love as a feeling. But love is intentionally caring or helping another person by doing something *regardless* of our feelings. Real servant leaders make choices about people first, and then the feelings follow. The Good Samaritan didn't necessarily *feel* like interrupting his travel plans or spending his hard-earned money on a complete stranger. He simply saw someone in need and he made a choice.

What you see when you look at someone determines how you serve. Many of us say we want to love others—but we see, feel, and move on. Servant leaders remember that someone with a chip on their shoulder may have scars on their back—so their approach is not judgment but loving action. Servant leaders serve people differently because they see people differently.

*Chris Hodges is founding and senior pastor of Church of the Highlands (www. churchofthehighlands.com) with campuses all across the state of Alabama. He co-founded the Association of Related Churches in 2001, and also founded a coaching network called GROW. In addition, Chris is founder and president of the High-lands College, a ministry training school that launches students into full-time ministry careers. He speaks at conferences worldwide and is the author of the books* Fresh Air, Four Cups, *and* The Daniel Dilemma.

# Chapter 15

# Compassion

## *The Heart of Servant Leadership*

### CRAIG GROESCHEL

*Craig Groeschel leads the church with the largest attendance in America—Life.Church. A few years ago he asked me to speak in Oklahoma City at a gathering of key staff from twenty-six locations. The meeting started with music—and the whole place quickly came alive with the most incredible energy I had ever experienced. I was scheduled to speak next and I could see it was going to be a tough act to follow! I learned that day the extent to which Craig and his wonderful organization live and lead with compassion—which, as he contends in this essay, is the heart of servant leadership. —KB*

RECENTLY I WAS driving home, running late for dinner, trying to make up some time on the back roads. I'd gotten to a stretch where there's literally nothing but a bunch of cows in a field and an occasional farmhouse or barn. (I live in Oklahoma, in case you were wondering.) I was in a big hurry, cruising along a familiar route, when I came to a stop sign and saw an unexpected sight. Right there, in the middle of nowhere, a woman was just standing beside the road.

I immediately thought, "I need to help her—she must've had car trouble and gotten stranded." But almost as soon as that thought came, it triggered a mini debate in my mind. *Maybe you should help her, Craig, but you're in a hurry. You're already going to be late for dinner, and your family's waiting for you. Besides, she doesn't look upset. She's probably there for a reason. Maybe she's just out for a walk. Maybe someone's meeting her there. She's not trying to flag you down or anything.*

Even with all of these justifications, I really felt I needed to help her.

I wrestled back and forth in this conversation with myself—for maybe a few seconds—then proceeded to drive right by without stopping. To this day, I still wonder what was going on with that lady. But even more than that, I wonder what was going on with me. I knew I should have helped her, but I just kept on driving. I still can't shake the failure I feel in my heart for not stopping.

Every time I remember that late afternoon, that missed opportunity, it reminds me of something at the heart of Jesus's ministry and at the very core of what servant leadership is all about: *Compassion.*

What is compassion to the servant leader? Compassion is not just a feeling; it's an action. It's allowing the emotion we feel to ignite the fire within to act—and to inspire others to act as well. To meet someone's need. To offer our help. To set an example for others. To do what Jesus did. To love how Jesus loved. To lead as Jesus led.

The Bible usually uses the Greek word *splagchnizomai* (splahgkh-NEED-zum-eye) to describe the kind of compassion we see in Jesus's life. *Splagchnizomai* means "to have deep sympathy"—literally a yearning in the bowels—to do something for someone else. Not surprisingly, every time we're told in Scripture that Jesus felt *splagchnizomai*, His compassion was immediately followed by action.

After the death of John the Baptist, Jesus "withdrew by boat privately to a solitary place" (Matt. 14:13), but the crowds followed Him. So what did He do? "When Jesus landed and saw a large crowd, He had compassion on them and healed their sick" (Matt. 14:14). In Mark's account of this same event, Jesus feels compassion "because they were like sheep without a shepherd" so He began teaching them (Mark 6:34). Moved by their need, He immediately began healing and teaching the people.

On another occasion, two blind men sitting beside the road called out to Jesus as He and His disciples were leaving Jericho (Matt. 20:29–33). The crowds following Jesus tried to shush the men. But Jesus was having none of it. Instead, He "had compassion on them and touched their eyes. Immediately they received their sight and followed Him" (Matt. 20:34). He felt so deeply that He had to act.

True servant leadership means you are called to care—not to just feel sorry for someone or feel sympathy or empathy—but to *do* something. Why? Because to say you care, and then not act, is to not care at all. True servant leadership cares. And because it cares, it must act.

If we're honest, even if we want to be models of servant leadership, we're still prone to choose our own agendas over God's. Just like my failure to stop for that woman on the side of the road, we get into mental arguments with ourselves where we justify all of our reasons not to act. We make excuses for ourselves when we really have no excuse for not loving others the way Jesus loves us.

Jesus did more than just model compassion in action. In Luke 10, an expert of the law came to Him and asked, "What do I need to do to be saved?" Jesus answered him, "Well, you tell me—what does the law say?" (I'm paraphrasing.) And the guy said, "Well, the law says to love the Lord your God with all your heart, all your mind, all your soul, and all your strength. And to love your neighbor as yourself."

So Jesus said, "You're right! Now go and do that."

But the guy wasn't finished. He had a hidden agenda. According to Scripture (Luke 10:29), "he wanted to justify himself." So he responded, "Okay, I will, but I've got to ask you something else first. If I'm supposed to love my neighbor, I need to know which neighbor we're talking about. Is it my next-door neighbor, or some random guy I meet on the street, or the woman I know who brings water from the well?" You or I might ask, "Are you talking about the people in the apartment next door? Or the single mom on my team at work? Or the barista who serves me my latte at Starbucks? *That* neighbor?"

Instead of answering him directly, Jesus told the parable of the Good Samaritan. (Chris Hodges shares this passage—Luke 10:30–37—in full in chapter 14.) It's about a man traveling from Jerusalem to Jericho who was attacked by robbers.

In short, the Samaritan took action to help the man when others didn't. Like Jesus, he *felt* something that compelled him to *do* something. He knew that compassion often interrupts our schedule. He knew that compassion chooses to act—that it bypasses whatever conversations are rolling around in our heads to justify our lack of activity. He didn't seem to mind the inconvenience or the expense, but even if he did, he didn't let it stand in the way of helping someone desperately in need. He knew that compassion—treating others like you would want to be treated—must include action.

I learned from my failure with the woman wandering at the intersection. Anytime that debate starts again in my mind—"You should stop and help." "No, I don't have time." "Blah, blah, blah . . ."—I now replace it with something much simpler: "Shut up! Stop. Get out. Make a difference."

God will move us with His type of compassion—*splagchnizomai*—if we will just *let* Him. If we want to lead like Jesus, we need to serve like Jesus. We need to understand that as followers of Jesus we are called to care. Every one of us can reflect the compassion and care of God. We're called to care for those in need—no matter who they are, where we are, where we're headed, or how late it might make us for dinner.

If you want to know the secret to servant leadership, it's pretty simple: Compassion changes lives.

*Craig Groeschel is the founding and senior pastor of Life.Church (www.life .church), known for the innovative use of technology in spreading the Gospel, which includes the free YouVersion Bible App. The church has brick and mortar locations in eight states as well as a burgeoning international partnership ministry of Network Churches. Craig speaks at conferences worldwide and has written several books, including* The Christian Atheist, Fight, From This Day Forward, *and his most recent release:* #Struggles—Following Jesus in a Selfie-Centered World.

# Chapter 16

# How to Spot Ideal Team Players

## PATRICK LENCIONI

*Pat Lencioni and I met early in his career when we were speaking at the same conference in Saskatchewan. After his excellent session, I went up to him and said, "You know the reason your stuff is so good and so useful? It all comes from the Bible." He said, "Really?" I had started the Lead Like Jesus ministry and recognized all of the positive things Pat was teaching were things Jesus had done. That began Pat's thinking about his faith and its relation to his work. Pat and I agree that everyone can be a servant leader—and as he will share with you, in order for that to happen it helps to have the characteristics of an effective team player. —KB*

WITH ENOUGH TIME, patience, and attention from a good manager, almost anyone can learn to become a team player. I believe that. I feel the same way about servant leaders.

Having said that, some people are better at teamwork than others. These are the kind of people who add immediate value in a team environment and require much less coaching and management to contribute in a meaningful way.

So, there are two obvious questions: What do these people look like? And how do we find them? As it turns out, they have three qualities, or virtues, in common: they are *humble, hungry,* and *smart.*

Before I explain each of those virtues, let me explain how this theory came about. Like so many of my ideas, this one surfaced as a result of my work with clients over the past twenty years. Whenever I worked with CEOs and their leadership teams to identify core values, I often was asked about the values of my own firm, The Table Group. When we revealed our three values, many of our clients would ask us if they could adopt those values for themselves.

Of course, we would say "no," explaining that they needed to come up with concepts that reflected *their* unique history and culture. We were a company oriented around teamwork and known for *The Five Dysfunctions of a Team*,[1] so the values of humility, hunger, and people smarts made sense for us. What we failed to realize was that our clients, almost all of whom were committed to the idea of teamwork, were drawn to our values because those were the building blocks of real team players.

## The Three Virtues: Humble, Hungry, and Smart

The three virtues seem quite simple, but require a bit of explanation:

> *Humble.* The first and most important virtue of an ideal team player is humility. A humble person is someone who is more concerned with the success of the team than with getting credit for their own contribution. People who lack humility in a significant way—the ones who demand a disproportionate amount of attention—are dangerous for a team. Having said that, humble team players are not afraid to honestly acknowledge the skills and talents that they bring to the team, though never in a proud or boastful way.

> *Hungry.* The next virtue of an ideal team player is hunger—the desire to work hard and do whatever is necessary to help the team succeed. Hungry people almost never have to be pushed by a manager to work harder because they are self-motivated and diligent. They volunteer to fill gaps and take on more responsibilities, and are eagerly looking around corners for new ways to contribute to the team.

> *Smart.* The final virtue of a team player is to be smart. This is not about being intelligent, but rather about being wise in dealing with people. Smart people understand the nuances of team dynamics and know how their words and actions impact others. Their good judgment and intuition help them deal with others in the most effective way.

As simple as these three concepts may be, the key to all this is the unique combination of all three virtues, which make a person an ideal team player. Unfortunately, when even one of these attributes is lacking in a significant way, challenges can arise.

For instance, a humble and hungry person who is not smart about people may accomplish a great deal but will often leave a trail of interpersonal destruction behind them. A person who is smart and humble but lacking in hunger will frustrate team members by doing only what is required and having to be constantly asked to do more. Finally, a team member who is hungry and smart but truly lacking in humility can have a devastating impact on a team. This type knows how to present themselves as a well-intentioned colleague, all the while looking out for their own needs. By the time team members figure this out, people have been manipulated and scarred.

How do you go about hiring ideal team players? It's mostly about knowing what to look for and probing in nontraditional ways. And what about people who already work on the team and lack one or more of the virtues? A big part of helping them improve is making sure they understand the concepts and know where they fall short. We've found that merely introducing this simple model to teams and allowing them to self-assess goes a long way toward improvement.

## Big Payoff

The impact of ensuring that members of a team value and demonstrate humility, hunger, and people smarts cannot be overstated. Most teams that struggle are not lacking in knowledge or competence as much as they are unable to access that knowledge and competence because of dysfunctional behaviors. A team full of people who are humble, hungry, and smart will overcome those dysfunctions quickly and easily, allowing them to get more done in less time and with far fewer distractions. My hope is that this approach will help leaders hire, recognize, and cultivate ideal team players in their organizations.

*Patrick Lencioni is the founder and CEO of The Table Group (www.tablegroup .com), a firm dedicated to helping leaders improve their organizational health since 1997. He is the author of ten business books that have sold nearly five million copies and been translated into more than thirty languages. His latest is* The Ideal Team Player: How to Recognize and Cultivate the Three Essential Virtues. *Pat has been featured in numerous publications including* Harvard Business Review, Inc., Fortune, Fast Company, USA Today, Wall Street Journal, *and* BusinessWeek.

## Note

1. Patrick Lencioni, *The Five Dysfunctions of a Team: A Leadership Fable* (New York: John Wiley and Sons, 2002).

# Chapter 17

# The Servant Leader Identity

## LAURIE BETH JONES

*I first became acquainted with Laurie Beth Jones through her book* Jesus CEO. *When she became involved with our Lead Like Jesus ministry, I quickly became a raving fan of not only her writing and thinking, but also who she was as a person. Leaders who are interested in serving rather than being served are not only comfortable with who they are, but also interested in finding out about the people they work with. After you read Laurie Beth's essay, the importance of understanding yourself and others will become clear to you. —KB*

AS A SERVANT leader, one of Jesus's clear strengths was that He had a clear and compelling narrative of who He was. He said, "I am the Good Shepherd" (John 10:11, 14); "I am the gate" (John 10:7, 9); compared Himself to "living water" (John 4:10–11; 7:38) and emphasized that He "did not come to be served, but to serve" (Matt. 20:28). This self-awareness of His strengths helped others quickly grasp in a visual way who it was they were dealing with.

The brain processes visuals sixty thousand times faster than words. When Jesus said the words "shepherd" or "water" or "servant," everyone in that culture had a clear image that came to mind. Had He, however, started stating His résumé or pedigree or paper qualifications, no doubt people would have wandered back off to the marketplace.

After my first book, *Jesus CEO*,[1] came out, I was often invited to coach and consult with leaders of organizations. When I would say to them "Tell me who you are," invariably they would begin to rattle off roles or titles. But when I would say, "Draw me a picture," silence would fall over the room. It was this lack of visual leadership identities that led me to create the Path Elements Profile, or PEP for short.

In Genesis, God uses four elements—*earth, water, wind*, and *fire*—in the creation story. Indeed, these elements are mentioned nearly two thousand times in Scripture. Jesus spoke frequently of, and to, the elements, for example comparing Himself to living water, or saying He had to come to "bring fire" (Luke 12:49). He even referred to two of His rowdiest disciples, James and John, as "sons of thunder" (Mark 3:17).

Here is a quick way to illustrate the different cultural values of each of the four elements:

*Fire* wants fast and visible results.

*Water* wants harmonious, long-term relationships.

*Wind* wants innovation and change.

*Earth* wants stability and order.

So, for example, when Jesus compared Himself to living water, His desire was to create a culture of harmony and respect for others, with growing relationships as a core value. A water leader understands that growth takes time and is willing to work below the surface, even invisibly, to make that happen.

A fire leader, on the other hand, values conflict as a refining process and wants to gain territory at nearly any cost. A fire leader wants visible results and wants them now. In many ways, this describes self-serving leaders to whom Jesus came to bring the perspective that great leadership had to do with both results and people.

Wind and fire move fast, and almost always have a visible impact. Earth and water move more slowly and tend to do their work underground.

Imagine what happens, then, when a fire leader lands in a water setting. The fire leader wants immediate results, using language like "My way or the highway." The water culture they inherited wants things to be done in harmonious ripples. Trouble ensues and steam rises. One or the other gives way or, better still, they create and develop a *both/and* relationship.

Or perhaps a wind innovative thinker is brought into an earth organization that likes the way things have always been done. A servant leader with a water temperament will take the time to listen, reflect, evaluate, and assess.

Leadership can come from any profile. While fires may tend to be the most likely to blaze a trail, if unchecked they can destroy the forest. While waters always seek to serve, without focusing on results it can turn into a country club. Earth leaders are masters at detailed planning but can also be overcome by analysis paralysis. Wind leaders can help an army set sail but, without proper harnessing, can stall or send them in multiple directions—sometimes just for fun. Consider the following examples.

King David, beloved by God, was a wind-fire leader who was given to high and low bursts of order and enthusiasm. One look at the Psalms and anyone can see how this elemental combination in a leader can lead to bold and sudden victories as well as near depression in a cave.

Solomon, in contrast, was more of a servant leader as a water-earth combination—the exact opposite of his impetuous warrior father. Solomon's first act was to send gifts to all surrounding territorial leaders rather than declare war. The tempo in Proverbs reveals an almost steady drumbeat of wisdom—do this and you get that—which is in great contrast to moody, haunting, exhilarating Psalms.

Whatever your God-created elemental makeup is will be reflected in all the work you do with a team. Jesus compared Himself to living water, and indeed when you follow His actions He acted very much like water in many ways. He said that His mission was to bring abundant life. That's what water does. He always sought the lowest place and, as a servant leader, told His disciples that honor is to be found in stooping to wash someone's feet as opposed to standing over their corpse with their head dangling in your hand (fire).

He did show upset in turning over the tables at the temple, but wind and water acting together create a powerful storm. He never wrote anything down, which would have been an earth characteristic. He told people to put away their swords and bless those who cursed them. This is definitely not a fire characteristic or response.

Likewise, you as a leader are going to do and teach things that reveal who you are elementally, thriving on bold initiatives and welcoming confrontation if it brings about change. If you are an earth leader, like Nehemiah, you will want to do things in a well-thought-out and measured manner—going about your work quietly, even being willing, as a servant, to get low in the ditches if it helps you see where the root problems are. If you are a wind leader, like Joshua, you will use your voice to blow the trumpets that bring those walls of Jericho tumbling down. You will say, "This is easy! Cross the river now!" and bring people across a river into the land that had been denied to them for forty years.

One of my greatest privileges as a consultant was working with a servant leader with a water temperament who inherited a fire/earth organization. Over fifteen years, I watched him turn silos into pipelines, drive decision making downward, and teach people ultimately that their greatest promise was taking care of others as well as one another.

Knowing which type of elemental leader you are can do much good for yourself and for those around you. Are you a fire leader, or more like water? More like earth, or more like wind? Jesus, as the greatest leadership role model of all time, obviously had flexibility to all four styles although in my opinion he was predominantly a water/wind combination. Most likely you are a powerful combination of two of the four as well. How about the people you work with? Do you have a sense of their type or combination of types? If you do, you can better serve them.

Remember, Jesus was very clear about his leadership style and adapted it to the special needs of his disciples. While he didn't attempt to change the styles of his followers, he helped them see other perspectives, which made one plus one greater than two. Are you clear about your leadership style and how it relates to the needs of the people around you? How can you help them bring their strengths to bear on the vision and direction your organization is working toward?

*Laurie Beth Jones (www.lauriebethjones.com) is an internationally recognized bestselling author, speaker, inspirational life coach, and trainer. A business development coach and consultant to CEOs and organizations, Laurie Beth's fourteen business books, written from a spiritual perspective, include* Jesus CEO; Jesus, Entrepreneur; Teach Your Team to Fish, *and* The Path: Creating Your Mission Statement for Work and for Life.

## Note

1. Laurie Beth Jones, *Jesus, CEO: Using Ancient Wisdom for Visionary Leadership* (New York: Hyperion, 1995).

# Chapter 18

# The Four Corners of the Leader's Universe

### HENRY CLOUD

*I first became an admirer of Henry Cloud through his writings. Then I met him as a presenter at a servant leadership conference and got to know him through our work in the field. He is not only a great human being but also one of the foremost thought leaders on servant leadership—as you will see when you read this essay. —KB*

HAVE YOU EVER met a friend for lunch, and to learn how you are doing they asked this question: "So, where are you?"

I'll bet you have. When you think about it, this is a really interesting question to ask someone to find out how he or she is doing. Obviously, the person knows where you are physically because you are sitting right in front of them. What they are *really* asking is where you are *on the inside*: in your heart, mind, and soul. The truth is, on the inside we are *always* somewhere. And because we are relational beings designed for connection with others, the place where we are inside always involves a state of connectedness or disconnectedness with others. Good or bad, we can't escape that we are relational in nature and that each moment we feel the results of how our relationships are going. Where we are in those relationships has a lot to do with how we perform and function; whether we thrive or stagnate; whether we win or lose.

In leadership, this is a big, big deal. Servant leaders are leaders who spend a lot of time asking themselves that very question about the people they lead: Where are they? Where are my people today—inside their hearts, minds, and souls? How does it feel for them to be here? How does it feel to be under my leadership? How does it feel to be on my team, or in my department or organization?

Servant leaders ask this question because research points to one conclusion: how people feel in their sense of connectedness with their leaders and peers is going to drastically affect whether they succeed or fail. They know this either because of their own leadership training, their life experience, or both. So they want to get it right.

But that brings up a question in the servant leader's mind: If I need to find my people's hearts, where do I look—where might their hearts, minds, and souls be at any given moment? Great question.

If we are looking for someone, it's good to have a map to know where to look to aid in our search. In working with leaders, I have found it very helpful to give them a map so that they can go on an active search for their people. There are only four possibilities of where the people you lead might be at any given moment. I call this map "The Four Corners."

Think of it this way. Picture a square map with four quadrants: three bad and one good. The people you lead will always be in one of these four locations—and it is a servant leader's job to find them and lead them into the only corner where they can thrive.

## Corner One: No Connection

This is the corner where someone feels like they are alone. In it all by themselves. It does not mean they have no people around them; they probably do. They probably have a boss or are on a team or surrounded by other colleagues. But to the real question of where they are in their hearts, minds, and souls, they feel very much alone. Disconnected. Not a part of things. Not listened to, encouraged, or supported. We know that this place is one where their engagement is lowered, motivation diminishes, suspiciousness and fear increase, and leaving becomes a greater option. Nothing good happens in Corner One—it is the place of detachment and isolation. Decisions are in silos, wins and losses are not shared and built upon, collaboration suffers, competitiveness is up and cooperation down. The experience of gaining meaning and purpose from work, of being on a shared mission with others, decreases. Not to mention, when these people are struggling in some way, the chances of getting any kind of help are very low. They feel as if they are on their own even if they are in meetings all day long.

## Corner Two: Bad Connection

Corner Two is the place where someone feels a connection with others, but the nature of that connection leaves them feeling bad about themselves. They feel not good enough. The phrase *nothing I do is good enough* goes through their head over and over. They feel inferior, flawed, judged, criticized, and a host of other really crummy feelings that diminish their performance, motivation, creativity, thinking, judgment, and other major ingredients for being able to win. They may try hard to gain the approval they are not getting; but after a while, they become defeated, resentful, and disengaged. Often, they will even become adversarial and divisive as they feel someone is against them and look for an ally against the enemy who makes them feel so bad. No one does well when feeling like they are not good enough. All of their performance tools—their hearts, minds, and souls—begin to decay. They just can't work well when they feel so crummy about themselves.

## Corner Three: Fake Good Connection

Corner Three is the place where people go to feel good when they find that being disconnected or feeling bad about themselves are not good options. They have to get some kind of relief, so they seek some way to medicate the bad feeling they had in the first two corners. They might look to connect with people who suck up to them and flatter them, those who will not tell them the truth and who agree with everything they say, even about other people. They are attracted to others who think they can do no wrong and they avoid everyone else, creating alliances that are not healthy. Some of these connections might even be illicit relationships or other destructive activities to make themselves feel better. They may become addicted to things like alcohol or food or the internet. Some get obsessed with needing to hear good numbers about sales or other metrics, driving their people for more and more performance, to make themselves feel good. Some seek awards, status, or promotions, as the addiction for feeling good is equated with being seen as good by others—smarter, stronger, greater—whatever it means to them. But this good feeling is shallow and not truly satisfying. It is like a sugar high—it always wears off.

## Corner Four: Real Connection

Corner Four is the place servant leaders want their people to be—the place where people feel genuinely connected with leaders and peers who are being honest and supportive with them. It is the corner where people can be honest and vulnerable about what they are going through—what they are thinking, discovering, or needing. It is the place where they can celebrate doing well, get help if they need it, increase learning, and thrive. They can be honest about what is working for them and what isn't, and are free to be curious and vulnerable. They find support and encouragement when they struggle and appreciation when they win. They are challenged and pushed to get better, but in a way that is motivating rather than controlling or diminishing. They have accountability, which makes them not only feel valued but also want to do well. Most of all, they feel they are winning with a team and an organization, for reasons that transcend their own interests—for a purpose larger than themselves. In Corner Four, hearts, minds, and souls thrive and prosper. Energy is up, brains are sizzling with creativity and innovation, collaboration is high, and people are fulfilled. As a result, outcomes are better. Because of the support, development, and accountability, how could that not be true?

## Leaders: Go on a Search and Ask Your People "Where Are You?"

I began with a question: Where are you? What if, as a leader, you saw this as one of the tools you could use each day—looking at your people and your teams and asking which corner they are in? What if you were on a mission to find out if they were in any of the three harmful corners so you could help them find Corner Four?

Are they in Corner One—isolated and disconnected? If so, what can you do to get everyone connected and feeling like they are an important part of the whole? Pull in those who have been disengaged and find out what caused it and how you can make it better.

Are they in Corner Two—feeling bad about themselves and discouraged? Find out what is making them feel that way. Are they hearing criticism more than encouragement? Address problems in a spirit of improvement instead of judgment. Is it something you are doing? Or is it their boss or someone on their team? Ask yourself, "What might I be doing to contribute to a culture of fear where people feel that they are not doing enough?"

Are they in Corner Three—always seeking to feel good in some way? Do they gravitate toward those who flatter them, always looking for praise or higher achievement? Are they addicted to success or position or drifting to unhealthy feel-good activities to medicate themselves? Ask yourself "How might I address their need to feel good in shallow ways by building them up in real ways so that they do not need constant adulation? How might I get them to see their weaknesses as growth opportunities instead of something to run away from? How can I make the culture an environment of learning instead of one where people feel they have to be perfect?"

Or are they in Corner Four—feeling connected, safe, supported, corrected, and held accountable in good ways? Are they feeling positively motivated and safe coming to you and the team when they are struggling? People in Corner Four see others as being *for* them instead of *against* them. They know there are people they can turn to for help and collaboration—their workplace is a place where their needs get met, even if they are confused or need clarity. When there are issues that need to be addressed, they know they will be listened to and those issues will be attended to. They feel energized by their relationships. What do you need to do to make sure Corner Four is happening? How can you help your people—or your entire organization—get to Corner Four?

A servant leader is someone who knows it matters where their people are at any moment, in any season. Servant leaders do not allow their teams to drift into disconnectedness, or be crushed under negative criticism, or hide behind flattery and happy talk. They seek to create real, supportive, yet highly accountable and challenging environments where people feel that their hearts, minds, and souls are engaged every day. If your team or organization can be a Corner Four place, where each time someone is asked "Where are you?" they answer "I am in Corner Four today," you will know you are a leader who serves your people well.

*Henry Cloud is a psychologist, leadership coach and consultant, and bestselling author of more than twenty books. He is highly regarded for his ability to connect personal and interpersonal development with the needs of business. Henry completed his PhD in clinical psychology at Biola University. His book* The Power of the Other *explains in depth his Four Corners concept and the leadership skills needed to produce Corner Four relationships.*

## Part Three

# Lessons in
# Servant Leadership

## What People Have Learned from Observing Servant Leadership in Action

- James M. Kouzes and Barry Z. Posner, in their essay "Finding Your Voice," emphasize that what earns the respect of your people is not your position, talent, or the tools and techniques you use—it's whether *you* are *you*.

- In her essay "A Lesson from My Father: Washing Feet," Phyllis Hennecy Hendry shares the most important lesson she learned from her father: selflessly caring for and serving others can change lives.

- In Neal Nybo's essay, "The Puddle Is Not the Problem," he shows how servant leaders must not only help their people identify problems but also prepare them to embrace necessary change.

- Jeffrey W. Foley, in "Five Army-Tested Lessons of Servant Leadership," describes how the lessons he learned while serving in the U.S. Army can help civilian servant leaders create that same winning culture in their workplace.

- In his essay "A Baptism of Servant Leadership," Erwin Raphael McManus illustrates how the choices we make to serve when nobody is watching in many ways can say more about us as a servant leader than the things we do for all to see.

- Jon Gordon, in "Little Things and Big Things," shares that there might not be a more important servant leadership role than that of a parent.

- Margie Blanchard's essay, "In Praise of Followership," emphasizes that the success of servant leaders often depends on their having followers who are willing to serve, too.

# Chapter 19

# Finding Your Voice

## James M. Kouzes and Barry Z. Posner

*I got to know Barry Posner when he was working on his doctorate at the University of Massachusetts where I was a professor. We reconnected when he teamed up with Jim Kouzes and they became one of the most dynamic duos in the field of leadership today. In this essay, Jim and Barry reflect on the nature of leadership and address the question of whether leadership is something that can be learned. The three of us agree that effective servant leadership is an inside-out job. All of the servant leaders I've had the pleasure to work with are comfortable in their own skin—in Jim and Barry's terms, they have "found their voice." Thanks to you both for validating that truth. —KB*

ONE OF THE most persistent myths in our culture associates leadership with rank. Another myth attributes leadership to talent. But leadership isn't a position or a special gift that only a few special people have.[1] It's an observable, learnable set of skills and practices available to everyone, anywhere in the organization.

We were making that case to a group of senior managers at a seminar when a hand shot up across the room. "I'd like to challenge that statement," said one participant. "I've been pondering this lately. Can anyone really learn to lead? If so, why do we seem to lack effective leadership these days?"

## That Special Leadership Something

Now why is that? What is it about leadership that constantly raises questions about the capacity to learn it? What is it about the concept of leadership that brings forth this question? Tell us, what is that unique something about leadership? What is the something else about leadership that can't be learned?

Here are a few representative responses to these questions from workshop participants: "Soul." "Spirit." "It's inside yourself." "Ethics." "Value system."

Is there anything on this list that you cannot learn? Maybe some of these things can't be taught, but can you learn them? You may or may not agree with what others said, but think about it for a moment. Soul? Spirit? Ethics? Values? Can you learn about your soul? Can you learn about your spirit? Can you learn what is right? Can you learn what you hope the future to be? Can you learn what gives you passion? Not for everyone. Not for society. But for you?

We bet you can. You won't find the answer in a workshop or a book, including the ones we've written. But if you search inside yourself, you will find your truth. As Ken Blanchard has said about servant leadership: "It's an inside-out job. It starts in your heart with who you are—your character and your answer to the question *am I here to serve or be served?*"

In his witty book *Management of the Absurd*, psychologist and CEO Richard Farson writes:

> In both parenthood and management, it's not so much what we do as what we are that counts. What parents do deliberately appears to make little difference in the most important outcomes—whether their children grow up to be happy or unhappy, successful or unsuccessful, good or evil. There is no question that parents can and should do worthwhile things for their children, but it's what they are that will really matter. . . . The same dynamic occurs in management and leadership. People learn—and respond to—what we are.[2]

Richard nailed it. All the techniques and all the tools that fill the pages of all the management and leadership books are not substitutes for who and what you are. In fact, they boomerang if thrown by some spin-meister who's mastered form but not substance.

We have been collaborating on leadership research for thirty-five years and we keep rediscovering that *credibility is the foundation of leadership*. It's been reinforced so often that we've come to refer to it as the First Law of Leadership: if you don't believe in the messenger, you won't believe the message. People don't follow your technique; they follow you—your message and your embodiment of that message. This is key for effective servant leaders.

In *Leadership Jazz*, Max De Pree, former chairman and CEO of the Michigan furniture maker Herman Miller, tells a moving story about being

with his prematurely born granddaughter during the first days of her fragile life. The nurse had advised Max and his wife to touch as well as talk to the tiny infant, "because she has to be able to connect your voice to your touch." That message, says Max, is "at the core of becoming a leader."[3]

Leadership credibility is about connecting voice and touch, about practicing what you preach, and about doing what you say you will do. But as Max makes quite clear, there's a prior task to connecting voice and touch. It's "finding one's voice in the first place."

## Soul Searching

Authentic servant leadership flows from the inside out. It does not come from the outside in. Inside-out leadership is about discovering who you are, what drives you to do what you do, and what gives you the credibility to lead others. Inside-out leadership is about becoming the author of your own story and the maker of your own history. Inside-out leadership is also the only way to respond to what your people want from you. And what is that? What they most want is to know who you genuinely are.

Finding your voice is critical if you are to be a servant leader. If you don't find your voice, you may find yourself with a vocabulary that belongs to someone else, mouthing words that were written by a speechwriter who is nothing like you at all. If you doubt the importance of choosing your own vocabulary, consider these phrases from the speech by a banking manager we observed during the course of our research:

- "You've got to watch out for the headhunters."
- "Keep your capital, and keep it dry."
- "We'll act like SWAT teams."
- "We're going to beat their brains out."
- "We won't tolerate the building of fiefdoms."
- "There will be only a few survivors."

Contrast them with these phrases from Anita Roddick,[4] founder of The Body Shop:

- "We communicate with passion—and passion persuades."
- "I think all businesses practices would improve immeasurably if they were guided by feminine principles—qualities like love and care and intuition."

- "What we need is optimism, humanism, enthusiasm, intuition, curiosity, love, humour, magic, fun, and that secret ingredient—euphoria."
- "I believe that service—whether it is serving the community or your family or the people you love, or whatever—is fundamental to what life is about."

What do these words communicate about the guiding beliefs and assumptions of the individuals speaking? Would any of these words be in your lexicon? Would you want them used in your organization?

Every artist knows that finding a voice is most definitely not a matter of technique. It's a matter of time and a matter of searching—soul searching.

We remember attending, with an artist friend, a retrospective of painter Richard Diebenkorn's work. Toward the end of our gallery walk, our friend turned to us and made this observation: "There are really three periods in an artist's life. In the first, we paint exterior landscapes. In the second, we paint interior landscapes. In the third, they come together into an artist's unique style—in the third period, we paint ourselves." We consider this the most important art appreciation lesson we've ever received. It applies just as well to the appreciation of the art of servant leadership.

When first learning to lead, you paint what you see outside yourself—the exterior landscape. You read biographies and autobiographies of famous leaders, you read books by experienced executives and dedicated scholars, you listen to podcasts by motivational speakers, you watch streaming TED Talks, and you participate in training programs. You accept job assignments so that you can work alongside someone who can coach you.

You do all this to master the fundamentals, the tools, and the techniques. You're clumsy at first, failing more than succeeding. But pretty soon you can give a speech with ease, conduct a meeting with grace, listen to others with openness, and praise an employee with style. It's an essential period; an aspiring leader can no more skip the fundamentals than can an aspiring painter.

Then it happens. Somewhere along the way you notice how that last speech sounded mechanically rote, how that last meeting was a boring routine, and how that last encounter felt terribly sad and empty. You awaken to the frightening thought that the words aren't yours, and that the technique is out of a text, not straight from the heart.

This can be a truly terrifying moment. You've invested so much time and energy in learning to do all the right things and you suddenly see that they are no longer serving you well. They seem hollow. You stare into the darkness of your inner territory and begin to wonder what lies inside. You say to your-

self *I'm not someone else. I'm a unique human being. But who exactly am I? What is my true voice?*

For aspiring leaders, this awakening initiates a period of intense internal exploration—a period of going beyond technique, beyond training, beyond copying what the masters do, beyond taking the advice of others. And if you surrender to it, after exhausting experimentation and often painful suffering, there emerges from all those abstract strokes on the canvas an expression of self that is truly your own.

## Your True Voice

The turning point in your development as a leader comes when you're able to merge the lessons from your outer and inner journeys. You awaken to the fact that you don't have to copy someone else and you don't have to read a script written by someone else. Unless it's your words, and your style, then it's not really you. It's just an act—you pretending to be you.

This leadership lesson is quite similar to what Anne Lamott, author of *Bird by Bird*, tells would-be writers in her classes:

> The truth of your experience can only come through in your own voice. If it is wrapped in someone else's voice, we readers are suspicious, as if you are dressed up in someone else's clothes. You cannot write out of someone else's big dark place; you can only write out of your own. When you try to capture the truth of your experience in some other person's voice or on that person's terms, you are moving yourself one step further from what you have seen and what you know.[5]

What's true for writers is just as true for leaders. You cannot lead out of someone else's experience. You can only lead out of your own.

To lead others, you have to learn about yourself. After all, if you are to speak out, you have to know what to speak about, and if you are to stand up for your beliefs, you have to know the beliefs you stand for. To do what you say, you have to know what you want to say. Authentic servant leadership cannot come from the outside in. It comes from the inside out.

So we'll have to amend what we said to the workshop participants. Yes, you can learn to lead, but don't confuse leadership with position or place. Don't confuse leadership with talent. And don't confuse leadership with tools and techniques. They are not what earn you the respect and commitment of your people. What earns you their respect in the end is whether *you* are *you*.

So just who *are* you, anyway? What a great question for aspiring, as well as experienced, servant leaders.

*James M. Kouzes and Barry Z. Posner (www.leadershipchallenge.com) are coauthors of the bestselling, award-winning book,* The Leadership Challenge: How to Make Extraordinary Things Happen in Organizations *and more than a dozen other books on leadership. Jim is the Dean's Executive Fellow of Leadership and Barry is the Accolti Endowed Professor of Leadership at the Leavey School of Business, Santa Clara University.*

## Notes

1. James M. Kouzes and Barry Z. Posner, *The Leadership Challenge: How to Make Extraordinary Things Happen in Organizations* (San Francisco: Wiley, 2012, 2017). See also their *Learning Leadership: The Five Fundamentals of Becoming an Exemplary Leader* (San Francisco: Wiley, 2016).
2. Richard Farson, *Management of the Absurd: Paradoxes of Leadership* (New York: Simon and Schuster, 1996).
3. Max De Pree, *Leadership Jazz* (New York: Currency Doubleday, 1992).
4. Anita Roddick, *Body and Soul: Profits with Principles—The Amazing Story of Anita Roddick and The Body Shop* (New York: Crown, 1991).
5. Anne Lamott, *Bird by Bird: Some Instructions on Writing and Life* (New York: Pantheon, 1994).

# Chapter 20

# A Lesson from My Father

## *Washing Feet*

PHYLLIS HENNECY HENDRY

*I first met Phyllis Hennecy Hendry when she invited me to speak at a December gathering of the Augusta, Georgia, chamber of commerce. She talked me into coming there for no fee by raising the possibility of playing golf at Augusta National, home of the Masters golf tournament. Being a golf nut, of course I agreed. Everyone I talked to in Augusta said that, as a leader, Phyllis was a 12 on a 10-point scale. So Phil Hodges and I lured her away from her job to be president and CEO of our Lead Like Jesus ministry. Read her essay and find out where Phyllis's servant leadership heart came from. —KB*

I OFTEN THINK back to the day my dad told me that God had called him to be a pastor. Even though he had worked as a construction supervisor all of his life, at age forty-eight, because he was a devoted follower of Jesus, he had been asked to help a large church in our community start a new church in another part of the city. He would be a bivocational pastor.

When my dad announced this to me, I remember wrapping my arms around his neck and telling him that I would help. I could never have imagined all the lessons I would learn as I helped. My greatest assignments were going with my dad to visit people in the community on Saturday mornings and playing the piano for the congregation on Sundays.

## Visits with Mr. Lunn

I will never forget our first Saturday visit with Mr. Lunn. He was a crotchety old man. I remember thinking that his wrinkles met in odd places around his face, especially when he smiled. Maybe that was why he didn't smile much. At first, it was amazing to my eight-year-old-mind that my dad wanted to visit this man every Saturday morning. On our very first visit, Mr. Lunn had made it clear he would *not* be attending my dad's new little mission church. But he did say we were welcome to visit him any time, so my dad took him at his word.

My dad and I began our Saturday mornings together at a small local restaurant, and then we would do our visitations—starting with Mr. Lunn. He and my dad would sit in rocking chairs on the front porch and I would sit on the steps. On our third visit, Mr. Lunn asked me if I wanted a grape Nehi drink—and of course, I did. He didn't seem so crotchety to me after that.

I don't recall my dad ever inviting Mr. Lunn to church again. I do remember the two of them talking about fishing and world news. They talked about a lot of things. Our visits always ended with Mr. Lunn saying, "Come back anytime" and patting me on the head.

I once asked my dad, "Why do we keep visiting Mr. Lunn since he said he is not coming to church?" My dad explained that visiting Mr. Lunn was one of the most important things we could do on Saturdays. He said, "We are washing Mr. Lunn's feet." I was really confused.

Then my dad reminded me about Jesus washing the feet of the disciples to show them that serving people was the way to do everything. And by visiting Mr. Lunn, we were serving him even if he never came to church. "Besides, I really like Mr. Lunn," my dad said.

## Something's Different

After months of regular Saturday morning visits, my dad heard from a neighbor that Mr. Lunn was in the hospital. We went immediately. He was so glad to see us—and I could tell something had changed.

When Mr. Lunn came home from the hospital, we took him soup and cornbread. My dad changed light bulbs and repaired minor things in his home. I sang to him. He smiled a lot more now—and instead of patting me on the head before we left, he would hug both my dad and me. He always said, "Thank you for coming."

Even though my dad did not mention coming to church, he did talk about Jesus, telling Mr. Lunn about the difference Jesus had made in his life.

Mr. Lunn sometimes asked questions, and my father patiently listened and responded to each one. I thought my dad was so smart because the questions seemed pretty hard to me.

As I mentioned, I served as the pianist for our little church even though I was only eight years old. I had been playing since I was five, but my repertoire was small. No one seemed to mind. One Sunday morning as we finished singing, I looked up from the piano to see my dad staring toward the back door of our church. A tear unashamedly rolled down his cheek.

I looked immediately toward the door and I could hardly believe it. There stood Mr. Lunn in his Sunday best. At the end of the service, Mr. Lunn walked straight down the aisle to my dad. Mr. Lunn told the whole church that morning that he didn't know the Bible well, but he did know that he wanted what the preacher had. He had come to understand that it was Jesus that made the difference. He said, "I want Jesus to live in me, too."

Several months later, Mr. Lunn became very ill. As my dad and I visited him in the hospital and at his home, we heard how much our visits had meant to him. We met his family and he introduced us as his "good friends." One day Mr. Lunn told me he had an important favor to ask of me. After a few quiet minutes, he asked if I would sing at his funeral. Of course, with tears flowing, I promised I would. I knew it would be the last way I could wash his feet, as my dad had taught me.

## Serving Changes Everything

My dad taught me the simple act of caring about someone and how serving people changes everything—literally. Even though he died more than thirty years ago, I remember his amazing example of service—not only to Mr. Lunn, but also countless others who always seemed to call in the middle of the night, knowing my dad would respond.

I often return in my mind to those hours spent with my dad, remembering how he listened, loved, and taught me. I know now that he was washing my feet, too.

*Under Phyllis Hennecy Hendry's leadership as the inaugural president and CEO of* Lead Like Jesus *(www.leadlikejesus.com), the organization has grown exponentially, equipping and empowering thousands of people around the world to lead as Jesus led. Phyllis is coauthor, with Ken Blanchard and Phil Hodges, of* Lead Like Jesus Revisited.

# Chapter 21

# The Puddle Is Not the Problem

## NEAL NYBO

*When the longtime pastor retired from the church my wife, Margie, and I attend—Rancho Bernardo Community Presbyterian Church—I volunteered to be interim coach in their transition of finding a new preacher. In the process, I got to know and appreciate Neal Nybo, the executive pastor at the time, as a wonderful pastor, writer, and human being. I think you will really appreciate Neal's creative mind in this essay about obvious "puddle" issues and hidden "cabinet" issues. —KB*

I WALKED INTO my kitchen to set something on the counter and found a puddle of water on the floor in front of the sink. The sink was dry. No one had been doing dishes. I got a sinking feeling (no pun intended) that the puddle was neither my real nor my most important problem. Cleaning it up would not resolve my situation—if I cleaned it up, the puddle would form again. My real problem was inside the kitchen cabinet. I was not eager to open it for fear of what I might find. Sure, it could be a small drip from a pipe I could tighten. But it also could be a stagnant pool damaging the interior of the cabinet or hidden mold that could hurt anyone who comes near it. The challenge and root issue—a leaky pipe—was completely out of sight in the cabinet. The fact was that before I could discover and address my predicament, I had to risk opening the cabinet door.

## Servant Leaders Help Open Cabinets

People and organizations face *puddle* problems on a regular basis. These kinds of issues are visible and relatively understandable. The solutions are known, even if they are not easy. For instance, I know a manager who regularly felt at odds with her supervisor over the allotment of time each of them received during their weekly team meeting. Her supervisor put a high priority on training and regularly used meeting time to teach insights from current leadership books he'd been reading. The manager had practical issues she needed the team to address. It was a recognizable problem with an understandable solution: reallocate time based on the needs of the team.

Unlike puddle problems, *cabinet* issues are not recognized so easily. These kinds of problems may be intentionally hidden or ignored by both leadership and staff. They are often not addressed directly—and when they are, the cabinet is opened and they become observable puddle problems that can be solved.

For example, the aforementioned meeting-time puddle problem led the manager—a servant leader who was as interested in her supervisor's concerns as her own—to approach things in a creative way. She pointed out to her supervisor the pattern of not having time in meetings to address issues they had agreed on. She asked him if they could work together to find a time management strategy that would address the supervisor's vision for regular training and also give the manager time to accomplish her agenda. The supervisor admitted that time management was a perceived area of weakness—a cabinet issue—for him. Secretly, he felt guilty because his inability to manage time often left his staff in a state of chaos. He had hoped that the leadership training might compensate for his lack of time management skills.

Dealing with the puddle problem by simply reallocating time in the meeting would not solve the hidden cabinet issue for the supervisor—it would just surface again or sprout a leak elsewhere. The manager suggested to the supervisor that he bring in a person to train everyone in time management, and also that he use the team meeting as a public forum for practicing his own skills. The supervisor announced to the team his intention to give the manager the time she needed in the meetings and stated that the team could hold him accountable to do so. The puddle was cleaned up and his potentially career-ending cabinet issue had begun to be addressed.

## Puddle Problems Tend to Be Technical in Nature

According to Ronald A. Heifetz and Marty Linsky, technical problems are issues people face on a regular basis for which they have known solutions.[1] For example, needing to lose five pounds after the holidays is a technical (puddle) challenge with known solutions. To lose weight, one eats less and exercises more.

Cabinet problems cannot be addressed by authoritative decisions. They require those involved to internalize a change before the problem can be resolved. For example, in the case of being overweight, much research has been done regarding stress eating. With persistent stress, the hormone cortisol builds up in our body and increases appetite. If stress is an unidentified factor in someone's weight gain, a puddle change like walking up the stairs at work instead of taking the elevator will not solve the cabinet problem—stress. A cabinet solution is often more complicated than a puddle solution—just as locating and fixing a leaky pipe is more complicated than wiping up a puddle on the floor.

Addressing adaptive challenges requires new ways of processing information and making decisions: experimentation, innovation, and changes in attitudes, values, and behaviors. It is vital that these most important and difficult issues be dealt with, but too often they are avoided. If servant leaders don't address them and lead their organizations through change, who will?

## Without Leadership, Cabinet Issues Can Escalate

Servant leaders need to help their people identify problems and prepare them to embrace necessary change. Regional executives lament the fact that relatively benign challenges too often blow up into large conflicts because no one onsite addressed the challenge in its early stages. In a personal email dated July 11, 2011, one such executive wrote: "Often we don't get notified of difficulties in local branches until after there is significant or public conflict. Instead of being able to work on prevention and resolution, we have to work on damage control, restoration, and recovery."

My experience is as much with churches as other organizations—and the problem of unaddressed cabinet issues is as pervasive among the sacred as the secular. In San Diego over a ten-year period from 1999 to 2009, five churches facing public, disruptive conflict saw average membership declines of 48 percent. In contrast, seven similar churches that did not experience public conflict experienced average decreases of only 6 percent. While financial and numeric losses are very real, imagine the added emotional and spiritual trauma that happens in faith-based organizations in tightly knit communities.

Every servant leader knows about or has been a part of an organization, family, or friendship devastated by conflict. I have counseled well-meaning people who were stymied by lack of personal knowledge and ability, and by organizational cultures that resisted exposing cabinet issues. I have realized that the life transformation we all seek is available as we live and work through our lives together over time—even amid the discomfort of conflict. Discovering and resolving challenges is a vital tool used by God to do deep, transformative work in human beings. As servant leaders we have the opportunity to bring this attention and resource to those we care about most.

*Neal Nybo (www.nealnybo.com) has been an ordained pastor since 1997. Neal came to ordained ministry out of a strong business career and a passion for communicating the great news of the kingdom of God. He is the author of* Move Forward, Shut Tight, *and* Discovering Your Organization's Next Step.

## Note

1.  Ronald A. Heifetz and Marty Linsky, *Leadership on the Line: Staying Alive through the Dangers of Leading* (Boston: Harvard Business School Press, 2002).

# Chapter 22

# Five Army-Tested Lessons of Servant Leadership

### JEFFREY W. FOLEY

*My father grew up in Highland Falls at the foot of West Point. However, when he graduated from high school, he decided to go to the Naval Academy in Annapolis. He retired as a rear admiral. Even though I am a Navy brat, I have a high regard for West Point graduates based on my visits to West Point as a kid. I met Brigadier General Jeff Foley, a hero of mine, through our Lead Like Jesus ministry when he volunteered to be chairman of our board of trustees. As you will learn from this essay, he learned a lot as a soldier. —KB*

IN THE WORDS of General Creighton Abrams, former U.S. Army chief of staff: "Soldiers are not *in* the Army. Soldiers *are* the Army."

To volunteer to willingly give up one's life as a soldier for a greater cause is perhaps the most profound example of servant leadership. Soldiers join the military for a host of reasons. One major reason soldiers choose to stay is the experience they share becoming a band of brothers and sisters—that special fraternity called the *profession of arms.*

For many folks not in this profession, there is a common misperception that the Army operates in a strict hierarchical structured environment. Non-Army personnel believe that command and control is exercised daily by those with the highest rank. There is some truth to that—especially during times of crisis when quick decisions need to be made. These are leadership matters of life and death.

However, for the vast majority of time when lives are not on the line, nothing could be further from the truth. In the Army, true leadership is not about being a master—it's about being a servant.

In a personal email, General Stanley A. McChrystal (U.S. Army, retired), former commander of U.S. forces in Afghanistan, shared with me a keen insight on servant leadership:

> Servant leadership is a term that I believe describes leaders whose actions and motivations reflect a selfless commitment to a cause, an organization, or their teammates. The key lies in intent more than in specific behaviors. It is an important distinction, because a leader's skills or effectiveness aren't a function of their underlying motivations—leaders can be exceptionally effective even when entirely self-centered or even evil in their intent. Servant leadership is a decision by any person to commit themselves to others in a way that subordinates personal gain to a wider sense of responsibility. I've seen it demonstrated by the humblest of soldiers whose personal presence is anything but stereotypical of our vision of leadership. And yet it brings a quiet dignity and underlying sense of purpose that inspires.

What follows are five tactics that represent valuable lessons about servant leadership I learned during my thirty-two-year career as a soldier.

## Lesson 1: Commit to Lead by Oaths, Values, and Creeds

New soldiers take an oath when enlisting in the U.S. Army: "I do solemnly swear (or affirm) that I will support and defend the Constitution of the United States against all enemies, foreign and domestic; that I will bear true faith and allegiance to the same."

In the mid-1990s, the Army embraced and solidified seven core values: loyalty, duty, respect, selfless service, honor, integrity, and personal courage. These values define expectations of behavior and are well defined, trained, and reinforced routinely throughout military life.

The Soldier's Creed reinforces the commitment to these values—another clear example of servant leadership:

> I am an American Soldier. I am a warrior and a member of a team. I serve the people of the United States, and live the Army Values. I will always place the mission first. I will never accept defeat. I will never quit. I will never leave a fallen comrade. I am disciplined, physically and mentally tough, trained and proficient in my warrior tasks and drills. I always maintain my arms, my equipment, and myself. I am an expert and I am a professional. I stand ready to deploy,

engage, and destroy the enemies of the United States of America in close combat. I am a guardian of freedom and the American way of life. I am an American Soldier.

With the help of a congressional nomination, I attended the U.S. Military Academy at West Point in 1974. While at West Point, three aspects stood out for me regarding servant leadership. The first was our motto: "Duty, Honor, Country." We learned on the first day of training that it is not about us. It is about something far greater: our nation and our comrades.

The second was our Honor Code: I will not lie, cheat, or steal, nor tolerate those that do.

The third aspect was the requirement to memorize Major General John M. Schofield's Definition of Discipline. General Schofield (a West Point graduate) addressed the Corps of Cadets on August 11, 1879. "The discipline which makes the soldiers of a free country reliable in battle is not to be gained by harsh or tyrannical treatment," said Schofield. "On the contrary, such treatment is far more likely to destroy than to make an army." Committing this definition to memory was one way to ingrain into our minds the dangers of toxic leadership, among other things.

Oaths, values, and creeds are not just words. They drive home the commitment to serve fellow soldiers and our nation—both greater causes than ourselves. They provide the foundation for the Army's culture.

## Lesson 2: Listen by Squinting with Your Ears

One of the most profound leadership skills in any organization is the ability to listen. My mentor, Major General Perry Smith (U.S. Air Force, retired), calls it "squinting with your ears."

Sergeants are the leaders of the enlisted branch of the Army. The origin of the term *sergeant* is from the Latin *serviens*, which means *one who serves*. So at the very core of the Army, the focus is on sergeants as ones who serve.

In 1978 I landed at Fort Bragg, North Carolina—home of the Airborne—on my initial assignment out of West Point. On the day of my arrival, I was met by the senior enlisted soldier of the battalion, Command Sergeant Major Tad Gaweda—a tough, battle-hardened veteran soldier and marvelous leader. He said to me that first day, "Every soldier has a sergeant. Don't ever forget that." The advice and keen insights I learned from listening to my sergeants paid huge dividends throughout my career, and continues to do so today.

The need to listen is not limited to sergeants, of course. You cannot help anyone if you do not listen with the intent of understanding. Active listening demands tireless practice. When I was able to set aside my ego, I learned tons from squinting with my ears.

## Lesson 3: Be Relentless in the Development of Leaders

The Army does not have professional privates or lieutenants. Soldiers either get promoted or leave—it is either *up* or *out*. Those who demonstrate leadership potential earn the opportunity to continue to serve.

The biggest differentiator between the U.S. Army and all others is the monumental investment in the training and leadership development of our professional noncommissioned officer (NCO) corps—our sergeants. We call our NCOs the backbone of our Army because of the monumental role they perform in leading, training, caring for, and motivating soldiers.

The development of officers is equally important.

The Army develops soldiers in three ways. First, millions of dollars are invested in professional soldiers through periodic formal training and education. Second, every Army unit is required to have an organic leader development program to help develop leaders. Third, all NCOs and officers help grow subordinate leaders through on-the-job coaching and mentoring. In the corporate world, these actions are referred to as *succession planning*. In the Army, succession planning is everyone's job, every day.

Servant leaders inspire people to grow while discovering their skills and unique gifts. Servant leaders do all they can to facilitate that growth by putting their people in positions where they can flourish.

## Lesson 4: Communicate Your Purpose and Intent

I recently discussed servant leadership and the Army with Bob McDonald, a 1975 West Point graduate, Army veteran, former chairman and CEO of Procter & Gamble, and most recently the U.S. Secretary of Veterans Affairs (VA). He shared with me his life's purpose: to improve lives. Servant leaders use this purpose—a mission larger than self—to motivate and inspire their team. McDonald worked every day to improve the lives of others at P&G and at the VA. This lesson, which he learned as a youth growing up in the Boy Scouts, was reinforced when he served in the Army.

Leaders need to understand the purpose and intent of their boss. When they do, they can better capitalize on bringing their own knowledge, skills, and abilities to bear in making good decisions in their lives.

One of the key roles of a servant leader is to be visionary, which means to communicate with precision about what is expected in the future or end state. In the Army's standard mission orders process, there is a specific place for what is called *commander's intent*. This is where the commander describes what constitutes success for the operation, linking the purpose to how the operation is envisioned to go down. When done well, this intent facilitates a shared understanding of what is in the mind of the commander.

I remember writing these valuable intent statements. Once clear understanding is achieved, the higher-level commander then becomes the servant by doing everything possible to enable the success of the subordinate commanders to meet that intent. This explanation is a bit oversimplified but it illustrates servant leadership in action. This same process is used at all levels of the Army including (less formally) down to sergeants who lead small teams.

## Lesson 5: Build Trusted Relationships

Building trusted relationships trumps everything when it comes to effective leadership.

True leadership comes to life when mutual trust exists between leaders and followers. Genuine trust happens when soldiers train, sweat, bleed, and sacrifice together in preparation for the ultimate test of combat. They are honest with each other. They hold each other accountable. There is an element of love and support that develops as soldiers of all ranks live life together. This unique esprit de corps is the special sauce that really separates great teams from good teams.

When there is a lack of trust in a military unit, the consequences are significant, possibly catastrophic: decisions are questioned, commitment evaporates, discipline erodes, and the unit becomes ineffective. It does not take long to create an environment of distrust.

When soldiers know their leaders have their backs, they trust them and will do anything for them.

Nowhere is it more critical to demonstrate the empathy and care for soldiers than when tragedy strikes. I learned when something tragic happens to a soldier to go to them and to the home of their family. I didn't need to worry about what to say; the family just needed to know that I cared. I visited many homes. I wrapped my arms around a lot of troops and families in need.

In the best units I served, I felt the love and support of those around me. I knew they would come to my aid if needed, just as I would them. The best leaders I have known have held trust as their highest priority.

## Summary: Putting the Lessons into Action

These five lessons are what I learned about how servant leadership contributes to a winning culture for the U.S. Army. Those who serve are volunteers and do so in support of a grateful nation. When the American people show their gratitude, it makes a difference because the soldiers know the people care about them.

To summarize how soldiers and their comrades in other services feel about serving in uniform, allow me to highlight a profound day in our recent military history. The date was July 4, 2008. The location was Camp Victory, the U.S. military headquarters in Baghdad, Iraq. On that day, 1,215 soldiers, sailors, airmen, and marines raised their right hand and pledged to continue defending the land of the free in the largest reenlistment ceremony since the all-volunteer Army was established in July 1973.

Why did so many troops choose to remain in uniform—and to do so in the combat theater where so many had deployed and sacrificed over seven years of constant conflict in Afghanistan and Iraq? I believe the servant leadership environment created by soldiers of all ranks was a principal contributor. And when you sacrifice and suffer in defense of America, you learn to love it more.

*Jeffrey W. Foley is president of Loral Mountain Solutions, Inc. (www.loralmountain.com), where he is a speaker and leadership consultant who coaches executives and helps them build high-performing organizations. He is coauthor of the book* Rules and Tools for Leaders, *now in its fourth edition. Jeff graduated from West Point and served thirty-two years in the U.S. Army, earning the rank of brigadier general. Throughout his military career he served in leadership positions around the world, always focused on the accomplishment of the mission and taking care of people.*

# Chapter 23

# A Baptism of Leadership

## ERWIN RAPHAEL MCMANUS

*Erwin McManus and I met when we were cohosts at a Lead Like Jesus simulcast. That was the beginning of my admiration for Erwin, not only as a preacher but also as a brother in servant leadership. What he has done with the creation of his Los Angeles-based church, Mosaic—a gathering place for broken people—is absolutely amazing. He felt if all of these people from different backgrounds and different walks of life could come together in a community of love, they could create a beautiful mosaic. Erwin's essay is a candid and personal story about a servant leader's struggle. —KB*

IT WAS A rainy Sunday morning and a rare day for me because I was in a suit. To be honest, *rainy* is an understatement. It was a torrential downpour where the streets were quickly turning into rivers. I had just finished speaking at a little church in the inner-city area of Dallas, and the prospect of getting to my car without being drenched was unlikely.

I watched as people ran through the parking lot using whatever they could find to cover their perfectly groomed hair and Sunday best clothes. I stood in a hidden corner wanting to avoid involving myself, as some people had taken the bus to church and were trapped by the storm.

My precious wife, Kim, pulled me out of the shadows and informed me we had been asked to chauffeur a group of high school students to their homes. I was not happy about being recruited. I felt I had already done my part by bringing a message of hope. (I'm not sure, but I may have even talked about the power of serving.)

Shortly thereafter, as we were driving through the rainstorm in our yellow Ford Pinto packed with teenagers, my wife suddenly yelled out, "Did you see that man?"

I said, "What man? I can't even see the road!" The windshield wipers were losing their battle trying to clear a view for me to drive forward. The car felt more like a boat as we pushed our way through the waters, causing waves as we advanced.

Kim insisted I stop to help the man who was caught in the storm. I genuinely never saw him.

I didn't want to see him.

"We need to take these kids home first," I said. "Then we'll go back and help the man if he's still there."

It took only a few minutes to make the rounds and get the crew to their homes. We were now fighting our way back to the street where Kim insisted the man had been standing. I looked and saw no one.

"There he is—you just passed him!" Kim shouted, as if I had done it on purpose.

Turning around in this storm would not be easy. I tried to convince her we should just go on home. She wouldn't have it. So I managed to turn around—and then I saw him in front of me: a homeless man trying to reassemble his shopping cart as his possessions floated in the flooded street.

Kim said, "We need to help him." Just so you know, my wife was about eight months pregnant with our first child at the time. I knew when she said *we* she did *not* mean herself and the baby. It was the royal *we*—which meant *me*, on her behalf.

Frustrated about having to take on a task I knew would be futile, I took off my suit jacket and jumped out of the car to help the man. While the rain poured down on us and the waters ran knee deep, I reassembled his broken cart and then helped him gather up his possessions—which to me looked like nothing more than garbage that was now soaking wet and worthless.

I will never forget the timing. The moment we were done, the rain suddenly stopped and the sun broke through. The sky was beautiful and clear.

The irony of this struck me as far too coincidental. Was this God's way of making a point, or simply His sense of humor?

After I spoke with the man and he assured me there was no other way I could help him, I slowly walked back to our car. I was drenched. I got in, closed the door, and quietly began driving.

I didn't even try to make eye contact with my sweet wife. I just wanted to make it home without having a conversation. But it was hard to ignore what was happening next to me in the silence. Kim was crying. So it was now dry outside and raining in the car.

I took a deep breath, thinking *Great, now she's crying. What did I do wrong?*

"Why are you crying?" I asked quietly, not really wanting to hear the answer.

It took a moment for Kim to catch her breath and find the words—words I will never forget.

"That was the greatest sermon you have ever preached."

Those words changed my life.

Frankly, I had always hoped my greatest message would be to an audience of thousands, not to an audience of one. Now I know better. Our message is *always* given to an audience of one—the person we are serving. In serving others, our message is our lives. We must live our message for our message to have life. To me, that's what servant leadership is all about.

The life of Jesus gave power to the words of Jesus. Jesus is the greatest leader the world has ever known because He is also the greatest servant the world has ever known.

*Servant leadership* is a peculiar and even unexpected combination of words. They would at first glance seem mutually exclusive. Pick one—but you can't be both at the same time. Or so it would seem. It also implies that there are many different approaches to leadership from which we can choose. After all, history is resplendent with examples of leaders we should have never followed.

The truth is, while everyone can serve, not everyone is equally designed to lead. I know in our egalitarian culture we want to pretend everyone is the same. But everyone is not the same. We all have influence, but the radius of that influence varies from person to person.

Some struggle to have a vision for their lives while others struggle because they have a vision for the world. You can maximize the influence you have been entrusted with, but the material of leadership is a rare combination of talent, intelligence, skill, and other unpredictable intangibles. All of this, forged together through the choices you make and the person you choose to become, has merged to make you the leader you are today. And here is the fundamental part of the problem: the more gifted you are to lead, the greater the temptation to forgo the calling to serve.

Leadership is a product of gifting. Servanthood is about character. The combination is what we would describe as *gravitas*. While leadership is clearly developed and honed, it is just as clearly forged from material you were born with. Your character is a different story. Here the material emerges out of your choices. You determine the depth of your capacity to serve.

Servanthood is completely independent of talent. While your talent may have a ceiling, your character does not. You can serve to your heart's content. And that is exactly the point—servanthood is a matter of the heart.

Leadership is the ability to move others in a common direction to accomplish a common mission. It is not limited or defined by why or where we are leading those who are following.

Servant leadership is about the *why*. It is about motive. Servant leadership isn't a strategy or an approach toward leadership. Servant leadership is the intention and the essence of our leadership. This is why it is so important to know how to serve before you learn how to lead.

Serving and leading change you. If you become a leader before you become a servant, you will use your talent to move people to fulfill your agenda regardless of their well-being. You will see and treat people as cogs in your wheel to move and use as you deem necessary.

If you become a servant before you become a leader, you will see your talent as a gift to be used for the good of others. You will see yourself as a servant to a higher calling; a more noble mission; a purpose greater than yourself.

The power of the servant leader does not come from their position but from their sacrifice. They are followed not because they are feared but because they are admired. Their gravitas is not based on their title or rank or status, but on their blood and sweat and tears. They have earned the right to lead because they have set the standard for what it means to serve. They choose to serve. They were chosen to lead.

This is the paradox of Jesus. Jesus rewrites the script of what it means to lead. He never asks more of His followers than He has given himself. He sets the standard: to lead is to serve. And only those who serve will ever be entrusted with leadership.

The way of Jesus is to serve. It is not a methodology or strategy. It is who God is. God is a servant. It is His essence.

That's why, when Jesus knew that all power and authority had been given Him, the first thing He did was tie a towel around His waist and wash His disciples' feet. This is what God does with His power. This is why God is both all powerful and all good. Absolute power does not corrupt absolutely, it reveals absolutely. With all the power in the universe, God still chooses the path of servanthood.

We tend to want God's power but not His character. Yet only when we embrace His character are we trustworthy with His power. Servant leadership understands that our calling is not to overpower but to empower.

Leadership is a privilege that should only be entrusted to those whose hands are callused and character is marked by the virtue of becoming a servant. He who serves greatly will lead greatly. And in the end, if you want to be great in God's kingdom, then become the servant of all.

Who we are in the rain, and the choices we make to serve when no one is watching, are all we will have to give to the world when we have our moment in the sun. The greatest leaders when the sun is shining are the greatest servants in the rain.

On the same day I was determined to stay dry, I found myself drenched. I didn't know it then but that day was my most profound baptism. It was my baptism of leadership.

The baptism of leadership is servanthood.

*Erwin Raphael McManus is an iconoclast known for his integration of creativity and spirituality. He is the lead pastor and founder of Mosaic, a church located in the heart of Los Angeles. He is the author of* The Last Arrow, The Barbarian Way, The Artisan Soul, *and several other books on spirituality and creativity.*

# Chapter 24

# Little Things and Big Things

## JON GORDON

*When Jon Gordon and I first met, I found out he was a fellow Cornellian. Then I heard him speak and I quickly realized we were more than Cornell brothers—we were kindred hearts. I think you'll feel the same way after you read his wonderful essay. Neither Jon nor I can think of a more important leadership role than being a parent, which Jon will demonstrate in this essay. What a blessing it is if you had a giving parent or two in your life who set the example for servant leadership. —KB*

WHEN I THINK of servant leadership, two images come to mind: Jesus washing the feet of His disciples, and my mom making me a sandwich.

It is written:

So He (Jesus) got up from the supper table, set aside His robe, and put on an apron. Then He poured water into a basin and began to wash the feet of the disciples, drying them with His apron. (John 13:4–5, MSG)

After He had finished washing their feet, He took His robe, put it back on, and went back to His place at the table. Then He said, "Do you understand what I have done to you? You address me as 'Teacher' and 'Master,' and rightly so. That is what I am. So if I, the Master and Teacher, washed your feet, you must now wash each other's feet. I've laid down a pattern for you. What I've done, you do." (John 13:12–15, MSG)

Jesus felt that no matter what your position is, your role is to serve. That was exactly my mother's philosophy. Even though she was my mother and I admired her, she was always serving me. She didn't have a self-serving bone in her body.

Ten years ago, I was taking a walk with my mom near her home in south Florida when I noticed she was getting tired. My mom and I always walked together. She was a fit walking machine who never got tired, so I knew something was wrong.

"Let's go back to the condo so you can rest," I said.

"No, I want to walk to the store so I can get some food to make you a sandwich for your drive home," she said. I was headed back to my home in Ponte Vedra Beach, and my mom thought I might starve to death without eating during the five-hour drive.

"Okay," I said, knowing she had her mind set. Growing up in a Jewish-Italian family, the one thing you didn't do was argue with Mom about food. To her, food and love were one and the same.

We continued walking and made it to the supermarket. As we walked back, I could tell she was getting more and more tired. When we arrived back at her condo, she was exhausted—yet the first thing she did was walk into the kitchen and make me a sandwich.

On my drive home, I ate her sandwich but didn't think much about it at the time. Now, ten years later, I think about that sandwich a lot because it was the last time I saw my mom alive.

My mom was battling cancer, which was why she was so tired. She didn't tell me how bad it really was, nor had she mentioned how bleak the odds were for her survival. She was fighting for her life—yet, on that day, her biggest priority was to make me a sandwich.

Looking back, I realize she wasn't just making me a sandwich. She was showing me what selfless love and servant leadership were all about.

At her funeral, many of her real estate clients and colleagues came up to me and shared countless stories of all the selfless acts of love my mom did for them as well. Turns out she served her work team and her clients the same way she served her family.

We often think that great leadership is about big visions, big goals, big actions, and big success. But I learned from my mom that real leadership is about serving others by doing the little things with a big dose of selfless love.

Making a sandwich and washing feet may not seem like exciting acts of greatness, and yet they are the very actions that move others to do great things and change the world.

When I think about Jesus and my mom, I think about what I can do to serve others. When I'm not on the road speaking, I'm devoted to helping my teenage children be the best they can be. I help my wife around the house and have even become skilled at doing laundry.

My company's mission is to inspire and empower as many people as possible, one person at a time. *One person at a time* means we will never be too busy to help one person in need. That's why I personally respond to anyone who emails me seeking advice after reading one of my books. I figure if Jesus can take the time to wash the feet of His disciples and my mom can make me a sandwich while battling cancer, I can surely find time to help someone who needs encouragement.

Serving others may not always fit our schedule, but it fits God's plan for our lives. God doesn't pick the best; God picks the most willing. If we are willing to serve in small ways, we'll change the world in big ways. It all starts with washing feet, making a sandwich, and other small acts of selfless love and servant leadership.

*Jon Gordon is the author of numerous books including* The Energy Bus, The No Complaining Rule, Training Camp, The Carpenter, *and most recently,* The Power of Positive Leadership. *Jon is a graduate of Cornell University and holds a master's degree in teaching from Emory University. He is founder of The Jon Gordon Companies (www.jongordon.com) where he lives his passion for developing positive leaders, organizations, and teams.*

# Chapter 25

# In Praise of Followership

### MARGIE BLANCHARD

*Margie and I have been married more than fifty-five years. She is
my mentor, my first love, and an unbelievable servant leader. We
started our company together and I was smart enough to agree
that she should be president. Nearly twenty years ago she stepped
down from the presidency to create and lead a think tank we call
Office of the Future, whose purpose is to ensure we are not
surprised by new innovations or technology that come along.
I think you'll find her essay on followership unique, considering
this is a book about leadership—but it's so applicable in today's
workplace. —KB*

DID YOU EVER think about the difference between the words *leader* and *leadership*? The *leader* is just one person, whereas *leadership* assumes both the person and their followers. In our world, we focus a lot of attention on the leader. That's who we want to be when we grow up. But the follower is the one who often does all the work. In fact, we spend much more of our time as followers in this world of work than as leaders—an estimated 90 percent of our time. If that's true, followership may be more important than leadership—particularly if the follower is a servant leader.

"A follower as a servant leader?" you might respond. "Yes," I would insist. A lot of managers we know would respond in the same skeptical way. In that regard, Ken and I teach a servant leadership course as part of a Master's of Science in Executive Leadership (MSEL) program we cofounded with the dean of the College of Business at the University of San Diego.

Prior to our weekend class, we ask the students to read *Insights on Leadership*, a book of essays on service, stewardship, spirit, and servant leadership edited by Larry C. Spears.[1] (Larry is the author of "Characteristics of Servant Leaders" in Part 1 of this book.) At the beginning of class, we divide the students into small groups and ask them to share with each other what they learned from the readings and what it means to them. We have them focus on five of the essays that we preassigned. Year after year, the essay that catches the students' attention the most is "Followership in a Leadership World" by Robert E. Kelley. Why? People don't think a follower can be an effective servant leader. Kelley suggests followership is often overlooked because most recognition and rewards go to leaders.

Kelley helped me think of all the times as a leader that I have been grateful for followers who do two things. One, they challenge my ideas and implementation style and help me get clarity on what I really want to happen and how to best execute it. Two, when I have a good idea, they are ready to help me implement it by beginning to problem solve some of the challenges my idea or initiative would likely face. The first involves *managing up the hierarchy* as a servant follower. The second is all about *serving as a direct report*.

## Serving Up the Hierarchy

One of the most common questions we're asked is "What do you do when you believe in servant leadership and want to implement it with your people, but the top manager has a command-and-control (hierarchical leader-dominated) philosophy?"

Our response is "You can comply, complain, confront, dust off your résumé, or become an effective follower."

The most common methods people use for dealing with a command-and-control leader are to *comply*—adapt to the flawed philosophy of top management—or *complain*—spend more time moaning and groaning to anyone who will listen than they spend doing their job. A few people will dust off their résumé and begin looking for a position elsewhere. Even fewer will confront the top manager—which, unfortunately, is not usually very effective. Why? Because they confront before they connect. In other words, they don't have a relationship with the boss before they deliver their feedback.

When attempting to influence up the hierarchy, it's important to remember that you have no position power; only personal power, at best. And when you give someone feedback with whom you have no real connection—I don't care how gently you give it—you will not build up your relationship.

I'll never forget years ago, when Ken was teaching an occasional course at a business school and a new dean arrived. The dean had written a lot about participative management—an early form of servant leadership. However, he didn't practice it. He was wheeling and dealing and making all kinds of top-down decisions without any participation from the faculty. Some of the faculty leaders individually decided to confront him about his inconsistent behavior—and yet none of them had ever really connected with this man prior to confronting him. He essentially threw each of them out of his office in turn.

Ken, who agreed with the direction the dean wanted to take the school but was concerned about his decision-making style, realized he had to develop a relationship with the dean before he could give him any feedback. Ken and I believe that building a relationship with someone is like having money in the bank. No matter how well it is done, giving someone feedback draws something from your interpersonal bank account with that person. As a result, you better have some good experiences in your account to draw from. Otherwise, using our banking analogy, you will need a mask and a gun— position power! Ken decided that since he didn't have any position power with the dean, he had better build up his interpersonal bank account before talking with him about the negative impact his style was having.

So, one day when he saw the dean in the hallway, Ken commented specifically on how much he admired the dean's writing skills. He said, "I'm working on a paper I hope to get published in a good journal. With your writing experience, would you have time to meet with me? I'd like to share my latest draft with you and get your feedback." The dean responded immediately: "I'd love to meet with you." When they met, the dean had all kinds of helpful feedback. At the end of a follow-up meeting the dean casually said, "Ken, how do you think we should deal with some of the jerks in this school?" The key word for Ken was "we." He knew he now had some money in his interpersonal bank account with the dean—personal power. So he felt free to talk to the dean about how a change in his decision-making style might help and knew the dean would listen without getting defensive. In retrospect, that's what a helpful, effective servant leader as a follower would do: put the good of the organization ahead of any ego needs.

## Serving as a Direct Report

Now let's look at the role an effective servant follower plays in helping leaders implement their good ideas. It's all about going somewhere—and it takes both the leader and the follower. My brother, Tom McKee, who is our company's chairman and CEO, once told me he evaluated people by the number of things they helped him move forward or even took completely off his plate! Sometimes I think it boils down to a leader creating a vision, destination, or initiative, and a follower understanding that vision and helping it come alive.

I remember a time when I was president of our company and got the idea that our leaders and managers needed to meet one on one with each of their direct reports for at least thirty minutes every other week. While the managers would be responsible for scheduling the meeting, what was different about these meetings was that their direct reports would set the agenda—talk about whatever was on their mind. It could involve having a sick child at home that required them to spend less time in the office, or a particular goal they were working on and needed some support and direction. This was an idea I had heard about from a very successful owner of three fast food restaurants who had the lowest turnover rate by far of any of the other restaurants in the chain. He credited his one-on-one meetings as a major factor in those results. When you think about it, why would a young person go down the street for a small increase in salary when they had an adult who really cared and was interested in them?

So here I was with my new idea for our company. I needed some believers that this initiative could take hold in our organization and that it would make a positive difference in a number of ways. I found a servant follower and we brainstormed and plotted and rounded up a few more followers to experiment with this new practice. As with any change, it was not easy or quick. Even though there were early successes, there were more excuses than there were meetings happening. And yet I continued on, creating various incentives and watching more managers catch on and become converts until one-on-one meetings were finally baked into our culture.

This never would have happened without the role of the followers. They were the ones who had to do something new. We need both servant leaders and servant followers to execute any change.

It goes without saying that leaders' ideas should be good ones—worth the time and effort both they and their followers are going to invest in making something new happen. Followers need to see a line of sight between a leader's ideas and some greater good for the organization and the people in it. In my example of one-on-one meetings, we were aiming for less isolation and more connection in the manager/direct report relationship.

I often hear that the world is in desperate need of great leaders—and I agree we are—but I also believe we need what Robert E. Kelley calls *exemplary followers*.[2] These independent critical thinkers are actively involved in serving the organization and making it as good as it can possibly be—an organization that achieves great relationships and great results. As an exemplary follower, each of us is tasked with listening more deeply to new ideas and being open to the possibility of being influenced. Exemplary followers look for the highest value of an idea and help their leaders sharpen their thinking. They look beyond the temporary awkwardness, inconvenience, and discomfort that comes with all change and they are willing to see new and needed resources that may be already in place—like other enthusiastic people willing to try something new. They need to resist the pull and comfort of *not* changing. When we hear statistics such as *80 percent of change efforts fail*, we need to realize that both leaders and followers have the responsibility to not let that continue to happen.

## Followers Get the Job Done

In research for The Ken Blanchard Companies done by our son, Scott, and colleagues Drea Zigarmi and Vicky Essary on the Leadership-Profit Chain,[3] they found that an estimated 85 percent of the execution of a vision or change initiative happens through followers. Followers create and refine product and service offerings; they market, sell, and fulfill these offerings; and they play key roles in solving problems. Today, job seekers are drawn toward organizations with followership opportunities that focus on developing people and encouraging their career growth. They are attracted to cultures that give them followership challenges that help them connect their day-to-day activities with a higher purpose: the mission, vision, and values of the organization.

When I was president of our firm, I used to evaluate my day or month on whether I was able to spend at least 50 percent of my time on opportunities and the future, or whether that 50 percent got eaten up by day-to-day concerns and problems that others should handle. For leaders and managers, in most cases—as we have emphasized—the work gets done by servant followers. Most jobs, even the role of president, have a followership component. In fact, the real key to promotion up the hierarchy might be effective followership.

When I talk about effective serving followers, I am not talking about people who are submissive, towing the line, taking orders without question, or playing inside the box of their job description. I'm talking about people who are committed to a higher cause than their personal gain. They are competent and credible people who constantly are looking for ways to grow. They are curious and they set high standards for themselves and others.

How does someone become an *exemplary follower* in Kelley's terms? He contends that "the best followers know how to lead themselves." We've felt that way for a long time. That's why Ken, Susan Fowler, and Laurie Hawkins developed a self-leadership program for our company that teaches people how to develop the mindset and skill set for getting what they need to succeed. When we say *succeed*, we mean not only personal success but also organizational success. Our belief is that leadership is not something you do *to* people—it's something you do *with* people. This encourages side-by-side leadership, not the old top-down leadership. Servant leaders today realize that they can't get much done without effective followers.

I have great respect for followers. I am one in 90 percent of my life. In the other 10 percent—when I attempt to lead—I am blessed by exemplary followers, and so is our organization.

*Margie Blanchard is cofounder of The Ken Blanchard Companies (www.ken-blanchard.com). A compelling speaker, author, entrepreneur, consultant, and trainer, Margie is a corecipient with her husband, Ken, of the Entrepreneur of the Year award from Cornell University. She received her bachelor's and master's degrees from Cornell and her doctorate from University of Massachusetts, Amherst. She is coauthor of three books:* The One Minute Manager Balances Work and Life, Leading at a Higher Level, *and* Working Well: Managing for Health and High Performance.

## Notes

1. Larry C. Spears, *Insights on Leadership: Service, Stewardship, Spirit, and Servant-Leadership* (New York: John Wiley and Sons, 1997).
2. Robert E. Kelley, "In Praise of Followers," *Harvard Business Review* (November 1988).
3. Scott Blanchard, Drea Zigarmi, and Vicky Essary, "The Leadership-Profit Chain," *Perspectives* (Escondido, CA: The Ken Blanchard Companies, 2006).

Part Four

# Exemplars of
# Servant Leadership

## People Who Have Been Identified as Classic Servant Leaders

- Ken Blanchard and Phil Hodges, in "Jesus: The Greatest Example of a Servant Leader," provide a worthy illustration of how the important thing about being an effective servant leader is not what happens when you're there—it's what happens when you're *not* there.

- John Hope Bryant, in "Andrew Young: Partner in Servant Leadership to Martin Luther King Jr.," relates how the relationship between King and Young remains an almost perfect example of a servant leadership partnership between two great men.

- In her essay "Pat Summitt: Steely Eyes, Servant Heart," Tamika Catchings captures how Coach Summit, while a fierce competitor, made sure her players always came first. She was a servant leader who focused on both results and people.

- Tony Baron, in "Dallas Willard: The Smartest Man I Ever Met," describes how his mentor inspired greatness with his servant heart as he humbly taught and encouraged people he met on his journey.

- In "Henry Blackaby: A Lifelong Servant Leader," Richard Blackaby shares how his father, Henry, the great pastor and writer, has always modeled that we do not lead organizations—we lead people. And when we impact people as a servant leader, we change the world.

- Jim Dittmar, in "Frances Hesselbein: To Serve Is to Live," describes an exemplary servant leader who, with grace and humility, through organizations such as Girl Scouts of the USA and the Drucker Foundation, has made a positive impact on thousands of lives.

- In his essay "Charlie 'Tremendous' Jones: A Sermon Seen," Mark Sanborn illustrates how "Tremendous" lived out the philosophy that the best servant leaders don't just *tell* us how to lead, they *show* us.

# Chapter 26

# Jesus

## *The Greatest Example of a Servant Leader*

### KEN BLANCHARD AND
### PHIL HODGES

*I'm a latecomer to the Lord. As a result, it wasn't until my early fifties that I started to really read the Bible and learn about Jesus. In the process, I realized He is the greatest leadership role model of all time. When I shared this insight with my colleague and friend Phil Hodges, who had been a spiritual guide of mine, he agreed— and together we cofounded the Lead Like Jesus ministry. In this essay we will focus on Jesus as the ultimate servant leader. —KB*

INITIAL INDICATION THAT Jesus is the greatest leadership role model of all time came to Ken when he was asked to be on Reverend Robert Schuller's TV show *Hour of Power* after *The One Minute Manager*[1] was released in the early 1980s.

As Ken remembers it, Dr. Schuller said, "I love *The One Minute Manager.* Why? Because I believe Jesus was the greatest One Minute Manager of all time."

"Really?" Ken said with a smile, never having thought of Jesus as a manager.

"Absolutely," said Dr. Schuller. "After all, he was very clear on goals with his disciples. Isn't that your first secret—One Minute Goal Setting?"

Ken said, "Yes."

Then Dr. Schuller smiled and said, "And you and Tom Peters didn't invent 'management by wandering around'—Jesus did. He wandered from one village to another. If He caught someone doing something right, He would heal them or praise them. Isn't One Minute Praising your second secret?"

"Yes," Ken repeated.

To finish his analogy, Dr. Schuller said, "And when people stepped out of line, Jesus wasn't afraid to give them a reprimand and redirect their efforts—after all, He threw the money lenders out of the temple. Isn't the One Minute Reprimand your third secret?"

Ken laughed and nodded, realizing he had a point.

What Dr. Schuller said about Jesus as a One Minute Manager got Ken thinking. So a number of years later, as Ken began to deepen in his faith, he started to read the Bible. As a behavioral scientist, he went straight to the Gospels—Matthew, Mark, Luke, and John—and the book of Acts because he wanted to know what Jesus did and how it impacted His followers. Ken quickly realized that everything he had ever taught or written about leadership, Jesus did—and He did it perfectly with twelve inexperienced people. He transformed his disciples into the first generation of leaders of a movement that continues to affect the course of world history more than 2,000 years later.

At this point, this is no longer just Ken's story. Why? Because when he shared his realization about what an incredible leader Jesus was with Phil, who had become an important spiritual guide, Lead Like Jesus[2] was born. The purpose of the ministry is to glorify God by inspiring and equipping people to lead like Jesus. That involves following His mandate to be servant leaders and to love others as He loves us. The goal of Lead Like Jesus is "Someday, everyone, everywhere, will be impacted by someone leading like Jesus."

When we (Ken and Phil) tell people that the greatest leadership role model of all time is Jesus, we get a lot of raised eyebrows. People want to ask what evidence we have—and we're glad when they do. A few years ago at a Lead Like Jesus live teleconference broadcast from Atlanta, Ken asked his cohost, the well-known pastor and author John Ortberg, "Why would you travel all the way across the country from your home church in Menlo Park, California, to teach people that Jesus is the greatest leadership role model of all time?"

A gifted storyteller, Ortberg smiled and said, "Suppose you were a gambler 2,000 years ago. Now I know some of you don't like gambling, but bear with me for a moment. Which of these would you have put your money on lasting: the Roman Empire with the Roman Army, or a little Jewish carpenter with twelve inexperienced followers?" Everyone in the audience smiled as John went on to say, "Isn't it interesting that all these years later, we still name kids Jesus, Mary, and Joseph, and we name our dogs Nero and Caesar? I rest my case."

While John got a big laugh, his point was well taken. Clearly, Jesus's leadership was effective. His church exists today—and the Roman Empire doesn't.

Regardless of your spiritual beliefs, you'll have to admit that Jesus of Nazareth was a model leader. In fact, He's the only religious leader we know who built a management team. He went out and gathered together inexperienced people when He could have recruited good preachers. None of the disciples He chose had the kind of background you would have expected Jesus to need. And yet, He built them into quite a team. For a long time, we have been saying that the important thing about being a leader is not what happens when you're there, it's what happens when you're *not* there. As a parent or business leader, you can usually get your kids or your work group to do what you want when you are there. The real test is what they do on their own when you're not there. After Jesus was physically gone, His disciples carried on quite successfully and made a difference in the world. How did He make that happen? He was a classic servant leader.

The first time Jesus defined greatness as service, not the way the world does, is found in Matthew 20. John and James's mother had gone to Jesus and essentially asked if, in heaven, one of her sons could sit at His left hand and the other one at His right hand. She obviously thought leadership was all about the hierarchy. After Jesus told her that her request was not for Him to grant, He approached the other ten disciples, who were miffed because this mother had asked for those places of honor before they did.

> Jesus called (His disciples) together and said, "You know that the rulers of the Gentiles lord it over them, and their high officials exercise authority over them. *Not so with you*. Instead, whoever wants to become great among you must be your servant, and whoever wants to be first must be your slave—just as the Son of Man did not come to be served, but to serve, and to give His life as a ransom for many." (Matt. 20:25–28)

We added the emphasis on "Not so with you" in that verse. Why? Because Jesus's call to servant leadership is clear and unequivocal. His words leave no room for Plan B. He placed no restrictions or limitations of time, place, or situation that would allow us to exempt ourselves from heeding His command. For followers of Jesus, servant leadership is not an option; servant leadership is a mandate.

Jesus wanted His disciples to get this important message: "Anyone who wants to be first must be the very last, and the servant of all" (Mark 9:35). And yet, while Jesus wanted His disciples to be servants of all, did He send them out to serve without a clear vision and direction? Absolutely not. He did not forget the *leadership* aspect of servant leadership.

Jesus established a compelling vision for His disciples.[3] First of all, He was clear about what business He and His disciples were in. He called them not just to become fishermen, but to a greater purpose—to become "fishers of men" (Matt. 4:19, NKJV). He established a picture of the future for His disciples when He charged them to "go and make disciples of all nations" (Matt. 28:19). Finally, Jesus identified the values He wanted to guide their journey, focusing first on loving God and then on loving their neighbors as themselves (Matt. 22:36–40).

Once His disciples had a compelling vision—they were clear on their purpose, where they were going, and what would guide their journey—Jesus shifted his role to the *implementation* aspect of servant leadership. This involved serving the vision by strategically turning the traditional organizational pyramid upside down. Now His focus was on inspiring and equipping His disciples to go out and support, encourage, coach, and facilitate other people hearing and committing to the good news.

Jesus symbolically told his disciples about this shift when He washed their feet at the last supper.

> You call me "Teacher" and "Lord," and rightly so, for that is what I am. Now that I, your Lord and Teacher, have washed your feet, you also should wash one another's feet. I have set you an example that you should do as I have done for you. Very truly I tell you, no servant is greater than his master, nor is a messenger greater than the one who sent him. Now that you know these things, you will be blessed if you do them. (John 13:13–17)

Patience is a core skill for servant leaders. Jesus had to be patient with His disciples as they moved from dependence to independence in their journey to become servant leaders. If servant leadership were easy, you'd think the greatest model would have had instant success with it. What is needed is patience, endurance, and consistent focus. We've said for a long time that implementing change comes more from managing the journey than announcing the destination.

In that light, it's interesting to note that when Jesus sent the twelve disciples out for the first time to spread the word, He gave them extensive basic instruction on where to go, what to say, what to do, and how to do it (Matt. 10:5–13). In other words, Jesus did not move to the implementation aspect of servant leadership, symbolized in His washing of the disciples' feet, until the vision and direction aspect of servant leadership was clear. It was not until the end of His ministry on earth just prior to His resurrection that Jesus felt He could delegate His role of servant leader to His disciples with the Great Commission.

> Then Jesus came to them and said, "All authority in heaven and on earth has been given to me. Therefore go and make disciples of all nations, baptizing them in the name of the Father and of the Son and of the Holy Spirit, and teaching them to obey everything I have commanded you. And surely I am with you always, to the very end of the age." (Matt. 28:18–20)

We began to wonder what prepared Jesus to become the greatest example of a servant leader and to prepare His disciples to be the same. After all, there's not much information in the Bible about Jesus from the age of twelve until He began His ministry in His early thirties. In fact, only two comments appear in the Bible that were made about Jesus during this time: "Isn't He the carpenter's son?" and "Isn't He the carpenter?" We do know He was a carpenter and that He undoubtedly learned the trade from His earthly father, Joseph. Recognizing those facts, we wondered in what ways working as a carpenter helped prepare Jesus to become a leader. We sought similarities between the work of a good carpenter and the work of a good servant leader—similarities we could learn from and apply to our own leadership. Here is a portion of what we discovered.

First of all, good carpenters see the finished product before they start a job. Similarly, good leaders have a vision of where they want to go before they start leading people. Second, good carpenters know how to work with various types of materials just as good leaders know how to work with various types of people. Third, good carpenters know how to use a variety of tools when dealing with different materials in developing a good finished product just as good leaders know how to use a variety of leadership styles when dealing with different people to help them become high performers.

How did Jesus's leadership of His disciples line up with these insights from carpentry and leadership? First, as indicated, Jesus did indeed develop a compelling vision for His disciples that motivated them after His physical time on earth ended.

Second, Jesus saw beyond current credentials to the long-range potential of those He called to become fishers of men. Getting to know His people and their strengths, weaknesses, and individual personalities was a key element of His leadership. As Jesus learned about His followers, they learned about and from Him.

Third, when Jesus first called the disciples from their ordinary occupations to become fishers of men, each brought his unique life experiences and skills to the new task—but absolutely no practical knowledge of how to fill the new role. During their three years under Jesus's leadership, the disciples were transformed from untrained novices to fully equipped, divinely inspired and spiritually grounded leaders able to fulfill the Great Commission. How did Jesus learn to do that?

We believe the experiences Jesus had learning the trade of carpentry provided Him with a practical model for helping people grow and develop. He used this model to guide the learning experience of His disciples and move them from call to commission. Why do we say that? In learning to be a carpenter—and in many other trades—people must move through four normal stages of learning: from novice, to apprentice, to journeyman, and, finally, to master teacher. To enable that kind of transformation, trainers or leaders would need to change their leadership style from directing—which is appropriate for learners at the novice stage (someone just starting out); to coaching—for an apprentice (someone in training); to supporting—for a journeyman (someone capable of working independently but lacking the confidence to teach others); to delegating—for a master teacher (someone highly skilled who has the competence and confidence to teach others).

This approach is very similar to the Situational Leadership® II model[4] that Ken referred to in his opening essay, "What Is Servant Leadership?" Both approaches suggest that effective leaders need to adapt their leadership style (amount of direction and support provided) depending on the development level (competence and commitment) of the person they are leading.

As we reflected on how Jesus helped His disciples journey from dependence to independence in becoming fishers of men, we noticed He moved over time from a directing leadership style when they were novices to a delegating leadership style when He felt they were ready to be master teachers. As we stated earlier, when Jesus sent his disciples out for the first time to spread the news, he used a very directive leadership style. He gradually changed His leadership style from directing to coaching to supporting. Finally, in Matthew 28:19, Jesus used a delegating style as He told His followers: "Therefore go and make disciples of all nations, baptizing them in the name of the Father and of the Son and of the Holy Spirit" without any further direction.

That, to us, is what servant leadership is all about: providing clear vision and direction, then rolling up your sleeves and doing whatever it takes to help your people be successful—live according to the vision and accomplish the established goals. In this situation, your people don't work for you, you work for them.

As Jesus said to His disciples, ". . . whoever wants to become great among you must be your servant . . . just as [I] did not come to be served but to serve" (Matt. 20:26, 28).

In this essay we've been talking about Jesus as the greatest example of servant leadership. But as we continue to pursue and learn about Him, we remain amazed but not surprised that He is so much more than a leader who served. In fact, we can't think of any attribute of leadership—whether it be serving others, casting a vision, building a team, motivating followers, or implementing change—that Jesus did not model for everyone as He trained His disciples.

*Phil Hodges worked in management for Xerox Corporation and U.S. Steel for thirty-six years. In 1997 he became a consultant for The Ken Blanchard Companies and in 1999 he founded Lead Like Jesus with Ken Blanchard. Phil is coauthor of five books including* Lead Like Jesus Revisited, Lead Like Jesus for Churches, *and* The Servant Leader.

## Notes

1. Ken Blanchard and Spencer Johnson, *The One Minute Manager* (New York: William Morrow, 1982, 2003). See also their *The New One Minute Manager* (New York: William Morrow, 2015).

2. Lead Like Jesus (www.leadlikejesus.com) is a ministry founded in 1999 by Ken Blanchard and Phil Hodges. It focuses on heart-centered, transformative leadership that equips leaders to effectively impact their own spheres of influence. See also Ken Blanchard and Phil Hodges, *Lead Like Jesus: Lessons from the Greatest Leadership Role Model of All Time* (Nashville: Thomas Nelson, 2005) and their *Lead Like Jesus Revisited* (Nashville: W Publishing, 2016).

3. For more on how to develop a compelling vision, see Ken Blanchard and Jesse Stoner, *Full Steam Ahead: Unleash the Power of Vision in Your Company and Your Life* (San Francisco: Berrett-Koehler, 2003, 2011).

4. For more on SLII see Ken Blanchard, Patricia Zigarmi, and Drea Zigarmi, *Leadership and the One Minute Manager* (New York: William Morrow, 1985, 2013).

# Chapter 27

# Andrew Young

## Partner in Servant Leadership to Martin Luther King Jr.

### JOHN HOPE BRYANT

*John Hope Bryant is truly a world changer. I'm looking forward to our first face-to-face meeting. I'm thrilled with his description of the servant leadership partnership between Andrew Young and Dr. King. I know you'll feel the same way. —KB*

"IT WAS NOT about me."

Andrew Young has said these words to me more times than I can remember. Parts of his story of selfless service are really being told for the first time here, on these pages.

The traditional narrative of our shared civil rights movement history of the 1960s—a period that helped to define the nation and the world we live in today—suggests that Dr. Martin Luther King Jr. led and affirmed the transformational changes of the twentieth century almost singlehandedly. In fact, this is not what happened. Like most great leaders in history, Dr. King had help. And in this man, Dr. King actually had a partner—some might call him a silent partner. He is Andrew Young.[1]

In 1972, Young was the first African American elected to the U.S. Congress from the South since Reconstruction. In 1977, he became the first African American U.S. ambassador to the United Nations under President Jimmy Carter. And in the 1980s, Young served as the transformational mayor of Atlanta for two terms. He is a recipient of the Presidential Medal of Freedom and the French Foreign Legion Award and holds more than 130 honorary doctorate degrees. But in the 1960s Andrew Young was a servant leader who helped increase the effectiveness and impact of a prophet of our times—one Dr. Martin Luther King Jr.

Anyone wanting clear and compelling evidence of this special and unique relationship in history need go no further than the photographs of the movement. A simple image search of these two names together—Dr. Martin Luther King Jr. and Andrew Young—will result in an amazing, compelling, and awe-inspiring consistency: Young is never actually looking at the camera. Nor is he looking at Dr. King. He is assessing the situation, surveying the ever-changing environmental landscape for threats against his friend, Dr. King. Most notably, he is constantly diminishing himself—his own presence—and in so doing is increasing that of his friend, Dr. King.

Andrew Young was the one who calmed the radical and often revolutionary nerves within the halls of the Southern Christian Leadership Conference (SCLC) and the offices of civil rights movement staff. He was the one who knocked heads with those on both the far left and far right around strategy within the civil rights movement, which enabled him to bring a balanced set of decisions for Dr. King (who disliked conflict) to choose from. Finally, Young was the one who negotiated with the business community behind closed doors after the marching was over.

It is this last role I choose to focus on in this essay: the role of the quiet cocaptain. Young was not an aide or a key supporter. He was the chief strategist and right hand of Dr. King during the most critical stages of the movement's success. Not only did he not seek credit or praise for himself back then, he has continued to shy away from that spotlight ever since. You see, Young never wanted to be Dr. King, nor did he want to share in Dr. King's much deserved success and acclaim. He only wanted to help him. Andrew Young was and is the very essence of a servant leader.

During the Montgomery Bus Boycott, Dr. King learned the power of the purse when he asked black riders to not board a bus unless they were allowed to sit in the front of the bus like everyone else. He suggested simply, "We shall not finance our own oppression." The riders stood down, creating their own makeshift taxi service for African American patrons going to and from work. This simple act of quiet defiance nearly bankrupted Montgomery's public transit system. Little did Dr. King or anyone else realize at the time that the African American community represented the majority consumer economy in many of those small cities in the American South. And when they stopped spending, it meant something.

Later on, Dr. King would combine this learning with a media-savvy strategy. King never marched after 2:00 p.m. as he knew reporters from the major networks needed time to get their canisters of film on a plane to New York City in time for the 5:00, 6:00, and 11:00 nightly news. After each day's successful march, Dr. King would ask Young (whom he called Andy) to trade his blue jean overalls for a business suit and go quietly to meet with the business leaders from each small town. It was always done carefully, behind closed doors.

In each of these small towns, following successful marches that dampened the downtown economy, Young would meet with one hundred business leaders. The premise was simple: if he could get one hundred prominent business leaders in a town to agree to any accommodation of social policy within their shops, stores and businesses, the mayor and local government would follow suit. And that is precisely what happened. Business leaders, impacted by a dampening of sales revenues and other challenges, were the first movers in every town in the American South. They would agree to take down the "Whites Only" signs atop water fountains, on dressing rooms, at soda fountain counters, and in the waiting rooms and seating cabins of private bus lines. Young never spoke of his successful negotiations in those back rooms for fear that it would draw attention toward himself and away from his leader, Dr. King.

It was not the local or state government that first integrated the American South, it was the business community. And this was achieved through a unique collaboration between two servant leaders and soldiers for good: Dr. Martin Luther King Jr. and Andrew Young.

The philosophy for negotiating with the business community—in this case, part of the oppressor class—was simple: "Talk without being offensive. Listen without being defensive. And always, always leave even your adversary with their dignity. Because if you don't, they will spend the rest of their lives working to make you miserable." Those are the words of my friend and mentor, Reverend Dr. Cecil "Chip" Murray. But they just as easily could have been written by Dr. King.

Dr. King believed oppressors needed to be left with their dignity and—more so—a dignified way out of their own predicament. King also believed that a minority group, having no military, bombs, bullets, or any real structural power to fight back with, needed as a matter of strategy to claim the higher moral ground in every situation, rallying the hearts and minds of a nation behind their noble calling. In this cause, Andrew Young became Dr. King's constant secret weapon. No wonder Young later became Ambassador Andrew Young. He was a global negotiator for good among all people.

In small town after small town, Dr. King would set it up and Andrew Young would help to pay it off as a matter of their shared strategy. Afterward, Young would hand any public success back to his friend and movement leader, Dr. Martin Luther King Jr. Their relationship remains an almost perfect example of a servant leadership partnership between two great men. It is also a mostly unrecognized strategy that brought about change to make the world we know today.

*John Hope Bryant (www.johnhopebryant.com) is an American entrepreneur, author, philanthropist, and prominent thought leader on financial inclusion, economic empowerment, and financial dignity. He is the founder, chairman, and CEO of Operation HOPE, Inc.; chairman and chief executive officer of Bryant Group Ventures, and cofounder of Global Dignity. Bryant is the author of* How the Poor Can Save Capitalism, Love Leadership, *and his latest,* The Memo: Five Rules for Your Economic Liberation.

## Note

1. To learn more about Andrew Young's work with Dr. Martin Luther King Jr., see Young's *An Easy Burden: The Civil Rights Movement and the Transformation of America* (New York: HarperCollins, 1996).

# Chapter 28

# Pat Summitt

## *Steely Eyes, Servant Heart*

### TAMIKA CATCHINGS

*I have never met Tamika Catchings but I followed her when she
played for Pat Summitt at the University of Tennessee. Pat and I
were speakers on a number of programs together and we came to
admire each other's servant leadership philosophies. Some think
servant leadership is soft management, but as Tamika will share
with you, that doesn't describe the way Pat Summitt served and
motivated her players. She was a fierce competitor but her players
always came first. When she passed away, the world lost a
great person and a great coach—but Pat Summitt's legacy as
a great servant leadership role model lives on through people
who learned from her and loved her—people like Tamika. —KB*

WHEN I THINK of servant leadership, I think of Pat Summitt.[1] Pat was my
basketball coach at the University of Tennessee (UT) from 1997 to 2001. And
I know I am speaking for all of the 161 young women who were fortunate
enough to play for her when I say that Pat was much more than our coach.
She was our friend. She was our mentor. She was our mother. She was our
inspiration. And she was a true servant leader.

Pat passed away on June 28, 2016, but she will be a part of me forever.
There's not a day that goes by that I don't feel her impact on my life.

Pat's professional record is legendary. During her 38 years at UT, she
coached the "Lady Vols" to 112 victories in NCAA tournament games, 18
NCAA Final Fours, and 8 National Championships. Her 1,098 total wins
still hold the record for the most wins of any Division 1 college basketball
coach—male or female. She received numerous awards including Naismith

Basketball Coach of the Century, the Arthur Ashe Courage Award, the Presidential Medal of Freedom—and let's not forget her two Olympic gold medals.

Pat's accomplishments on the court are what we hear about a lot, but she was so much more. Basketball sidelines around our country are filled with coaches at all levels who can point directly to Pat's influence as the reason they are where they are today. She put herself out there every day for her players, her fans, and just about anyone who was willing to look beyond those steely blue eyes to get a few moments with her. It was never a big deal for her to serve others. I don't think she saw it as a big thing to come in early, stay late, or to do any of the extra stuff she did—it just got done. Her players would never think *Wow, I can't believe she just did that.* Pat was our superwoman. We just knew where there's a will, there's a way and she was going to get it done, whatever it was.

I grew up in a basketball family. My father, Harvey Catchings, played in the NBA for eleven years. Soccer was my first organized sport, followed by softball, and then basketball in the third grade. My sister, Tauja, played basketball in college and beyond. My brother, Kenyon, was a stellar basketball player in high school before he was sidelined with Crohn's disease. I played for Pat at UT and then played for fifteen years in the WNBA for the Indiana Fever until I retired in September 2016.

I was in the eighth grade when I first laid eyes on Pat Head Summitt. I was home from school, sitting on the couch channel surfing, and suddenly it happened. Those icy blue eyes were staring at me from the screen, and in that moment I was completely transfixed and unable to turn away. While the players dressed in orange were going up and down the court, my gaze was fixated on the lady with the eyes. She was stomping up and down the sidelines, yelling to her team, staring them down and demanding respect. I loved it! I was drawn to it. My first thought was *Whoa! That lady is intense!* But my next thought was *Wow, if I ever get good enough, I want to play for her. It would be the best thing ever.* I don't know how much more of the game I watched, but I had been mesmerized by that woman. One minute she would be shooting that steely glare and the next minute she would be smiling and grabbing one of the players in a bear hug. That was the day I started thinking about going to college, wearing that orange uniform, and playing for the lady with icy blue eyes.

Just two years later, the recruiting process began for me. I received all types of offers to different schools, but somehow even as a youngster I didn't get caught up in any of that. As I thought about where I wanted to play, I was looking for somebody who had the same values as my mom and dad—the values I had been raised with. There was one coach who had all of those values and more: Coach Pat Summitt.

I remember the day during my junior year of high school when Pat sat in my living room for a home visit, telling me what it would be like to have me playing on her team. It was so cool. The thing I loved the most about her visit was that she didn't promise a specific amount of playing time, or that I would start or even have a chance to play. She said she treated all her players the same—they had to earn their minutes and their position on the team. She expected everyone to strive to be their best, every single day. And she told me she would help make me the best player I could be. That's the thing I loved the most—being challenged.

So I chose Tennessee and Pat. Reading my acceptance letter, which came directly from Pat, was a dream come true. It was something I had hoped for since the day I saw her laser blue eyes glaring back at me from my TV screen.

Coaches at other schools I had visited had shown a clear leniency toward their players. But Pat was strict and her expectations were high for everyone. Her players knew what they were getting into when they came to play for her—it was going to be a lot of work. But when you want to be the best, you know what you have to put out there. Most of us had come out of high school as stars with numerous titles and accolades, but we were now all on the same level. So if a player came in acting like a diva, Pat would put her in her place really fast. "If you're going to play for me, these are the things I expect," she would say. She wanted our all.

Every day, Pat drilled into us her team-first philosophy: it's not about you—it's about the team. Every game was a team effort. It's just like life: you need your people around you to be successful and to help you get through it. Despite her legendary glare, stomping, and shouting, Pat's ultimate goal and purpose was to help each of us be better—not just better players, but better people. Isn't that what servant leadership is all about?

Pat challenged me in ways I had never been challenged before, and I loved it. I had never worked as hard as I worked in her practices during those years. Practices were always competitive between the players—even bloody at times! But off the court, we were family. Pat made sure there were no grudges held. She always had us practice against male players because she was always thinking about the game and how she could best prepare her team. It was never about girls vs. boys—Pat knew if we practiced against people who were quicker, stronger, taller, and more athletic, it naturally would condition us to be better players. She always said, "You've got to practice against the best to be able to play against the best." After going through Pat's practices, the games were almost easier.

Emblazoned on the wall in our locker room at UT was a list with the title "The Definite Dozen." They were Pat's rules for success—her blueprint for winning, not just in basketball but in life. She saw these ethical principles, developed through her years as a coach, as the reason for her success. And every year she drilled them into her team. The Definite Dozen were:

1. Respect yourself and others
2. Take full responsibility
3. Develop and demonstrate loyalty
4. Learn to be a great communicator
5. Discipline yourself so no one else has to
6. Make hard work your passion
7. Don't just work hard, work smart
8. Put the team before yourself
9. Make winning an attitude
10. Be a competitor
11. Change is a must
12. Handle success like you handle failure

Pat wanted us to be the best at everything we did—not just basketball. Yes, she focused on the game and wanted our best on the court. But she also wanted our best in the classroom. She wanted our best when we went out into the community. She continually pressed all of us to be great players, great students, and great people. When I go back to values, that's what stood out for me. She wanted me to be the best *me* I could be. She didn't want me just because I was a good basketball player—it went way beyond that.

I was born with a hearing disability and wore hearing aids at a very young age. Since I never really knew anything else, I didn't give it much thought until I started second grade in a new town. The other kids made fun of me relentlessly, laughing at my big, clunky hearing aids and the way I talked. So one day when I was walking home from school, I threw those hearing aids as far as I could into a field full of tall grass. My parents weren't happy and decided not to replace them. I didn't care; I was free! And I didn't wear hearing aids again—until Pat got involved.

Like many great leaders, Pat had an open door policy. If we had something going on in our personal lives we wanted to share with her, she was there.

And it went both ways: if Pat was curious about something, she wasn't shy about finding out what she needed to know.

One day after practice, Pat asked to speak with me. Along with our athletic trainer, Jenny Moshak, we sat down in the training room and Pat began asking me some seemingly random questions.

"Tamika, when people can't see clearly, what do they need?"

"Glasses," I said, oblivious to what was happening.

"And when someone walks with a limp, what do they need?"

"I guess sometimes they need to wear something inside their shoe?"

The questions continued. And then:

"And when people can't hear, what do they need, Tamika?"

I suddenly realized why we were having this talk. *Oh man, she got me!*

"They need . . . hearing aids," I said with a smirk.

Pat told me she had called and spoken with my mom. She had noticed more than once that I hadn't heard something she'd said, and she wanted to find out if there was anything she needed to know. Of course, my first thought was how mad I was at my mom. But Pat had a message for me that day that I'll never forget.

"Tamika, think of where you want to go, what you want to do, and who you will be one day. You'll have so many opportunities to impact people's lives. You'll be able to show kids who are going through the same thing you did when you were younger that it didn't stop you—and that they, too, can do anything to reach their dreams. You'll be able to encourage parents who have a child with a disability. You don't get it right now, but you have so much to offer. One day by using your voice you will make a difference in so many lives. You need to start preparing for that right now."

I got the message, immediately began speech therapy, and was fitted for new hearing aids. Pat was right, of course. She was always right.

Pat was honored when they dedicated the Pat Summitt Plaza and statue at UT in 2013—but she kept saying, "It's not about me, it's not about me." And I said, "Pat, it *is*. We all are where we are and have had the success we've had because of you." But that was Pat. She was an extremely humble person who never gravitated toward the spotlight. She would always turn it around and shine it on her players. That's the kind of person and the kind of leader she was—a servant first.

After I graduated from Tennessee and went to the WNBA, Pat and I stayed close. I looked to her for support and direction navigating the ups and downs of professional basketball. She was always only a phone call away. From the beginning, Pat seemed invincible to me. But, well, life shows us differently.

There are still days when I can't believe she's not physically here. It hits me at the weirdest moments. But then something snaps me out of it. It's almost like Pat's there telling me she's okay—"Catch, you got this." I know I would not be the person I am today without her presence in my life. There will never be another Pat Summitt. But her legacy shines bright through the players she coached, the staff who worked tirelessly around her, and the many fans and people across the globe who Pat encouraged and inspired. While we don't get to see her every day, her memory will live on forever.

*Tamika Catchings played basketball for Coach Pat Summitt with the University of Tennessee Lady Vols from 1997 through 2001. She was a member of the 1997 National Championship team at UT, and is a four-time All-American. Tamika retired from WNBA basketball in September 2016 after spending her entire fifteen-year professional career with the Indiana Fever. She was the WNBA MVP in 2011 and took the Fever to their first WNBA Championship in 2012. She is the founder of the Catch the Stars Foundation, which provides and promotes fitness and literacy programs for underserved youth. In 2016 she published her autobiography,* Catch a Star: Shining through Adversity to Become a Champion. *Following her love for tea, she purchased Tea's Me Café in Indianapolis in 2017 and has plans to franchise the company.*

## Note

1. For more information on Pat Summitt, read her autobiography (with Sally Jenkins): *Sum It Up: A Thousand and Ninety-Eight Victories, a Couple of Irrelevant Losses, and a Life in Perspective* (New York: Crown Archetype, 2013).

# Chapter 29

# Dallas Willard

## *The Smartest Man I Ever Met*

### Tony Baron

*I first met Tony Baron when he was running the Servant Leadership Institute at Datron World Communications. As I got to know him, I realized he was not only a wonderful teacher but also a great author and speaker. When Tony volunteered to write an essay about his mentor, Dallas Willard—a classic servant leader I had always wanted to meet—I was excited. I believe Tony has captured the essence of the amazing servant leader that Dallas was. When you read this, I think you will agree. —KB*

THE SMARTEST MAN I ever met was my doctoral professor at Fuller Theological Seminary. He taught a class on spirituality and ministry during a two-week seminar held at the Mater Dolorosa Catholic monastery in the hills of Sierra Madre. It was a lackluster topic, to be sure, but a fairly typical one for graduate school. The title of the class did not do justice to the richness I experienced during my time studying in that beautiful retreat setting under the guidance of Dr. Dallas Willard.[1]

Some may not be surprised that I call Dallas the smartest man I ever met, assuming it is due to his academic qualifications. He held a Doctor of Philosophy degree, specializing in epistemology—how it is that we know what we know. Besides his work at Fuller, Dallas taught philosophy for nearly fifty years at the University of Southern California, where he was voted Outstanding Faculty Member by the student senate. He was well loved and widely respected as a professor. I suppose it's also possible I refer to him as the smartest man I ever met because of his many writings on philosophy and spirituality, which offer readers a glimpse into his genius.

I call Dallas Willard the smartest man I ever met for this reason: I have never known another human being who was so integrated with the ways of Jesus, the icon of servant leadership (Mark 10:45). He understood how to live life as our Father in heaven designed us to live it. No one I ever met epitomized servant leadership more than my professor and friend.

## The Role of a Servant Leader

To paraphrase Robert K. Greenleaf, I believe a leader must be a servant first.[2] Servant leaders must leave people they are serving better off emotionally, physically, spiritually, or psychologically for having had encountered them. Servant leaders must also seek what is good and true and model and dispense wisdom on how to live life in the context of one's surroundings.

Dallas Willard lived out three dimensions of servant leadership that profoundly changed my life as a professor, pastor, parent, coach, and person. He inspired greatness, he was a humble teacher, and he was a compassionate encourager.

## Dallas Willard Inspired Greatness

Most leaders inspire greatness in others through their words. After all these years, Martin Luther King's "I Have a Dream" speech still moves us. A profound sermon or speech often compels us to be more or do more. Through words, we are motivated to think bigger and live with greater purpose—to be a better person, a more effective servant leader, or a more obedient follower of Jesus.

Some leaders inspire greatness beyond their words—their daily lives demonstrate the richness and weight of their words. They live and speak what is true. We find ourselves marked by the authenticity of their statements and won over by their convictions. Leaders of this caliber inspire greatness because they align their words with their actions. They convey wisdom with kind justice toward others and great responsibility toward God. They have an instinct for what is important in life. They are mindful about what needs to change to make the world better. Nelson Mandela and Mahatma Gandhi come to mind. More than their words alone, their *lives* stir greatness in others. In the same way, Dallas Willard inspired people to make a difference in the world. The ripples can be seen in the very public lives of theologians such as Richard Foster and J. P. Moreland and pastors such as John Ortberg. Tens of thousands of students, faculty, clergy, philosophers, scholars, church members, and truth seekers have been inspired by Dallas Willard, and I am among them.

## Dallas Willard Was a Humble Teacher

No one can be a transformational teacher or servant leader without humility. Arrogant teachers may provide knowledge to their students, but rarely wisdom. Humility is the honest appraisal of one's gifting without competitive comparisons to others and with full recognition that God is the provider. In essence, humility is personal power under control.

It is often said that ego stands for Edging God Out, and I would agree. But I would also say that an unhealthy ego is Edging *Growth* Out. Humility demands that we be lifelong learners of worthy things.

What made Dallas Willard such a gifted and humble teacher was that he was a seeker of truth and knowledge; a servant to his Lord for the benefit of others; and a sage for all those willing to hear and learn how to live "on earth as it is in heaven." Dallas incarnated what he imparted.

## Dallas Willard Was a Compassionate Encourager

I will never forget the opportunities I had to visit one on one with Dallas. He had a way of making me feel as if I were, at that very moment, the most important person in the world. Someone else with his impressive intellect might make the other person nervous or the give-and-take of good conversation difficult, but not Dallas. His gentle demeanor was consistent with his remarkable listening skills and warm eye contact. He genuinely cared about each person as an individual.

Before I met Dallas, my close friend Keith Matthews, also a teacher in my doctoral program, had already told him about me, my work, and a little bit of my heart. Dallas knew I was an Anglican priest serving as senior pastor of a Southern California church. Although the church was healthier than ever in its hundred-year history, I was physically tired and at times would experience spiritual burnout. The numbers were growing, the people seemed responsive, but I wondered if the church was really making disciples of Jesus for the world or just better church members for the parish. After five and a half years, I was wondering if I could continue to be an instrument of God—and if I was the problem.

As I talked with Dallas, it didn't take long for him to get to my heart. My tears flowed freely. Dallas touched my hand and looked me in the eyes.

His words were encouraging and refreshing water to a dry soul. I was truly nourished by them. I suddenly understood that I was called to stay at that ministry and continue on. It was as if Jesus Himself had told me that He was pleased with my ministry. No exaggeration—the burnout totally evaporated in that moment.

I had several conversations with Dallas in more casual settings over meals and in front of other friends. He always encouraged me with a touch, a look, or a voice that expressed "I believe in you."

I knew I was not alone. Many people called Dallas a dear friend simply because he was available to listen and pray with them. When I became part of the faculty at Azusa Pacific University, he told me he was pleased. His affirmation was timely and dear to me. It confirmed to me that becoming a professor was the next natural step in my journey as an apprentice of Jesus.

Thirteen years have passed since I took Dallas's course on spirituality and ministry. I still miss him deeply. His life and ministry continue to impact me in profound ways.

As I get older, I continue to prune my library and give books to my students, friends, and family. My wife has graciously managed to make room in our home for 1,500 books. Needless to say, I have not given away any books written by Dallas Willard. I need them.

Once when clearing books from storage, I discovered a note from Dallas. It was kind, positive feedback about one of my major doctoral papers. I believe it was a divine appointment by God to recover this note when I did, because I had been questioning my skills as a writer—and at that moment reading these words made me feel as if I were sharing my struggles with Dallas face to face:

> Dear Tony, You are an excellent writer in every respect. . . . Your paper is a profound meditation on the experience and use of silence by a disciple. . . . You are very strong on both depth of understanding and originality of ideas. . . . Thank you for being one of the best contributors in class.

The note was a great boost at a time when I was wrestling with how to communicate leadership and spiritual formation ideas with originality and understanding. Dallas encouraged me to keep expressing my thoughts in writing.

Dallas had this kind of effect on countless others. When he passed away, the Willard family opened an invitation on their website to anyone who had been impacted by Dallas. They encouraged people to share their thoughts and stories. Hundreds of people posted. Time after time, the posts spoke of his ministry of encouragement while sharing transforming truth. Dallas Willard, as a servant leader, was a compassionate encourager.

## Dallas Willard's Passage into Heaven

Dallas often described death as a transition from one room in the house to another. He even surmised that when his time came, it may be a while before he realized he had died. On May 8, 2013, the servant leader who changed hundreds of thousands of lives in his seventy-seven years on earth passed permanently to another room.

Dallas Willard inspired greatness and demonstrated compassion and humility as he taught and encouraged people he met on his journey. I am sure he is still learning and growing in the presence of the Lord. I would like to think he has been promoted from an Apprentice of Jesus to a Master Apprentice—although in my mind he already had achieved that status here on earth.

Although barely able to speak in his final moments, Dallas uttered two last words: "Thank you." I am told by those who were there that they were unsure what he was grateful for—although, of course, there were many things. Was it his wife, Jane? His family? His life? No one knows for sure. However, it wouldn't surprise me if this humble servant leader was simply responding to Jesus at the heavenly gates after hearing our Lord say, "Well done, good and faithful servant. Enter in the joy of your Master."

*Tony Baron (www.drtonybaron.com) is a professor at Azusa Pacific University and an internationally recognized speaker, writer, and consultant on the subject of creating servant leaders and transforming churches and corporations. He also serves as scholar-in-residence for Center for Executive Excellence (www.executive excellence.com) and is the author of six books. Tony holds a double doctorate in psychology and theology, is board-certified in forensic medicine, and is a diplomat in the American Board of Psychological Specialties.*

## Notes

1. To learn more about Dallas Willard, visit www.dwillard.org.
2. See Robert K. Greenleaf, "The Servant as Leader" (Atlanta: The Greenleaf Center for Servant Leadership, 1970).

# Chapter 30

# Henry Blackaby

## *A Lifelong Servant Leader*

### RICHARD BLACKABY

*I have worked with and been inspired by Henry Blackaby, who is highlighted here by his son, Richard, as a true exemplar of servant leadership. Henry's book,* Experiencing God, *coauthored with Richard, has impacted millions of people. One of Henry's key philosophies is "Find out what God is doing, and then join in." He helped me realize that I shouldn't be praying for God to support my agenda, but rather figuring out if my agenda supports His. Henry also convinced me that "God doesn't call the qualified; He qualifies the called." Thanks, Richard, for sharing your wonderful father with us all. —KB*

"LEADERSHIP IS ONE of the most observed and least understood phenomena on earth." Thus James MacGregor Burns introduced his seminal work on leadership, titled *Leadership*.[1] I would add that within the field of leadership studies, few philosophies are cited more often—and more incorrectly—than servant leadership.

I recall talking with a minister to college students who proudly informed me that he was teaching his students lessons on servant leadership. He related how he had taken his protégés to a downtown location where they had served soup to the homeless. This man, while sincere, was misguided. Service is not identical to servant leadership. Not everyone who serves is a leader—while, paradoxically, no true leader leads without serving.

In 1977, Robert K. Greenleaf published his influential book *Servant Leadership: A Journey into the Nature of Legitimate Power and Greatness*.[2] In it, he wrote "A new moral principle is emerging which holds that the only authority deserving one's allegiance is that which is freely and knowingly granted by the led to the leader in response to, and in proportion to, the clearly evident servant stature of the leader." Greenleaf challenged the prevailing command-and-control approach to leadership by asserting "the servant-leader is servant first." He went on to suggest that "the best test, and difficult to administer, is: Do those served grow as persons? Do they, *while being served*, become healthier, wiser, freer, more autonomous, more likely themselves to become servants?"

Servant leaders primarily do two things. First, they enhance the lives of their people. Despots use their people and drain them of their vitality. Servant leaders inspire, enable, and bless those they work with. Second, servant leaders develop organizations that not only achieve their mission but also benefit those who participate in it, whether they are employees, shareholders, or customers. As Max De Pree observes: "The goals of the organization are best met when the goals of people in the organization are met at the same time."[3] Unlike notorious CEOs who plunder their companies for profits or callously discard employees to improve the bottom line, servant leaders build healthy organizations that enable their people to thrive. Without a servant's heart, leaders will not properly care for their people; absent of leadership skills, leaders will be unable to benefit their people over prolonged periods.

Society has been inundated with reports of high-profile leaders who led selfishly, greedily, unethically, and ultimately illegally. Yet, despite regulatory laws and a cacophony of moral indignation broadcast by the media, the disturbing trend continues. What is needed is a fresh understanding of, and appreciation for, servant leadership.

Servant leaders can thrive in any walk of life. Robert K. Greenleaf led in that manner as he worked for one of the largest companies in America. Abraham Lincoln once claimed he would tend General McClellan's horse if he would win victories for the Union. In these pages I want to introduce you to the servant leader I know best: my father, Henry Blackaby.[4]

Henry Blackaby began his career as an unassuming, unlikely leader. Born in Canada, he was shy and soft spoken. After migrating to California to attend graduate school, he became the pastor of a troubled little church in the San Francisco Bay area. Gang violence, murder, and drugs were rampant in the blue-collar community. Yet my father's church began to regain hope and to grow. When the crime rate dipped significantly, the local police attributed much of the credit to my father's humble congregation. His second church was in Los Angeles. The congregation had endured a devastating split in which it had lost numerous members. Once again, the congregation began to regain its health. In both churches, my father felt called to leave after hope and vitality had been restored (and, I might add, shortly after his congregation finally brought his salary to a livable level).

It was in his third congregation that Henry Blackaby eventually began to garner attention. Faith Baptist Church in Saskatoon, Saskatchewan, only had ten members remaining when it called my father as its pastor. The church had posted a "For Sale" sign and determined that if my father rejected their invitation it would disband. Years of bickering and decline had brought the congregation to the brink of extinction. Again, my father restored healing, hope, and health to the congregation. Attendance grew. The building was remodeled and expanded. Joy and laughter filled the previously vacant hall-ways.

Throughout his career, Henry Blackaby led in a twofold manner. First, he always sought to ascertain the big picture. Where was this organization to go? What were the possibilities? Having an unbounded faith in God, my father claimed that if God were as powerful as Christians claimed He was, then nothing was impossible. In the early days, operating in a dilapidated building with a handful of bickering members, my optimistic father sounded more like a lunatic than a leader. But something astounding always happened in organizations led by my father. One would look in vain for his cutting-edge marketing strategy, innovative use of media, or enlistment of prominent investors. Yet it would always happen: hope, excitement, and expectation, along with radically transformed lives, inevitably resulted from his leadership.

At Faith Baptist Church, university students began attending in droves. As those enthusiastic students were trained, they were dispatched across the province to begin new churches. During the twelve years my father led the church, his modest congregation began thirty-eight mission congregations. But he was not merely a visionary. He was a servant. I recall numerous occasions when he brought college students to our home and spent the evening speaking into their lives. At times those young, aspiring ministers would fail and end up in our driveway or around our dinner table. My father poured his life into the people he led. Many of those people are prominent leaders today.

My father repeated his servant leadership style when he assumed the role of denominational leader. While without formal authority over fellow ministers, he exerted enormous influence in their lives by both serving and inspiring them. As a result, over the years he exercised profound influence over others.

Henry Blackaby has been invited to speak at the United Nations, the White House, and the Pentagon. He has mentored CEOs of *Fortune* 500 companies. He has traveled to 115 countries and spoken to their leaders. He has never possessed significant financial resources to distribute, nor has he had the power to dispense promotions or bonuses. My father's greatest resource has always been himself. People want to be with him. People have traveled across the country to seek his counsel, or to just be around him.

I have heard more than one aspiring leader ask my father the secret to his influence. I'm not sure my father fully understands it to this day. He has always had an unparalleled belief and confidence in God, and he instills that faith in others. He has that uncanny ability—possessed by all great leaders—to make the people around him better. He raises people to greater heights through his encouragement and personal example.

We live in an age that is desperate for servant leaders. In the long run, servant leaders exert enormous influence. My father certainly has, not only with our family but with people around the world. Perhaps it's because he has always understood that, ultimately, we do not lead organizations—we lead people. And when we impact people, we change the world.

*Richard Blackaby (www.richardblackaby.com) is president of Blackaby Ministries International (www.blackaby.net) and lives in Atlanta, Georgia. He travels internationally, speaking on spiritual leadership, and regularly ministers to Christian CEOs as well as church and family leaders. He has authored or coauthored more than thirty books—many with his father, Henry.*

## Notes

1. James MacGregor Burns, *Leadership* (New York: Harper and Row, 1978).
2. Robert K. Greenleaf, *Servant leadership: A Journey into the Nature of Legitimate Power and Greatness* (Mahwah, NJ: Paulist Press, 1977).
3. Max De Pree, *Leadership Jazz* (New York: Currency Doubleday, 1992).
4. To learn more about Henry Blackaby, visit www.blackaby.net/about-us/bmi -team.

# Chapter 31

# Frances Hesselbein

## *To Serve Is to Live*

### JIM DITTMAR

*I met Jim Dittmar when he was directing the Servant Leadership
Institute at Geneva College just outside of Pittsburgh. Every year
he brought in outstanding speakers who had a heart for servant
leadership. Frances Hesselbein was one of the best. I got to know
Frances even better through her role at the Drucker Foundation.
Despite her amazing accomplishments, she exudes humility.
When Marshall Goldsmith interviewed Frances recently and asked
her the key to her success, she said it was her blood type—
"B positive." When you read Jim's essay on this legendary servant
leader, you'll see why that is true. —KB*

FRANCES HESSELBEIN[1] WAS CEO of Girl Scouts of the USA from 1976 to 1990;
cofounder in 1990 and CEO of the Peter F. Drucker Leadership Institute (re-
named the Frances Hesselbein Leadership Institute in 2012); recipient in
1998 of the Presidential Medal of Freedom; and one of *Fortune* magazine's
"World's 50 Greatest Leaders" in 2015. The complete list of Frances Hesselbein's accomplishments, awards, and honors would take your breath away. Yet
the reason she is so admired, respected, and loved by people from around the
world has little to do with the tributes she has received. The reason is all about
who she is—as a person and as a leader.

"The awards are not what's important in life," says Frances. "You have to
have values that are the basis of all you do. You have to live your values. After
all, leadership is a matter of how to be, not how to do."

I have had the privilege of knowing Frances as a friend for nearly fifteen years. During the times that I have visited with her, watched her speak

and conduct meetings, observed her interactions with a variety of people, and listened to others speak about her, I have reached the same conclusion as many others: Frances is a humble, energetic leader of influence. She is a masterful change agent whose character resonates integrity, steadfastness, civility, and trustworthiness. In her often quoted mantra, "To serve is to live," she embodies the qualities that set her apart as an exemplar of servant leadership.

Frances describes her day-to-day life of service this way: "Every day I find a way to make a difference, to help someone, even if I don't know them. And then at night I ask myself 'What did I do today that helped someone, some group or organization? In what ways did I make a difference in someone's life?' I never fail to ask that question at the end of the day."

How did Frances Hesselbein develop into the exemplary servant leader she has been for decades—one who serves, values inclusion, breaks down cultural barriers, and works tirelessly for the greater good? What happened early in her life that had such a formative influence on her character and behavior? In answer to these questions, what follows is a portion of her story that is about humble beginnings, life-shaping experiences, rich familial influence, and walking through opened doors.

Frances grew up in Johnstown, Pennsylvania. After graduating from high school, she enrolled in the Johnstown Junior College, University of Pittsburgh. She later married John Hesselbein and they had a son, also named John.

Frances's hometown experiences were a crucial source of personal development: "As I look back, everything I learned in Johnstown prepared me for my life in leadership. Growing up and going to school with children whose fathers, grandfathers, and great-grandfathers had come to Johnstown from all over the world to work in the coal mines and steel mills gave me exposure to and an appreciation for a rich diversity of cultures."

The journey that eventually led to Frances becoming the CEO of the Girl Scouts USA was a circuitous route—one that began in a way that she never imagined would lead to the organization's top role. In 1960, Girl Scout Troop 17—thirty 10-year-old girls who met in the basement of the Second Presbyterian Church—was disbanding. Their leader had left to become a missionary and no one had stepped forward to replace her. Frances was invited to be their volunteer leader. She declined the offer several times before finally agreeing to "do it for six weeks, until we find a real leader," she thought. What was to be a six-week commitment continued until all of the girls had graduated from high school, six years later.

In 1970, Frances was asked to become the executive director of the Talus Rock Girl Scout Council and she accepted. In 1974, she agreed to take the same position with the Penn Laurel Council in eastern Pennsylvania.

Other doors of leadership opportunities in Johnstown also opened to Frances. In 1970, Frances was appointed the chairman of the Johnstown United Way campaign, the first time a woman had held the position in Johnstown or the United States. Responsible for leading its most important fundraising effort of the entire year, Frances immediately gathered a coalition of labor union and steel mill executives to help secure its success. Together, they mobilized the region to raise the highest per capita level of financial giving of any United Way campaign in the nation.

Besides these experiences in Johnstown, Frances's family was very influential in helping shape her character and her perspective on life and leadership. Of her father, Frances states: "His example of writing and storytelling, his sense of history and our heritage, and his love of family and service walk around me. I think of him every day and am grateful to a soldier, 'an officer of great character and courage,' who adored his children; understood the power of love, language, and example; and tried to prepare Trudy, John, and me for a life well lived—a life of service."

Another example of significant influence, which Frances calls her "defining moment in life," came when she was visiting her grandmother, Mama Wicks, who lived in South Fork, Pennsylvania. Frances was very close to her grandparents and spent considerable time in their home while growing up. In Mama Wicks's home, two beautiful Chinese vases stood on a shelf above a large pipe organ. Frances was very fond of these vases and often she would ask her Grandmother Wicks if she could play with them or simply touch them. Each time her grandmother would say no. During one visit, when Frances was eight years old, she again pleaded that she be allowed to play with the vases. Her grandmother took her aside, sat down with Frances and told her this story:

> "Long ago, a Chinese laundryman named Mr. Yee lived alone in a small shed near our home. Each week he picked up your grandfather's shirts and brought them back in a few days, washed, starched, and ironed perfectly. Mr. Yee wore traditional Chinese dress—a long tunic and a cap with his hair in a queue. Some days your mother and her sisters would come home from school crying that bad boys were chasing Mr. Yee, calling him bad names, and trying to pull his queue.

"One day there was a knock on the kitchen door. When I opened it, there stood Mr. Yee with a large package in his arms. I asked him to come in and sit down, but he just handed me the package, saying, 'This is for you.' I opened the package and in it were two beautiful old Chinese vases.

"I said, 'Mr. Yee, these are too valuable, I can't accept them. Why do you want me to have your beautiful vases?' He said, 'Mrs. Wicks, I have been in this town for ten years, and you are the only one who ever called me Mr. Yee. They won't let me bring my wife and children here, and I miss them too much, so I am going back to China. The vases are all I brought with me. I want you to have them.' There were tears in his eyes as he said good-bye."

At the age of eight, that story taught Frances the lesson of respect for all people and became the basis for her commitment to diversity and inclusion.

Another major source of influence for Frances was her friend and mentor, Peter Drucker, whom she first met in 1981. She had been invited by the chancellor of New York University to hear Peter speak. After meeting and speaking with Frances, Peter became deeply involved with the Girl Scouts USA, met its leaders, and shared his management insights with them for the next eight years. For Frances, it marked the beginning of a mentor relationship that lasted until Peter's death in 2005.

Their regard for one another was mutual. During an interview, Peter was once asked who was the greatest leader he had ever known. His answer? "Frances Hesselbein." "Oh, you mean in the nonprofit sector," the interviewer replied. Peter countered, "Frances could manage any company in America."

After having served as executive director for the Talus Rock and Penn Laurel Girl Scout Councils, in 1976 another door opened for Frances—this time an invitation to interview for the position of CEO of Girl Scouts of the USA. Frances describes that experience:

I never would have applied on my own. For 67 years, they had never brought up someone from within the organization. I didn't want to be interviewed but my husband was marvelous. He said, 'I'm driving you to New York—it's the perfect job for you.' So I went and interviewed, and because I was not interested in the job, I was very open and relaxed. Finally, they asked me, 'If you did take this job, what would you do?' I gave them this almost revolutionary, total transformational plan. Two days later, I got the call: Come to New York. It was July 4, 1976, and for the next 13 years, as CEO of Girl Scouts of the USA, I never had a bad day.

So Frances and her Girl Scouts of the USA leadership team set out to make the changes necessary for the organization to thrive well into the future. They applied leadership principles Frances had acquired through her experience learning by doing as a local Girl Scout leader, as well as the lessons of life taught to her by her family and friends and, later, by her mentor, Peter Drucker. Frances and her team worked to establish organizational structures and a culture that encouraged shared authority and decision making, emphasized a spirit of service, and, above all, embraced inclusion.

For Frances, inclusion meant replacing hierarchical, top-down authority with a model of shared governance and decision making that utilized the input of Girl Scout leaders nationwide. Frances called this model *Circular Management*. It meant finding ways to encourage girls of all races and ethnic backgrounds to become Girl Scouts. It meant making sure that adults in Girl Scouts leadership included members of those same racial and ethnic backgrounds.

To attract such diversity among the Girl Scouts and help girls and leaders in five racial and ethnic groups find themselves in Girl Scouting, Frances adopted a marketing and recruiting approach that spoke respectively to each of these groups. For example, five recruitment posters were created, each one featuring a Girl Scout and her leader who were either African American, Asian, Caucasian, Hispanic, or Native American, with a scene and a message that were culturally specific. The effect of this effort was very positive and resulted in doors being opened to girls and leaders that had not been opened before.

Frances also felt that the Girl Scouts of the USA was seriously out of date. When she was appointed CEO in 1976, she realized the program handbooks in use had not been revised since they were originally developed in 1964. To address this concern, she brought together a team of outstanding contemporary writers, researchers, and illustrators to create new program handbooks that were relevant to the young girls of the mid-1970s. These handbooks were heavy in math, science, and technology. And throughout each handbook were illustrations that represented the diversity of girls who were members of local Girl Scout troops.

All of these changes and more transformed the Girl Scouts, whose mission is "To help each girl reach her own highest potential," into an energized, relevant, inclusive, and growing organization that embraced the future with a hopeful sense that Girl Scouts of the USA could make a real difference in the lives of its troop members. As a result, by 1990, Girl Scouts had grown in number to 2.3 million members with 788,000 adult leaders.

At the last gathering of national Girl Scouts leaders before Frances retired, Peter Drucker was in attendance. As part of her final goodbye to all those in attendance, Frances and Peter were to engage in a dialogue while sitting on the auditorium stage. As they prepared to begin their presentation, Peter said to Frances, "We've played a trick on you. I'm going to interview you." As the interview neared completion, Peter told Frances, "A portrait of you will be hung in the hall of this beautiful facility (the Edith Macy Conference Center in New York). What shall the brass plate on it say?" Frances answered, "I hope it will say that I never broke a promise." "No," Peter replied, "It will say, 'She kept the faith.'"

Frances has indeed kept the faith. She has kept the faith of all those whose influence helped to make her the person she has been throughout her life. She has kept the faith while walking through doors opened to her. And she continues to keep the faith as she lives to serve.

This statement from Frances delightfully captures the themes of her life of service:

> Leadership is not a destination; it is a journey. And along the way we find fellow travelers to share the journey. We open doors that tell us where we should be—and then, once we have served, we close those and then we open new doors.

*Jim Dittmar is president and CEO of 3Rivers Leadership Institute (www.jimdittmar.com/home), which provides leadership development and training that is transformational. Utilizing insights gained over the past thirty-seven years as a leader, teacher, and trainer of working professionals, Jim creates learning experiences that are exceptional in content and interactive and engaging in process. He is excited about his new book,* A Leadership Carol, *coauthored with John Stanko.*

## Note

1. To learn more about Frances Hesselbein, read her autobiography: *My Life in Leadership: The Journey and Lessons Learned along the Way* (San Francisco: Jossey-Bass, 2011).

# Chapter 32

# Charlie "Tremendous" Jones

## *A Sermon Seen*

### MARK SANBORN

*It warmed my heart when Mark Sanborn, whom I've shared a speaking platform with a number of times, decided to write an essay about Charlie "Tremendous" Jones. Charlie's positive attitude had a major impact on my faith and my life. I'll never forget the last time I talked to Tremendous, just before his death from cancer. I said, "When you get to heaven, will you tell us what it's like?" Tremendous was weak but his answer illustrated what kind of guy he was. "I wouldn't have the words to describe it! If I did, you'd probably commit suicide!" Thanks, Mark, for sharing about such a great servant leader—my friend and mentor, Charlie "Tremendous" Jones. —KB*

EDGAR GUEST WAS born in England but moved to the United States where he became known as "The People's Poet." He penned more than 11,000 poems, which were syndicated in 300 newspapers and collected in more than 20 books. One of his best-loved poems is a classic familiar to many called "Sermons We See." In it he says, "I'd rather see a sermon than hear one any day / I'd rather one should walk with me than merely tell the way."

Servant leadership is about being a *sermon seen*; about living out an inner philosophy. The best servant leaders don't just *tell* us how to lead, they *show* us. And I don't think I ever saw a better sermon about servant leadership than my friend Charlie "Tremendous" Jones.

Many recall Charlie as a powerful speaker and successful author. His book *Life Is Tremendous* has sold more than two million copies since 1967.[1] When Charlie spoke, people listened in rapt attention. His booming voice and physical interaction with the audience were his trademarks. Charlie had the gift of engaging the brain by appealing to the funny bone, and few who experienced one of his live presentations ever forgot it.

He is probably best known for his declaration: "You will be the same person in five years as you are today except for two things: the people you meet and the books you read."

Charlie combined his love of books, leadership, and learning with his speaking and publishing career. Charlie founded Executive Books (now Tremendous Life Books) as a way to get affordable and uplifting books into as many hands as possible. He leveraged the service provided by his book company into an ongoing conduit for philanthropy: a percentage of the earnings each year goes to support the charities and organizations that were near and dear to Charlie's heart.

Here are a few reasons why I think Charlie was an exemplary servant leader.

## Charlie Was Larger Than Life

I dedicated my book *The Encore Effect* to Charlie, and in it I referred to him as "larger than life."[2] In the best sense of that phrase, Charlie demonstrated that we can live life larger than we are. He was a role model of a life lived large, and that is the legacy he left to us all.

Charlie lit up a place when he entered. I'm sure some people, upon first meeting Charlie, wondered if he was for real. We have all met people whose enthusiasm or mannerisms were an act. Charlie was the real deal. His enthusiasm was contagious and, frankly, irresistible. Over the years I've seen many cynics won over when in Charlie's presence. It was impossible not to get caught up in his tremendous spirit.

## Charlie Had a Passion for Others

Charlie's love of books was second only to his love of people. I smile thinking of how he would present someone with a good book: he'd hold it to his chest, sigh delightedly, and gently kiss the cover before he'd hand it over. You knew you were getting good stuff. I don't think we can ever count how many people fell in love with books because of Charlie or had their lives changed through a book he encouraged them to read. Charlie's great love affair with books was because he knew the power of books to dramatically impact the reader's life.

He loved and accepted everyone, even people who were mean to him. It is easy to like nice people. Charlie proved that you can love even the unlikable. He especially loved babies and little children. It was hard to get through a store or other public area without Charlie stopping to interact with and kiss the little ones he encountered.

If you ever tried to pray for Charlie, especially as he was battling his cancer, he'd admonish you to save your prayers for somebody who really needed them. "You might get to heaven before I do," he'd boom, "so don't pray for me." His unique and humorous perspective proved that Charlie was more worried about others than he was about himself—the mark of a true servant leader.

## Charlie's Highest Desire Was Service

Charlie was never about Charlie. He was all about Jesus, and therefore he was all about others. He lived out what he felt was his mandate: to demonstrate Jesus—the greatest servant leader of all—to everyone he met.

I believe ambition and leadership are two different things. Ambition creates benefits for the ambitious; leadership creates benefits for the greater good. While an effective leader enjoys benefits, servant leadership always benefits others—the larger community. Charlie's ambition was channeled into how he could serve others.

Charlie lived modestly when he could have enjoyed a much more lavish lifestyle. That's because he'd rather give—or "return," as he said later in his life. One great example is the joy he found in taking friends to a favorite factory outlet store where you could get an amazing deal on quality clothing. Once there, you learned that Charlie purchased far more for others—shirts, ties, and other dress clothes to give to missionaries—than he ever did for himself.

## He Was Congruent

There was no distinction between Charlie's professional life and his personal life. His faith infused everything he did. While some may not have agreed with Charlie, nobody could question his sincerity. He was serious about his work but always had fun. He loved to sing and laugh and he enjoyed the simple pleasures as much as the big ones. And his greatest joy was in helping others have fun.

Charlie dedicated the lower level of one of his buildings as a Christmas room, full of seasonal delights that could be enjoyed by people year round. He found great joy in bringing underprivileged children to visit so they could experience the Christmas message. The room was filled with easy-to-play instruments and Charlie often conducted makeshift performances by giving everyone an instrument and asking them to play.

## He Was a Conduit

To me, Charlie was a conduit of Jesus's love. It gave him superhuman energy, amazing patience, incredible compassion, and unlimited grace. Because of Charlie, I'm a better husband, father, son, brother, friend, and Christian.

Author, teacher, and preacher Samuel Brengle said, "The final estimate of men shows that history cares not an iota for the rank or title a man has borne, or the office he has held, but only the quality of his deeds and the character of his mind and heart." The quality of Charlie's deeds and the character of his mind and heart made him the most effective sermon seen—a servant leader who realized his greatest purpose and joy by putting others ahead of himself and loving them unconditionally.

*Mark Sanborn (www.marksanborn.com) is president of Sanborn & Associates, Inc., an idea studio dedicated to developing leaders in business and in life. He is the author of eight books including* The Encore Effect, You Don't Need a Title to Be a Leader, *and his national bestseller,* The Fred Factor. *Mark is a noted expert on leadership, team building, customer service, and change.*

## Notes

1. Charlie "Tremendous" Jones, *Life Is Tremendous* (Wheaton, IL: Living Books, 1968).
2. Mark Sanborn, *The Encore Effect: How to Achieve Remarkable Performance in Anything You Do* (New York: Crown Business, 2008).

## Part Five

# Putting Servant Leadership to Work

- In "How Servant Leadership Has Shaped Our Church Culture," Miles McPherson, pastor of Rock Church in San Diego, describes how love as the central theme has caused this servant leadership-based church to flourish.

# Chapter 33

# Treat Your People as Family

C O L L E E N   B A R R E T T

*One of the most enjoyable writing experiences I've ever had was coauthoring* Lead with LUV: A Different Way to Create Real Success *with Colleen Barrett, former president of Southwest Airlines. The airline industry, in its history, has lost money. But Southwest Airlines, year after year, has turned a profit. Why? Because Colleen and founder Herb Kelleher have always had servant leadership in their veins. You'll see it in the way she insists on capitalizing words such as Mechanic, People, Customer, and Leader! This essay is about Southwest's servant leadership story. —KB*

OVER THE YEARS, all of our Leaders at Southwest Airlines have tried to model Servant Leadership. Herb Kelleher, our Founder, led the way clearly—although I don't think he even knew what the expression "Servant Leadership" meant until we told him. To be honest with you, neither did I, until my friend, the visionary leader Ann McGee-Cooper, introduced me to the book *Robert K. Greenleaf: A Life of Servant Leadership* by Don Frick.[1]

But while our recognition of the term *Servant Leadership* might have come late, for over four decades Herb and I have said that our purpose in life as Senior Leaders with Southwest Airlines is to support our People. To us, that means treating People as family. To quote Herb's foreword to the book I coauthored with Ken Blanchard, *Lead with LUV*:

> Most people are looking not only for monetary security but also for psychic satisfaction in their work. That satisfaction is provided in our personal lives by the love and affection of family and friends. Why shouldn't a business simply be an enlargement of our circle of family and friends?[2]

How does that play out for us at Southwest?

First of all, we want each of our People to realize they have the potential to be a Leader. They can make a positive difference in anybody's work and life, regardless of whether they are in a management position. So we try to hire Leaders, no matter what role we want them to fill.

Second, our entire philosophy of Leadership is quite simple: treat your People right, and good things will happen. When we talk to our Employees, we tell them:

> You are the most important Person to us. You are our most important Customer in terms of priority. Therefore, we're going to spend 80 percent of our time treating you with Golden Rule behavior and trying to make sure that you have an enjoyable work environment where you feel good about what you do, about yourself, and about your position within this Company. But if we do that, what we want in exchange is for you to do the same thing by offering our Passengers—who are our second Customer in terms of priority—the same kind of warmth, caring, and fun spirit. If you do that consistently, our Passengers will recognize how significantly different this is from the behavior they witness at other businesses, and they will come back for more.

## The Quadruple Bottom Line

As you can tell, to me a Servant Leader's energy is focused not on just the financial bottom line, but also on these three bottom lines: being the *employer of choice*, *provider of choice*, and *investment of choice*.

I think the entire success of a Company begins with being the employer of choice. We try in every way to let our Employees know they are important and are empowered to make a positive difference on a daily basis. That's one of the reasons why, in our corporate headquarters in Dallas, there is a huge inscription on the glass elevator wall in our lobby that says:

> The People of Southwest Airlines are the creators of what we have become—and of what we will be. Our People transformed an idea into a legend. That legend will continue to grow only so long as it is nourished—by our People's indomitable Spirit, boundless energy, immense goodwill, and burning desire to excel. Our thanks—and our love—to the People of Southwest Airlines for creating a marvelous Family and a wondrous airline!

We are concerned not only about our People, our Customers, and our financial well-being, but also about how we give back to the community. We have always encouraged our People to be active in their communities. We want them each to be the citizen of choice. So in many ways, we focus on the *quadruple* bottom line: being the *employer of choice*, *provider of choice*, *investment of choice*, and *citizen of choice*.

## Three Serving Values

The highest priority for all of our Employees is safety, which we never compromise. Beyond that, we have identified three key values—Warrior Spirit, Servant's Heart, and Fun-LUVing Attitude—that we want our People to engage in every single day.

While having a Warrior Spirit is about being competitive, it's not in a warlike way. Basically, it means that you have to have a fighting spirit to be successful. You want to be the best, work hard, be courageous, display a sense of urgency, persevere, and innovate. You want to be a winner. People don't want to work for a loser. You want to win at what you set out to do. That's why we can still turn a plane around faster than anybody.

It's similar to one of the two character traits that Jim Collins, in his book *Good to Great*,[3] used to describe great leaders: will, or resolve. It's the determination to follow through on a vision, mission, or goal. The focus is on giving your all to get the best result so everyone wins—your People, your Customers, your owners, and the communities in which you serve. We think there's nothing wrong with wanting to be the best at what you do.

Our second value is a Servant's Heart, which is the core of knowing how to lead with love—or LUV, as we spell it at Southwest Airlines. (LUV is Southwest Airlines' symbol on the New York Stock Exchange. The airline first started flying out of Love Field in Dallas. At Southwest, LUV continues to be the common spelling of the word love, which is used, along with the symbol of a heart, in marketing, correspondence, and décor throughout the organization.)

When we interview, hire, and promote, we're looking for People who are Servant Leaders—no matter what title or position they are going to hold, they have to want to serve. They need to have a Servant's Heart—a passion for serving others. We want all of our Employees to follow the Golden Rule, adhere to our basic principles, treat others with respect, put others first, be egalitarian, demonstrate Proactive Customer Service, and embrace the Southwest Airlines family. As a result, while we obviously wouldn't hire a Pilot who can't

fly, we also wouldn't hire Pilots who think they are a big deal and more important than the rest of our People or our Customers. Our Pilots have even been
known to help clean cabins in our planes when there is a time crunch between flights.

Our third day-to-day value is a Fun-LUVing Attitude. I can't tell you how
hard we worked on the proper descriptive we wanted to use. We ended up
with "Fun-LUVing" to once again highlight our LUV symbol on the New
York Stock Exchange.

Basically, a Fun-LUVing Attitude means just that: we want to *enjoy* our
work life as much as we do our home life. We want to show each other and
our valued Customers that we care about them, and we want them to feel
like extended family members while they are in our presence. We have fun,
we don't take ourselves too seriously, we maintain perspective, we celebrate
successes, we enjoy work, and we are passionate Team players.

Our Fun-LUVing Attitude is personified by our Flight Crews. They are
always thinking of creative ways to make flights interesting and fun for our
Passengers.

For example, we received a letter from a Customer who told us that
before her flight left the ground, one of our Flight Attendants made an announcement that the Flight Crew had had a long day and they were tired.
For this reason, instead of passing out the peanuts they were going to put them
in a pile at the front of the plane and when the plane took off, the peanuts
would slide down the aisle and everyone could grab a packet. Passengers
laughed and thought he was joking, but then they saw him dump a pile of
packaged peanuts into the center aisle. Sure enough, during the steep takeoff
all of the peanuts began to slide toward the back of the plane. Everybody
started laughing. People in the aisle seats grabbed peanuts and passed them
over to other Passengers who stretched out their hands.

Do I have to say anything more about the Fun-LUVing Attitude of our
People? I think a lot of them must have colored outside the lines as children.

## The Leadership Aspect of Servant Leadership

The strategic, or *leadership*, aspect of Servant Leadership, which is the responsibility of the hierarchy, is rounded out with short-term goals and initiatives
that tell our People where they should put their attention right now.

At Southwest, we have annual goals and initiatives we want our People
to always have top of mind. But those things are tied to the big picture that
we want them to also focus on continuously—that we are in the Customer

Service business and happen to fly airplanes, we want to democratize the airways, and that everyone, every day, needs to live our values of safety and having a Warrior Spirit, a Servant's Heart, and a Fun-LUVing Attitude.

## The Servant Aspect of Servant Leadership

When it comes to the *servant* aspect of Servant Leadership, Herb was my role model. He had no trouble philosophically inverting the traditional pyramidal hierarchy. To him, once everybody knew where we were going, what we wanted to accomplish, and what our values were, he worked for our People and our Customers.

One of our relatively new Leaders once told me that his best example of a Servant's Heart was something he saw Herb do at one of our Spirit parties. Spirit parties are held once a year at different fun locations where everybody has lots of space to move around and visit. This Leader happened to be standing near the doorway when Herb entered the room. He'd heard about what a "rock star" Herb was with our People, but he still marveled over what he saw.

He watched Herb talk to a Mechanic in worker's clothes for at least fifteen minutes—even though there were literally hundreds of People circling Herb for his attention. Herb never looked over the guy's shoulder to see who else might be there, and never diverted his eyes from this man while they were talking. Herb was courteous to everyone who was trying to shove the guy out of his space so that they could fill it, but he gave this man his time. It was clear to this new Leader that Herb had no hierarchical concerns—he was completely interested in what the Mechanic was trying to tell him. That had a profound impact on this Leader, and he remembers it to this day. He has been with us more than twenty years now.

Not only do we serve and care about our People, but we empower them to use common sense and good judgment. Yes, we have written rules and procedures, and you can go look at them, but we say to our folks every day, "The rules are guidelines. We can't sit in Dallas, Texas, and write a rule for every single scenario you're going to run into. You're out there. You're dealing with the public. You can tell in any given situation when a rule should be bent or broken. You can tell because it's simply the right thing to do in the situation you are facing."

Our folks are marvelous about handling all kinds of situations with our Customers. We have had Pilots pay for hotel rooms because our Customers were getting off at different cities than they intended for the night, and the

Pilots could see that the people needed help. They don't call and ask, "Is it okay? Will I get reimbursed?" They do these things because that's the kind of People they are.

When our People realize they can be trusted and they're not going to get called on the carpet because they bend or break a rule while taking care of a Customer, that's when they want to do their best. Our People understand that as long as the decisions they make are not illegal, unethical, or immoral, they are free to do the right thing while using their best judgment—even if that means bending or breaking a rule or a procedure in the process. Servant Leadership and empowering your People is not soft management. It is management that not only gets great results but generates great human satisfaction for both our Employees and our Customers.

*Colleen Barrett (http://bit.ly/2uI0lv8) is president emeritus of Southwest Airlines. She joined Southwest in 1978 as corporate secretary, serving in VP and executive VP roles before becoming president and COO in 2001. She stepped down as president in 2008. Colleen has been the recipient of many notable awards over her career including the Tony Jannus Award in 2007 and the prestigious Wright Brothers Memorial Trophy in 2016.*

## Notes

1. Don M. Frick, *Robert K. Greenleaf: A Life of Servant Leadership* (San Francisco: Berrett-Koehler, 2004).
2. Ken Blanchard and Colleen Barrett, *Lead with LUV: A Different Way to Create Real Success* (Upper Saddle River, NJ: FT Press, 2011).
3. Jim Collins, *Good to Great: Why Some Companies Make the Leap and Others Don't* (New York: HarperBusiness, 2001).

## Chapter 34

# Developing and Using Servant Leadership in the Military

### ROBIN BLANCHARD

*Robin Blanchard is the daughter of my cousin, Bob, who was one of the top school superintendents in the country, finishing his career in Portland, Oregon. Watching her father as a leader motivated Robin to become a great servant leader herself. I think you'll realize in this essay that she accomplished her goal through serving our country in the military. —KB*

RECENTLY, WHILE LOOKING through documents my mother kept from my childhood, I found an aptitude test I had taken in the seventh grade. My highest score was in leadership. Who would have known then that I would follow a path leading to the honor of serving as the first female brigade commander in the Washington National Guard!

I have always felt drawn to serving others. Some in the military did not always support my servant leader philosophy. But they didn't understand that a servant leader has flexibility—although we always put our people first, we are able to be very directive when necessary. No discussion is needed when a military leader says, "Take that hill and hold it." Soldiers must move out quickly to accomplish whatever they are directed to do. They are dedicated to the mission of protecting this nation's freedoms and will always do their best to that end. However, followership must be earned. Some leaders win the hearts and minds of their soldiers and have comments made about them such as "I would follow them anywhere." Other leaders find that their people only follow them when it is required—or when someone is watching.

What's the difference? I would posit that some leaders understand servant leadership and some don't. A servant leader must be technically competent; but to motivate others they also must earn trust and respect. Before a leader can have success on the battlefield—when orders must be followed quickly or someone might die—they already must have earned the hearts and minds of their troops. That takes a servant leader.

During my twenty-eight years practicing servant leadership in the military, I realized two critical things about leading others: (1) People need to feel valuable; and (2) People need to be equipped for success.

## Let People Know They Are Valued

I wanted my people to know I valued them. I worked hard to ensure this by praising them, empowering them, and always being focused on them during interactions. Equipping these people for success meant ensuring they were well trained for new positions and always understood what was expected of them.

Praise is important for everyone—it's part of what makes people feel valued. The significance of sincere, specific praise cannot be overlooked by leaders. It lets direct reports know you are paying attention and also gives them a road map for exactly how they should behave in the future.

During my deployment in Kuwait, I attended a high-powered, rank-heavy meeting. Picture a large room with a U-shaped table arrangement facing a screen with the commanding general sitting in the center. The majority of those sitting in the first row were general officers ranging from one to three stars. Since I was a commander, even though I was only a colonel, I sat in the first row. It was quite intimidating. My plan was to keep quiet, observe, and learn.

Several times during the meeting, the commanding general asked for comments or suggestions. Although I had passed on speaking several times, at one point I could not sit silent anymore. I explained with passion what I believed to be the issue and solution. Although to everyone else in the room it was simply another comment in a sea of comments, for me it was anything but normal. The experience left me shaky and nervous. I was proud I spoke up but wondered how many people thought I was a complete idiot. The commander had acknowledged my comments and solutions as something to consider, but an emotional mind goes to crazy places when intimidated. To my surprise, my boss, a two-star general, found me during a break, praised me for my input, and explained in detail what he liked about my comments. Having received that praising, for the rest of the meeting I freely gave my input and contributed to solutions.

Remember that no matter how senior or junior you are in the workplace, praise releases the recipient's creative genius—and organizations reap the benefits.

Another essential part of valuing people is to trust them and strive to earn their trust in return. Trust is vital up and down the chain of command—maybe even more so for members of the military who deal regularly with life-and-death situations in combat. Soldiers feel valued when their leaders prove they will back them up. In aviation, we call that "having (the person's) six." In an aircraft, the direction you are moving is considered twelve o'clock and behind you is considered six o'clock. I always tried to have my soldiers' six, because a person will be motivated at work when they feel safe to use all of their abilities and take some risk. Risk often results in great revelation that should not be missed; in fact, most innovation begins with someone taking a risk. There is a downside, however: everyone makes mistakes—and they can be significant. How a servant leader deals with those mistakes is key. I tried to defuse and collaborate when mistakes were made. To me, this meant defusing the stuff coming from the people above me who were frustrated with the team's mistake, and then collaborating with my people to solve the problem. A servant leader asks the question *How can I help?*

One summer when I was commanding a training battalion in Yakima, Washington, I was tested on how much I trusted my soldiers. As a traditional guardsman, I did not work full time, so I relied on soldiers who were full-time employees managing the courses taught in Yakima. The most senior soldier on the ground in Yakima was my sergeant major. He was a competent soldier who had blended together a training staff of combat arms soldiers and support soldiers to effectively manage the rigorous course schedule.

When his first call came, I had no idea it would be the start of a very difficult summer. The conversation went something like this:

"Ma'am, we have a problem."

"Okay, Sergeant Major, what is it?"

"During the live night fire last night, the tracer rounds ignited the grass on the range. Before we knew it, 600 acres had burned."

I quickly replied, "Is anyone hurt?"

He said "No. Range control and the base commander are all in the loop. I just wanted you to know what happened."

At this point, the conversation went a bit deeper. Suffice to say that the summer was not starting well—but I supported my soldiers.

I must preface the next call with an explanation. In the military, when a sensitive item is lost, it is very bad. Entire installations can be shut down until the item is found, and people often lose their jobs over this type of mistake. Examples of sensitive items are weapons, devices that allow sight in the dark, and explosives. Now, I will continue.

The next phone call came a few weeks later.

"Ma'am."

"Yes, Sergeant Major."

"We have a problem."

"What is it?"

"We lost one of our borrowed night vision goggles. That is, we *think* we lost it. It's not here in the armory and we are currently checking with the unit that loaned us the goggles."

Again, a significant conversation ensued with questions and suggestions back and forth.

Ultimately, the goggles were found. The mistake was due to poor accountability when the goggles were borrowed—one had been left in a bag in the corner of the loaning unit's supply room. This begs the question *Why were the goggles not accurately counted at the time of issue?* This problem, among several others, was addressed during the course of the investigation into the mistake. Even with this mishap, I kept my focus on my soldiers.

The summer was going from bad to worse. I traveled to Yakima and had a face-to-face conversation with the sergeant major, in whom I had a lot of confidence. He assured me he had everything under control and was putting corrective measures in place.

When the third call came, it was all I could do not to wince.

"Ma'am."

"Yes, Sergeant Major."

"Let me first say, there were no injuries. However, while transporting the M4 rifles to Seattle, the truck broke down just before entering the armory and there was an accidental discharge."

This means that one of the M4 rifles fired off a live round. It is routine when transporting weapons to have live ammo—however, it should never be chambered unless a threat is imminent. Naturally, a lengthy conversation ensued. A mistake is one thing, but three errors in one summer is something else.

Later that day I received a call from my boss, who was not happy. He is normally a calm man, but today that trait disappeared. Let's just say this time there was no praising involved—and I did not have much backside left after the conversation.

My three-hour drive to Yakima to meet with the team was filled with strategizing how to remedy the situation. My boss had been very clear: "You have a leadership problem over there. Get it fixed!"

I could either fire everyone—or think of a better solution. When a person is not performing, and it has become obvious they will *never* perform in that position, a reassignment to a more aligned position could be an option. But sometimes sharing the person with the competition is the only option. A servant leader must make the decision. In this situation, I believed in my soldiers. I was convinced they had simply hit a few difficult situations and, with support, I knew they could turn the situation around. I chose to defuse and collaborate.

I brought all the leaders and instructors together and we strategized how to make things better. I guided them when necessary, but mostly I listened and encouraged. An interesting side note to this story is that almost all the soldiers in the room were male combat arms and had never worked for a woman. This naturally made it a bit tougher, but at the end of the meeting, the soldiers had solutions they intended to implement.

It worked. During the rest of my command of that unit, the soldiers worked harder than I had ever seen anyone work. They were rewarded with no more major mistakes. The unit passed all accreditations with excellent ratings.

On several occasions over the years since that assignment I've run into soldiers from that unit, and their reaction is always the same. "Ma'am, you had our six that summer, and we will never forget it." If you want to motivate people, make sure they know they can trust you.

## Equip People for Success

People must be equipped in order to succeed. Therefore, a servant leader must ensure that people know what is expected of them, understand policies and procedures, and receive whatever training is needed.

My fifteen-year-old son's first job was working as a day camp counselor for the city parks and recreation department. He was so excited to have a real, paying job. But after a month, his motivation went down. When I asked him what was wrong, he said, "Mom, I don't think they are going to pay me."

I said, "What do you mean? You haven't been paid?"

He nodded sheepishly.

I said, "Call your supervisor and ask what is wrong."

He said, "Maybe I misunderstood and I'm not going to get paid." Poor guy, he felt terrible.

I said, "Call her."

When he called, her response was, "Did you submit your time card?"

"What's a time card?" he asked.

When people don't know policies and procedures, it can cause frustration and be very demotivating. Too often, orientation of new employees is not given much emphasis. Because a servant leader seeks to equip their people, employee orientation is a critical element to ensure continued motivation.

Servant leadership is the best way to lead. Everyone needs to feel valued, and whatever you do toward that end will be motivating. I show my people I value and trust them by giving them sincere and specific praise, empowering them, and ensuring I am focused on them, not on myself. Equipping people for success is just as important. I seek to ensure my people know policies and procedures, are aware of my expectations, and are trained for their job.

Throughout my career, my most rewarding experience has been seeing my people succeed. And that is the goal of every servant leader: to care more about the success of others than your own.

*Robin Blanchard owns and operates Blanchard Consulting (www.blanchardconsulting.biz) in the Washington, DC, area. She is also a senior trainer with The Ken Blanchard Companies, facilitating both civilian and governmental organizations across the United States. She retired as a colonel after twenty-nine years of service with the Washington Army National Guard. She has a master's degree in strategic studies from the U.S. Army War College and an MBA from Grand Canyon University.*

# Chapter 35

# Leading Is Serving

## DAVE RAMSEY

*I've always been a big fan of Dave Ramsey. When he spoke at a leadership conference I was part of a few years ago, I was fascinated by his thinking. He has a unique way of making complicated topics like finance simple and interesting. With his popularity, he certainly could think of himself as a big deal—successful people often are used to being served rather than serving. But that's not the case with Dave. Why? Because he realizes, and will share in this essay, that with success comes the responsibility to serve. —KB*

I'VE SPENT A lot of time thinking about what God's done in my business over the past two decades. This thing has literally grown from a one-man show on a card table in my living room into a team of more than 550 superstars doing work that's changing lives. It's crazy! I always knew God was going to do some big things with our stuff, but the level of talent and commitment He's brought alongside me over the past twenty years has totally blown my mind.

As I tried to put all those experiences into my book, *EntreLeadership*,[1] and as I thought about all the stories that have led us to where we are, one concept kept coming to the surface as the key to our success: servant leadership. That mindset changes how you do just about everything.

## Servant, Not Subservient

Back at the start of my career, when I was a young hotshot looking to make my mark in business, I attended just about every leadership seminar that came to town. That's something my parents taught me. Even back when I thought I knew *everything*—which is another way of saying young and stupid—I still soaked up information from everyone around. There was always something new to learn.

So when as an adult early in my career I came to know Jesus, I started checking out Christian leadership speakers and authors. I remember when I was sitting in one of those seminars, the guy on stage said something like, "The greatest leaders are always servant leaders." My first reaction was *You have got to be kidding me. If I wanted to be a servant, I'd go work for someone else. I want to be my own boss!* Now that I get to teach and speak on leadership pretty often, I see the same reaction on other people's faces. In corporate America, the gap between *servant* and *leader* is about the size of the Grand Canyon!

Here's the problem. When some leaders hear *servant*, they think *subservient*. That is, they think servant leaders bow down to the whims of their teams. They mistakenly think that a servant leader only takes orders and acts like a doormat at the front door of the business—trampled on by everyone who walks in. That's way off the mark, but it's something I watch young leaders struggle with every time I teach on this topic.

## Servant Leaders Are Powerful

I get so frustrated at the false notion that servant leaders are weak, timid figureheads with no power. Was Jesus timid when He went head to head with the pious religious leaders of the day? Was He weak when He drove the moneychangers out of the temple? No way! He served His people far more than anyone else ever has, but He always maintained His strength. The truth is, servant leaders are powerful. We are warriors for our people, and we act to defend the culture from anything that would tear it apart.

When I call out a salesperson who is only making half the calls he is supposed to make, I'm serving him, because his income will always be limited by his weak performance. When I immediately fire someone who was sexually inappropriate with a coworker, I'm serving that coworker and everyone else in the building by removing a cancer. When I enforce our strict no-gossip policy with a new team member, I'm serving them by helping them understand the environment that we all enjoy around our place.

When I lead a staff meeting, invite a great devotional speaker, help plan our annual Christmas party, or authorize a pay increase, I'm serving my team. When I do a month-long media tour to promote a new book or go through endless hours of meetings with the city trying to get building permits approved for new office space, I'm serving my team. Serving them as I lead them doesn't really change *what* I'm doing; it changes *how* and *why* I'm doing it.

## A Heavy Responsibility

I remember the day this lesson really clicked with my son several years ago when he was still in high school. We had just arrived at our annual company picnic. When I say picnic, please don't picture a traditional, corporate America, get-in-and-get-out kind of deal. This thing was huge. We rented out an entire park facility, and we had giant inflatable bounce houses, slides, zip lines and other games all over the place. There were kids running, screaming, and playing *everywhere*.

We've got a pretty young team, so we've got a lot of young families. For this particular picnic, that meant we had ninety-seven kids under the age of ten running around. As the president and CEO, I'll admit it was pretty humbling walking across that park. As I felt that responsibility wash over me, I looked over at my son, Daniel, and realized this was a perfect opportunity to teach him what it means to be a servant leader.

I said, "Daniel, look across this field. What do you see?" He laughed and said he saw way too many little kids. I smiled and said, "Yeah, there are ninety-seven kids here under age ten that are the children of our team members. Do you know what that means?"

He shook his head. "Nope, but I bet you're going to tell me."

I said, "Those kids' parents make a living, have a future, and those kids have a future partly because of how I act. If I misbehave in my personal life, if I fail in areas of integrity, if I screw up, it will mess up a ton of lives. As a servant leader, I understand that I am at least partially responsible for those little kids."

He hung his head a little and said, "Dad, that much responsibility is kind of heavy."

He was right. It is a heavy responsibility. But what I got to tell him that day was that he—even as a teenager—shared that responsibility with me. I explained that if he went out and acted crazy, he could impact those kids' lives just as much as I could. If he went out and got drunk, got into a car accident, and killed someone, we'd get sued and some of those team members could end up losing their jobs. As my son, he gets to enjoy the benefits of our success, but he also shares in the responsibility of servant leadership. He needed to know, even as a teenager, that the decisions he makes and the actions he takes have an impact.

## Leading Is Serving

If there's one big key to servant leadership, it's pretty simple: put other people first. It kind of sounds like the Golden Rule, doesn't it? Your team will share your values, so make sure you're modeling what you want them to emulate. That means no executive perks and no ivory towers. Maybe it means eating lunch in the company break room every day and getting your own coffee every morning. If there's an all-hands-on-deck emergency, make sure *your* hands are on deck too.

Show your team by your actions that leading *is* serving. Look for every opportunity to show them that, although you're in charge, you're all in this *together*.

*Dave Ramsey (www.daveramsey.com) is a personal money management expert, a popular national radio personality, and bestselling author of several books including* Financial Peace, The Total Money Makeover, *and* EntreLeadership. *Ramsey Solutions provides biblically based common-sense education and empowerment that give hope to everyone in every walk of life. The Dave Ramsey* Show *is heard by more than fourteen million listeners each week.*

## Note

1. Dave Ramsey, *EntreLeadership: 20 Years of Practical Business Wisdom from the Trenches* (New York: Howard Books, 2011).

# Chapter 36

# Serving from an HR Perspective

## SHIRLEY BULLARD

*Almost twenty years ago, we were blessed to talk Shirley Bullard
into creating and developing the HR operation in our company.
I don't know many people who are as competent and caring as
Shirley. This essay will show you the important servant leadership
role that HR has in both good times and bad. Thanks, Shirley, for
being the great servant leader you are. —KB*

I FIND THAT I am still surprised at how long I have been working in the field of HR (human resources)—it's been more than forty years. I got into HR completely by accident when someone told me they thought I would be good at it. Back then, I did not know much about the field except that HR professionals hire and fire people. If that had been the extent of the role, I would have been long gone by now—but it is so much more than that. Those who think HR is a place where situations are black or white, right or wrong, or "do this, don't do that" typically do not last long. The first encounter with a hostile employee can leave even the best HR professional shaken and applying for any job just to escape another unpleasant confrontation. However, once I got my start, I never looked back.

Why have I stayed in HR? Because I truly enjoy working with and helping people. It is not the field or profession that is so unique—it is every individual and every encounter. I like understanding what makes people do the work they do. I enjoy the thrill of watching people develop and grow. I like making a connection with someone and figuring out how to make them the "star" in our encounter—how to put them first, meet them where they are, and help them move forward toward a positive way of thinking, acting, being, and believing. That is HR at its finest.

It is also one of the core elements of being a servant leader—putting other people's needs ahead of your own. Without this mindset, your actions can be viewed as self-serving. Putting others first balances the acts of service and leadership. A serving mindset is part of the fiber of who you are. You *want* to serve and you do it instinctively, which is why you never tire of it.

When asked to share a story about servant leadership from an HR perspective, several came to mind. What makes these memories endearing to me is that other people involved have freely shared their perspective and their personal gratitude for my encounters with them. All involve putting the other person first while exercising leadership.

Oftentimes in HR there is no script for what you will encounter; there is no rule or policy that you can rely on; there is no clear-cut plan of what to do or not to do. But with a mindset of "I am here to serve," you can get through even the most challenging event with grace. Notice I did not say "without angst, second guessing, or fear." These are real emotions that exist for any leader who finds themselves encountering a situation that is unfamiliar territory.

This was the case for me in October 2007. The event: wildfires of epic proportions were racing through San Diego County. For nearly four days, a combination of extreme draught conditions, temperatures in the 90s, and rapidly shifting Santa Ana winds kept the fires moving, playing hopscotch across freeways, and rapidly consuming trees and homes in their paths. For those of us who were there to experience it, there seemed to be no end in sight. What direction will the winds blow next? Is a fire coming our way? How did they all start? What already had been destroyed? Like most citizens, I got my answers from the news.

What was being called a rural brush fire when I went to bed that Sunday evening became a deadly inferno in only a few hours. In many different communities, people's lives were upended as they were awakened in the middle of the night to the smell of smoke and a reverse 911 call with a recorded voice telling them to evacuate their home and move to a safer location. For some people in those early hours, a safer location meant our offices at The Ken Blanchard Companies.

The first call I received was from my assistant, who had stayed up all night watching the deadly paths of the fires and was letting me know that a major freeway had been closed down. In fast succession, call number two came from our facilities manager, reporting that some of our people and their loved ones and pets had taken refuge in one of our buildings. I did not need to wait for a third call. I was up, dressed, and speeding to the office. The first person I met was our facilities manager, who had secured the campus and now wanted to know what to do about those who had taken shelter in our offices. I corrected him instantly—we needed to think about what to do *for* those people.

I knew I needed to go to be with them, because I had not experienced the trauma this group had been through that morning: being uprooted by the sound of law enforcement telling them to get out of their homes and get out *now*. As I remember, there were about fifteen people, including children with tears in their eyes. Some had brought along pets, who were panting and confused. I gave hugs to everyone I knew and got introduced to the others. My next task was to get them food and anything else they needed to be more comfortable. I asked for names so I could label the various items for when I returned. This also helped me learn the names of the folks I did not know.

Next was communication. I had to get word to all of our people in the local area that they were not to come to work today but were to focus on caring for their families and their safety. I needed to give them information about where the fires were in relation to our offices, to ask them to report in and let us know they were safe, and finally to reassure them that I would be back in touch with more updates. I had to do it in a way that would spur necessary action but not panic. I also had to communicate to a greater audience of our associates who were outside of San Diego about what was happening locally and how they could help. I had to do all of this over voicemail—the only mass communication tool available to me in those wee hours of the morning.

My continuing mission was to put others first—to let them know what we knew, to give them some sense of what to do next, and to give them hope. Luckily, most employees thought to check voicemail. In addition to my communication, Ken Blanchard—our company's chief spiritual officer—left a voice message for everyone from Florida, where he and his wife, Margie, were at the time. He gave us all an update as to what was happening with his family, as some had been directly impacted by the fires.

Here's a transcript of my first message from Monday, October 22:

> Good morning everyone. This is Shirley with a global message to all of the employees of the Ken Blanchard Companies. This is of particular importance to those who work in Escondido. By now I'm sure you've all heard about the fires raging in the city and county. While our office will be open, I am asking all employees who work locally to please remain at home today—particularly those of you who are in areas that the fires are moving toward, those of you who have been evacuated, and those of you who have children in a school district that has closed. If you have the ability to work from home today, please do so. There will be an email out regarding emergency

information. Also, you know that you can dial 211 to get updates in the county with regard to what is happening with fires around the area. I am asking all employees in the area to please check in with the front desk to let them know that you are okay and to let them know where you will be today in the event that we need to get in touch with you. I also am going to ask that you please check your voicemail at the end of the day, and we will have instructions on what will be happening on Tuesday, October 23. As soon as we know the whereabouts of all employees, we will put out a message letting everyone outside of the area know what's happening at the company. Please check your email later for a message, and also check voicemail later this evening for instructions for Tuesday.

Later that morning, I informed everyone that our offices were officially closed for business and that some of our people were using them as temporary housing. I was happy to report that we had heard from most of our local people and everyone was safe. And I asked for continuous prayers for everyone who had been affected by the fires.

For the next few days, sleep was not a high priority as I knew it was my responsibility to stay on top of what was happening and communicate both good news and bad news to our people. The bad news was that Ken and Margie Blanchard's house had burned to the ground and was a total loss. To make things worse, because the San Diego airport had been closed due to the fires, they wouldn't be able to get a flight home from Florida until later in the week. Fortunately, out of more than 160 local employees, only one other house was lost. That was a blessing, given the fact that more than fifteen hundred homes were lost in San Diego County as a result of four separate fires burning at the same time. The evacuation of more than five hundred thousand people was one of the largest in the history of our country. The city responded beautifully as people reached out to help one another, offering assistance of every kind.

Dealing with this kind of a crisis isn't in anyone's job description. But as the head of HR, I was the caretaker of the people in our organization during this tough time. I had to rely on my instinct and my desire to serve. There were many rewards, though. One thing I was encouraged and pleased about was our company spirit, which was stronger than ever during this time. I was also grateful for my colleagues who stood beside me as servant leaders, putting the needs of others first. While the amount of property lost was staggering, our employees and their families were safe.

Through this experience, I realized once again that being a servant leader is more about serving than leading. You need both to be effective—especially when there is no script.

*Shirley Bullard is chief administrative officer for The Ken Blanchard Companies. She joined Blanchard as vice president of HR and chief personnel officer in February 1998. Shirley's prior industry experience included ten years at the Poway Unified School District as director of personnel support services and more than fifteen years with the U.S. Navy as a civilian employee. She received her juris doctorate from Thomas Jefferson School of Law in San Diego.*

# Chapter 37

# It's How You Treat People

## James H. Blanchard

*When Jim Blanchard was chairman and CEO of Synovus Financial,
it was honored by Fortune magazine as the #1 Best Company to
Work For in 1999 and was later admitted into a newly created Hall
of Fame. Why? Because, as I learned when I was asked to work
with Synovus a number of years ago, Jimmy and his management
team all were—and still are—humble servant leaders. As you read
his essay, you'll see why I thought it was important to include Jim's
story. He and I are not related, but I would be happy to adopt him
because of his caring heart. May Jim's dream be your dream and
his hope your reality. —KB*

## The Intent to Serve from Day One

It's never too late for a leader to stand up in a bad culture and decide to build
a great one. Fortunately, I didn't have to do that. The seeds of the servant leadership culture at Synovus go all the way back to 1888 when the founders of
Columbus Bank and Trust Company were in the cotton mill business.

One day when a woman was working on a loom in the mill, her skirt got
caught on the machine. The hem ripped and her life savings came spilling
out onto the floor. To her, the hem of her skirt was the safest place to keep
her money. That day, the founders decided they could do better for their employees—so they started a bank that would serve as a trusted place for their
workers' life savings.

The idea of serving people was not an add-on to the Synovus culture. On
the contrary—it was the very DNA that spawned its existence. The culture
began the moment that woman's savings spilled onto the floor.

## Taking It to the Streets

What began as a mission of service to employees expanded to a commercial bank with a mission of service to customers. By 1957, CB&T had become a major player in the community by doing what it did best: serving people with integrity. Into that environment my father, James W. Blanchard, entered as president. He embraced the service culture easily because that was who he was—someone who always pushed for excellence and strived for the next level of success, but never at the expense of others. Let me give you an example.

When my father was named president of the bank, we learned it would require a move to Columbus, Georgia, from our home in Valdosta—175 miles away. I was about to be a junior in high school and didn't want to move. My father didn't shut me down; in fact, he said, "Okay, in a few months when it gets to be that time, we can look at getting you an apartment here for your junior and senior years." When the time came, I found myself saying, "So tell me more about Columbus!"

Being a great leader, my father accomplished his desired outcome: I was ready to do what he wanted and it felt like my idea. I think he even would have rented that apartment for me, but he didn't have to. His openness to show me that my needs mattered gave me the freedom to see the move for what it was—a better opportunity. But don't overlook the fact that at the same time my dad was caring for us, he was making the move to the next level. He was going to Columbus.

The blend of caring for people and driving for more was shown throughout the next era at CB&T. My father took the existing service culture being delivered to CB&T's customers to the next level: outward, into the broader community CB&T served—the Chamber of Commerce, the United Way, the Association of the United States Army, and other organizations. Employees learned how to create new banking relationships and the entire community gradually became part of the customer family as well.

The people of Columbus took a liking to CB&T and its approach to doing business. My father had solidified the service culture with his successful drive to develop relationships in the community. Then, right in the middle of his incredible career, Dad's life was cut short. He died of lung cancer in January 1969.

When the owners of the bank approached me about becoming the new president, I left my law practice and took my father's place. When I accepted the position, I inherited the culture my father had so deliberately enhanced from the one that had existed since the bank's founding. Throughout the

1970s my colleagues and I took that culture forward, emphasizing the great tradition of service and community involvement, and grew the bank substantially.

Focusing on business performance always went hand in hand with mindfully serving our people and the community. It drove our growth and made Synovus an inspiring place to work. As we acquired more banks, I realized something: it was hard to transport a culture and overlay it on other cultures. But it had to be done. We wanted this culture to be built into all of our banks. It required us to systematize culture building as a strategy. We got very intentional about it and saw it as a key differentiator for our business.

While our strategy was moving our growth forward, I always knew it was our culture that made it happen. At some point in the early 1980s, the patriarch of the bank, Bill Turner, came into my office with a book Robert K. Greenleaf had written on servant leadership. Bill tossed the book on my desk and said, "Jim, this is exactly what we have been doing. We just didn't know what to call it!"

## Open to Outside Help, Focused on Internal Strategy

We knew we wanted to become the finest financial institution in the world and that the key would be a very focused strategy toward that end. Our culture was great, but we wanted more—so we needed to learn more. About that time, I met Ken Blanchard. He helped us understand what servant leadership looks like. He taught us that leaders must see themselves on the bottom of an upside-down pyramid—that's where they serve the entire organization using their power, resources, influence, and everything else leadership affords. Ken and other leadership experts helped us learn how servant leadership concepts fit into running a successful business.

A few criticized us, saying the approach was too soft and permissive. So we had to prove it was the exact opposite—that people who were loved, respected, and prepared would perform better. Servant leadership led to higher performance and there was nothing permissive about it—we loved our people *and* we expected high performance. I believe that if you truly care about someone, you will not only love them but also expect the best from them and hold them to it.

There's no doubt that servant leadership is by far the best way to see business results. But this is important: we did not implement a service culture for the purpose of getting people to perform better or for a better bottom line.

We did it because it was the right thing to do—a worthy goal in and of itself. It is simply the way people should be treated.

We created a new position in the company and filled it with one of our top marketing officers, Nancy Buntin. Nancy had a genuine heart for our culture and a steadfast love for our team members. Part of her job was to come into my office on a regular basis, ball up her fists, and remind me about our culture and always taking care of our people first. You see, it's natural for a CEO to get caught up in financial performance, owner demands, politics, etc.—to get spread thin on important matters and forget to tend to the most significant job of all. Nancy made sure I never drifted away from the people who gave their best to a company that loved and appreciated them.

Nancy was a big part of our continued progress. Over the years, others played huge roles in our journey: Lee Lee James, Rob Ward, Alison Dowe, Marty Stephens, Lisa White, Stephanie Alford, Susan Charron, and many more—and, of course, our senior executives who never wavered.

In 1996 we established a series of initiatives called the People Development Exponent (PDE), designed to raise each individual's development to a higher level. We implemented it from top to bottom with a lot of structure. This was not merely a new program—it would be a way of life. PDE required major changes from our team members, whose loyalty and passion was our ultimate secret sauce. We oriented all new employees to the concepts and let them know they would be expected to conform to it as an element of the Synovus culture.

As part of PDE, we instituted best practices in human performance and spent a lot of time on leadership training and development. We knew this culture was something our leadership team was going to have to model and support, so we poured a lot into developing our leaders and future leaders. Our team knew we were serious because we put emphasis on training people in not only business and banking, but also in culture and leadership. In fact, the most serious move we made may have been the establishment of our Leadership Institute—an executive leadership training program of equal caliber to programs at Harvard, Stanford, and other top universities.

Another major effort was our Tuesday morning company-wide meeting, which included business updates and strategy information as well as a culture segment, which I hosted. I spent my time drumming in the importance of treating people well and building a servant leadership culture. I knew this repetitive message directly from the CEO was key. People need to know what matters most to their leaders—and when the message is supported by actions, programs, performance reviews, training, celebration, promotion, and reward, they get it.

Like any other business strategy, we knew for this culture initiative to have results we would have to measure it, hold people accountable to it, train to it, and deliver it. So we created an evaluation system that included financial components to the metrics on culture as well as feedback from employees, customers, and stakeholders. You have to treat culture like a business plan: everything you do for financial performance must be done for culture as well.

## A Surprise

By 1998 we were doing well. People were thriving, growing, and fulfilled. We continued to acquire more banks and financial companies and bring them into our culture. Performance was thriving as well. We were setting records and were at the top of the industry in almost every metric.

Then we got a surprise—we learned that what we were doing had been noticed by people outside the company. We were named the #11 Best Company to Work For by *Fortune* magazine. What a thrill! We celebrated and were so happy—but the coolest thing was that our people were happier that we had that kind of culture than they were that we got an award for it. We all *wanted* to be this way. Some thought we should have made a bigger deal of it PR-wise, but we knew doing the right thing was its own reward—it's not about trying to get attention and turning it into a marketing trophy. We had accomplished this for real reasons and we did not want that to change.

Then one year later, in 1999, it happened again—except this time we were at the top of the chart: *Fortune*'s #1 Best Company to Work For! What an incredible validation that was for our people—for everything we were doing for each other. It made me so proud of everyone and so fulfilled to be at Synovus. And we celebrated again. This time, a thousand people came together for the celebration and I was presented the award on behalf of all of us. True to our culture, I came in directly from a quail hunt, was late to the celebration, and walked on stage in hunting clothes! I think people loved it. It was a great example of how just being real was at the heart of who we wanted to be. Real people taking care of each other. And at the same time, we were one of the very best financial institutions in the world. It felt great!

Although we kept the celebration alive for a while, we didn't forget our real purpose—to continue this kind of culture for our people. I told everyone I was proud of them and wanted them to know I would be doing everything possible every day to make Synovus even better and more humble. I told them every day we wanted to be more and more like Chick-fil-A. I love that company and I knew it could be done.

We continued to strive for and maintain a culture where everyone was treated with respect no matter their status or ability to help us. We treated people the way we would want to be treated and we told stories about how to treat others. One of my favorites came to be known as "the bedbug story."

A Southern gentleman was traveling by train from Atlanta to Washington. When he got into his berth on the train, he realized the bed was loaded with bedbugs. After he returned from the trip, he wrote to the CEO of the railroad and told him of the experience. He was sure the CEO would take action. Sure enough, he received a nice letter from the CEO who assured him that the problem had been addressed and would never occur again. The customer noticed that the CEO's letter was attached to the customer's original letter. To his surprise, handwritten across the top of his original letter were the words "Send this [blankety-blank] the bedbug letter."

Unfortunately, this is an example of the way people are still treated by too many businesses. Insincere. Uncaring. Too busy to take time to listen.

We wanted our people to care for others sincerely and without hypocrisy, so the bedbug story was used a lot. We even joked about it when debating with each other, saying, "I'm going to send you the bedbug letter." It became part of the fabric of our culture to remind each other of the importance of sincerity.

Driving on, we created working groups around every element of the culture. Team leaders were responsible for holding their teams to cultural development. Our cultural trust committee met each month, with leaders rotating each year, to hold the company accountable for walking the talk. Our performance ratings were always at the top levels of the industry. I told our people if we didn't make our numbers and stay at the top, I would be gone and they would have to get used to another CEO! Our culture was the starting point. It was sacred.

## You Have to Prune

No garden grows to be beautiful without pruning weeds, infected and dead branches and plants, and the like. If things are not healthy, changes are necessary.

Our pruning process began with my telling everyone we would not tolerate behavior that was inconsistent with our cultural goals. I made it clear that if anyone's manager was not treating them well, they should have a conversation and get it worked out—and if they couldn't, they should come to me. I promised to deal with the situation and said, "If I don't deliver on this promise, you have no reason to ever believe anything else I say."

It became my mission to free our workplace of anyone who was holding our cultural goals back. Senior leadership, including myself, decided we would not keep any manager we would not be willing to work for ourselves. When someone treated us well but didn't treat their people well, we called it "salute the flag and kick the dog."

As part of the process, we always invited the manager to get better at leading. It was their choice. Often when a boss caused problems and one of their people talked to them or came to me, the problem would end. But if it came down to it, I would say to the manager, "I don't care how good you are at your job, or numbers, or financial performance. If you mistreat people, you are not suited for this company. Period."

Over about a year or so, we saw nearly two hundred people, mostly managers, depart. Some retired, some left because they didn't like what we were building, and some tried to change but couldn't. Many others remained important players on our team. Every time someone who had mistreated people left the company it was like a fresh wind blowing. It was an important time for our company and our people. Our people would often say, "How come it took you so long?"

Let me stress that this process was not just about behavior. Nice people who don't perform aren't good for your culture, either. We made it clear that everyone had to carry their share of the load. The goal is to have leaders who embrace the culture and are totally committed to the shared vision, mission, strategies, and aspirations of excellence and high performance.

## From the Top

Most people would like their workplaces to have the culture I am talking about. Many look for and find companies that are like this—but many don't. Why does it happen sometimes and not others? One word: leadership. The leadership at the very top has to want this culture, see it as a key priority, live it, resource it, train to it, review to it, have accountability and metrics to drive it, and then enforce and reward it when it happens.

Top leadership has to do all of these things, consistently, and then celebrate the achievement just as if it were finance or performance related. Leaders have to confirm that the culture is important by highlighting it at every opportunity and by showing others what will be noticed and rewarded.

Also, leadership must be united. One of the most important drivers of success at Synovus was that the entire senior executive team embraced the strategy and cultural goals. When leaders are unified around a goal like this, others cannot divide or sabotage you.

## Never Done

When we got to be the #1 Best Company to Work For in America, you would think we had arrived or at least would be tempted to sit back on our laurels. *Fortune* magazine created a Hall of Fame and put us there. It was very rewarding. It was again a great validation of our aspirations and our actions.

What continues to be my belief is this: even if you win awards, you are never done. Someone asked me how they could hit the finish line like we did. I thought about it and said, "You don't ever hit it." When it comes to treating people the way you want to be treated, it is not for a contest—it is forever. So Synovus just keeps going. I loved the journey and still do, even though I have been retired from Synovus for years. Great people! Great results! Great memories! A great team effort! It was a golden era. Of all of the accomplishments I was involved in over my long career, the pursuit of a servant leadership culture at Synovus was my greatest and most favorite satisfaction.

*James H. Blanchard (www.jordanblanchard.com/james-blanchard) began his service with Synovus Financial Corp. in June 1970. He served as CEO of Synovus from 1971 until being named executive chairman of the board in July 2005. He retired from Synovus in October 2006. In 2011, he partnered with the Jordan Company, a Columbus-based real estate and investment firm, to create Jordan-Blanchard Capital, where he currently serves as chairman, board of advisors.*

# Chapter 38

# How Servant Leadership Has Shaped Our Church Culture

## MILES MCPHERSON

*I first met Miles McPherson when he was in the early stages of building Rock Church. I admired his vision, values, and incredible energy to make a difference in the world. If we had more servant leadership churches like the Rock, the world would be a better place. I love you, Miles, and I'm proud of what you are doing in the world. —KB*

WHEN I WAS asked to write about how the culture at Rock Church—the church I pastor—has been shaped by servant leadership, I decided to ask a few people on our staff what they saw:

- Everett told me that when one of our pastors is on call and a pastoral need arises, they excuse themselves from business meetings to pray and minister with the hurting person.
- Carissa said her supervisor refuses to identify as such, instead labeling her as a teammate. He even calls himself Huckleberry—you know, like Tom Sawyer's sidekick—a reminder to his team that he's here to *serve* his team.
- Before regular duties on Sundays, Pastor Pauly comes in with *Dawn Patrol*, an eight-person team that arrives at 4:40 a.m. and sets up every—yes, *every*—room in our building that will be used for ministry.

There's a lot going on at our church, so I didn't know about some of this stuff until I asked. But that's the awesome thing about servant leadership: once it has become a fundamental component of organizational culture, it permeates every department, sneaks into every office, and defines every leader.

I came to San Diego in 1982 to play for the Chargers in the NFL. For the first few years, I was living a wild life, running around, doing drugs, and getting into all kinds of trouble. I met a lot of people who—like me—were empty, hurting, and self-medicating their pain with all kinds of vices.

When God got ahold of me, He turned my life upside down—and eventually He led me to start Rock Church in 2000. We made *pervasive hope* our explicit vision. That doesn't just mean hope in every facet of life, it means hope on every street corner! Every place that a sinner can go to treat their pain—bars, strip clubs, movie theaters, crack houses, etc.—that's where they need to be confronted and overwhelmed with the compelling force of hope.

And 1 Peter 3:15 says there is hope in us. *We* are the vessels through which the hope of the gospel moves!

God gifted me as an evangelist—and I can do a lot—but my reach and influence is tiny compared to the combined potential of all the people in our church. With a vision of pervasive hope, I had to become an *empowerer*. My job expanded as I realized that to actually take hope to every geographical location of San Diego county, I needed to make it my mission to serve, energize, and enable the people in the congregation to proclaim hope wherever *they* go.

But how do you get more than *fifteen thousand people* on board?

Well, Jesus—who is, without question, the best leader ever—gave us a perfect model of servant leadership. Fully human, but also fully God, Jesus washed the feet of His disciples. It was an expression of kindness and intimacy, but also a radical dramatization of God's valuation of power and authority. If God's Son *chose* to stoop, serving sinful men—including the one who would betray him to his death—who are we to expect to be served? Jesus himself didn't come to be served, but to serve, giving his very life as a ransom for many.

I realized that if I wanted to see hope in every hurting corner of San Diego, and if I wanted to activate, inspire, enable, and empower our congregation to do that, I had to model service.

So we came up with the "Do Something Church" model. It consists of four main steps: count, walk, ask, and love.

First, we *count*. I love this one because I'm a numbers guy. *What* we count is something we call *symptom centers*. These are the places people go to find temporary and fake relief for the pain of their sin. We count the liquor stores, the strip clubs, the abortion clinics, the hospitals, the adult bookstores, the foster care centers, etc. Anywhere a person's pain can lead them, we want to know about it and count it.

Then we *walk*. We drive across town or walk across the street and just show up at their front door. We attend their meetings. We call them. We get in touch, one way or another.

Then we *ask*: "How can we help you?" Every year we go to our mayor and ask what we can do for the city with *x* amount of volunteer hours. We went to the fire and police departments and found out they could use grief counseling for victims and chaplaincy for their teams.

And finally, we *love*. This is the most powerful step in servant leadership. It's the fruit—the reward—for all the work that goes into the first three steps. And, most important, leaders: it's the heart—the essence—of your message. If you don't have love, you're just a sounding brass, a clanging cymbal. If you don't have love, you're just hype. If you don't have love, you have nothing.

So keeping in mind the vision—*pervasive hope*—and the four simple steps by which we make that vision a reality—*count, walk, ask*, and *love*—we decided to let volunteer team members lead our outreach ministries. Whatever God put on their hearts, we wanted to get behind it! And because they saw us lead through service and love, they were all about it. We currently have 178 volunteer-led outreach ministries, ranging in activities from visiting prisons to hiking to teaching Spanish and feeding the homeless. It's an amazing workforce! They're out on the front lines, serving and loving people who would never walk through our doors on their own.

Nearly 17 percent of San Diego's children live in poverty, making Christmastime tough for parents and children alike. *Pain*. So in 1997 I decided to start Toys for Joy, where we give toys, food, and the hope of the Gospel to people in need. More than 4,500 volunteers came out in 2016—our twentieth anniversary—and Toys for Joy had four locations around San Diego. We gave away 25,410 toys and 12,000 bags of groceries—and 490 people got free haircuts. Even more important, 3,440 people received prayer and 3,803 made a decision for Christ! *Love*.

Back in 2007, Southern California was hit with some terrible wildfires. Whole communities were consumed overnight. People lost everything. *Pain*. We decided to open up our church building to emergency responders and law enforcement, and turned it into an evacuation center for people displaced by the fires—and they came in by the thousands. Among them were 122 senior citizens from a retirement community in Spring Valley. They got meals, clothes, a bed to sleep on, and a little bit of hope in their darkest moment. *Love*.

In 2009, we went to our mayor and—by faith—pledged a whopping 100,000 community service hours. Over the last eight years, we've been able to give our city 1,820,232 community service hours. In 2015 alone we donated 221,979 hours, saving San Diego taxpayers an estimated $4,128,710 by coordinating large, city-improving events. *Love.*

A little over a year ago, my wife heard people talking on TV about how some of the cops in San Diego didn't have trauma plate kits—which are used to treat critical gun wounds. *Pain.* I called the chief of police that same day and asked how we could help with that. She gave me an estimate, and we brought it to the church and other community partners. In a few weeks we were able to give law enforcement seven hundred kits. A few months later I met a young officer who was shot in the neck on duty. Guess what? One of those trauma kits saved her life, and brought her home to her husband and baby. *Love.*

San Diego is a military hot spot, with thousands of families relocating for training or deployment—often facing separation and the looming threat of tragedy. *Pain.* So we do an event called Boots Off. In 2016 we served 1,887 people from the military community, 25 of whom made a decision for Christ. We also gave away 500 backpacks with school supplies, served 1,668 lunches, and provided 913 free services like massages, haircuts, and computer services. *Love.*

Through servant leadership, God has blessed us with grace in San Diego and has opened doors for us to minister in ways we never could have imagined. Service is nothing more than an expression of love. And it is absolutely necessary for effective leadership and maximum influence for change.

> Though I speak with the tongues of men and angels, but have not love, I have become sounding brass or a clanging cymbal. And though I have the gift of prophecy, and understand all mysteries and all knowledge, and though I have all faith, so that I could remove mountains, but have not love, I am nothing. And though I bestow all my goods to feed the poor, and though I give my body to be burned, but have not love, it profits me nothing. (1 Cor. 13:1–3, NKJV)

If you want your influence to grow, *love.* If you want to be a better leader, *love.* If you want your work to matter, *love.* If you want to be more like Jesus Himself, *love.*

*Miles McPherson (www.milesmcpherson.com) started Rock Church (www.sdrock .com) in San Diego in 2000. Today, attendance at the Rock stands at more than fifteen thousand people who attend in person as well as through online streaming, radio, and TV. In 2013, Miles initiated Do Something Church, a community outreach ministry. Miles played NFL football for the San Diego Chargers from 1982 to 1985. After he left football, he worked as a youth pastor for Horizon Christian Fellowship in San Diego and enrolled in Azusa Pacific University's School of Theology, receiving his Master of Divinity degree in 1991. He has writ-ten several books including* God in the Mirror, Do Something, *and* Bad to the Bone.

## Part Six

# Servant Leadership Turnarounds

## How Servant Leadership Can Dramatically Impact Both Results and Relationships

- Art Barter, in his essay "Out of the Flames, into the Light," shares a dramatic story about purchasing Datron World Communications when it was in trouble and how he used servant leadership as the strategy for turning the operation around.

- Cheryl Bachelder, in "Serve the People," tells the story of how implementing servant leadership completely transformed Popeyes Louisiana Kitchen during her tenure as CEO.

- In "Waste Connections: A Servant Leadership Success Story," Rico Maranto shows how the influence of top management can make servant leadership come alive—and create great relationships and results in the process.

- Garry Ridge, in "Don't Mark My Paper, Help Me Get an A," describes how servant leadership motivated him to create a win-win performance management system for his organization, WD-40 Company. To him, helping people get an A is servant leadership in action.

# Chapter 39

# Out of the Flames, into the Light

## ART BARTER

*Art Barter and I met when I spoke at his church a number of years ago. He was intrigued when I talked about Jesus as the ultimate model of servant leadership. Having recently taken over Datron World Communications, Art decided servant leadership would be his strategy for turning the operation around. You'll enjoy this essay describing how he put servant leadership into action. —KB*

EVERYTHING SEEMED TO be against our company, Datron World Communications. I had brought our management team together to lay out a plan for recovery. They looked at me—their new leader—eager to hear the next steps that would pull us out of the flames. Datron had just been dragged through an agonizing eight-month criminal investigation by the Department of Justice (DOJ). The investigation focused on the Foreign Corrupt Practices Act (FCPA). They wanted to see if anyone in our company had bribed foreign officials to obtain or retain business. To be accused of misconduct had been exhausting and, frankly, scary. It certainly had taken its toll on me as well as all of Datron's employees.

As I looked at my management team I knew that, after everything the organization had been through, the first impulse for any prudent leader would be to insist that everyone put their back into it and work as hard as they could. We needed to make sure everything stayed on track; otherwise, we could all lose our jobs *and* our company.

But I didn't want business as usual. Based on our experiences during the DOJ investigation, there had to be a better way to run a company—and to live a life. Ken Blanchard had taught me about a concept called *servant leadership.* We decided to use it as the foundation for how we managed the company going forward.

Was this revolutionary approach possible? Would my team embrace it?

## Servant Leadership: Your Highest Ideal Becomes Your New Bottom Line

At Datron, the proverbial rubber had now hit the road. Could this same generosity of spirit—this servant's approach to leadership, giving up a personal agenda to help someone else achieve their higher aspirations—actually work in a manufacturing company? More important, could it work at a company that was in turmoil? At this juncture, the problems appeared too daunting to overcome.

Before me, Datron had been owned by a large defense contractor who had acquired it several years earlier. The leaders there had high hopes that we might help them get into the international marketplace. However, the relationship began to unravel when an acquisition offer for our parent company came in. The buyer began their normal due diligence regarding Datron. Shortly after their inquiry was complete, I was informed that several of my staff members and I were considered *subjects* in a criminal investigation. The DOJ had stated, in no uncertain terms, that they didn't know if I was innocent or guilty.

I had been with Datron for nearly seven years and I knew we had done nothing wrong. This news and the process we were about to go through were overwhelming. Our parent company, along with the acquiring company, began an intense, protracted probe into Datron's company affairs for the previous five-year period.

No one had done anything along these lines. We were in full compliance. Still, it was unsettling to be under a microscope, not knowing if there would be additional accusations. The threat of prosecution was ever present.

When an organization is going through something like this, every employee is on edge. They all want to know what's going on. After the subpoenas began to fly, I called an all-hands meeting. I told our employees that I believed the truth would set us free. "It's real simple," I said, "just tell the truth." Several of us went one step further and formed a group that met each morning to pray for the truth to be revealed and also for the individuals involved with the investigation.

After the investigation had gone on several months, we became aware of the acquiring company's desire to use the DOJ investigation to negotiate a lower price per share for the acquisition.

Finally, the investigation came to a close. We had proved what we knew all along: nothing illegal or even questionable had been done. The DOJ suggested only that a few of our administrative procedures be improved.

Yes, this investigation had put us through a long, dark nightmare. But then came a new opportunity. Our parent company's CFO notified us they wanted to sell Datron.

My wife, Lori, and I decided we wanted to buy it. It was a tremendous risk, as Datron was in the red and hemorrhaging money at the time. And while I had worked in management, I had never owned a company. But I believed in the business and in the customers we served. Although Lori and I didn't have the personal wealth to purchase the company, we were able to work an owner-financing deal and we took the plunge.

Miraculously, on our *first day* of ownership the company collected on some customer accounts early—resulting in close to $5 million in the bank *by the end of the day*!

Lori and I spent several months discussing what type of an organization we wanted Datron to be. We were committed to running the company like it had never been run before. We wanted to exercise values that were different from those of most other organizations. We realized that a servant leadership style—which I had originally learned about from Ken Blanchard—was the only option. It was a matter of being obedient in our faith.

The actual practice of servant leadership is not some arduous rule or some overwhelming, difficult exercise. It is a life-giving, life-freeing mindset that releases people. This approach operates by one overarching ideal: caring about people. When you treat individuals with dignity and respect, you unlock their vast potential. This thoughtful attention is not for just my employees—it extends to their families. As the leader, I'm responsible for all of those families: the moms and dads who get up every day and sacrifice their time to work at Datron, away from their kids. Mine is not a burdensome obligation. Rather, it is a joy that servant leaders are privileged to experience every day of their lives.

As we began our journey, we contracted with an outside consulting firm to help us define the purpose and mission for the company. We came up with a very simple mission and purpose statement that is still in place today: *A self-sustaining, profitable communications company which positively impacts the lives of others today and in the future.* After we rolled out our new mission and purpose statement, we moved our focus to learning about and implementing servant leadership.

## Servant Leadership Doesn't Stop at Your Company's Door

I didn't want the focus of our company to simply be profit. I felt the real bottom line had to be people. That meant a couple of things. First, we had to throw out the organizational chart. I think org charts only reinforce the positional leadership model. The principles of servant leadership turn that model upside down. A true servant leader's attitude is to put their employees above and ahead of themselves.

The next key component was to put our families ahead of our work. For most leaders, that's a nice thought; however, many believe it would detract employees from their work and productivity would decline. Nothing could be further from the truth. Of course, most of us at Datron had been so caught up in the DOJ investigation that our families ended up at the bottom of our priority list during that time. In essence, they had been sacrificed for the good of the company. I needed to change that.

You can imagine how this new philosophy was received by my management team, who knew the shaky ground we were standing on. If anything, they felt we needed to strengthen our organizational chart to include accompanying areas of responsibility, not abandon it. And our families could remain on the back burner so that we could stay focused at work.

Adding to the challenge was the psychological state many of our employees were in. The DOJ investigation had taken a real toll on people. The accusations had made some feel as if they were witnesses under interrogation lights. Some leaders had become so afraid they were paralyzed and had difficulty making decisions again for fear they would make a mistake.

Lori and I believed servant leadership could help us not only heal, but thrive. So we boldly moved forward.

We made several misjudgments and mistakes. One of the most important things I learned in those early years was that people transform from traditional leaders to servant leaders at a different rate. They may have the desire to take the journey, but they move at different speeds and have varying ideas about what servant leadership really is.

I found my role to be similar to a caretaker managing several different kinds of fruit trees. Some shot up and produced fruit right away. Some required more patience and a little more pruning. But the ever-expanding result was each tree coming into its own and flourishing. Along the way, I had many experiences that inspired me and helped confirm that we were on the right track. I remember visiting the CEO of a large software firm on the East Coast. As we sat in his conference room, he told me that his daughter had just gone into labor and he wouldn't be able to spend much time with me that day. His daughter's needs came first. This care for families extended to all his employees. He said his primary job was to ensure that when the employees left their jobs at the end of the day they not only wanted to come back the next morning, but also felt they were fulfilling a greater purpose by being there.

Little by little, we continued to implement servant leadership throughout Datron. I remember the day we announced this new approach to the entire company. We played a video that included interviews with some of the managers and workers who had gone through our servant leadership training. I wasn't quite prepared for what I was about to watch. In the interviews, people talked about the impact of servant leadership not only in their work environment but also in their personal lives. As I watched, my eyes began to tear up. I couldn't speak. People were giving to others—truly placing others' needs ahead of their own. And as they gave, others gave to them. It was a living example of what's possible when people take time to listen and care for one another.

Thus began an upward spiral of ever-expanding goodness that permeated the organization. It didn't stop when people left work each day. They were so inspired they began to apply servant leadership principles at home. They shared how difficult relationships in their marriages and families were being transformed. And guess what? As this higher ground was being activated and achieved, we began to see phenomenal growth in our financial bottom line at Datron. We obtained record revenues, margins, profits, and cash flow. And in late 2016, Datron was awarded a record contract of $495 million.

## Taking Servant Leadership to the Real World

As I move into the future, I have a vision to share servant leadership with the world. I want to teach the principles—but even more important to me is to provide the strategies and tools for implementation of those principles. As a practical manager, I want to help leaders and companies implement and apply servant leadership to the everyday, real-world challenges in their organizations. I want to share the challenges we've faced, the pitfalls to avoid, and the ultimate success that is possible. We created the Servant Leadership Institute (SLI) to do just that. SLI is a leadership development organization that focuses on the implementation of servant leadership. Today we have an international audience of practitioners and seekers, wanting to lead from their hearts, who—through servant leadership—help people through the unfolding of their life events.

As I've traveled over the last four years talking about servant leadership, I've found that people at all levels within organizations desire a better way of managing and leading. Now is the time for us to make a difference in this world through servant leadership. I trust that many will come to enjoy the journey, relish the challenges, and experience the life-transforming results of servant leadership in the people they touch. It's my hope that organizations around the world will choose to move out of the flames and into the light. God bless everyone.

*Art Barter (www.artbarterspeaks.com) is the owner and CEO of Datron World Communications and the founder and CEO of the Servant Leadership Institute. Art began his career working for the Walt Disney Company. He then spent more than twenty-five years with several manufacturing companies before joining Datron in 1997. He is passionate about servant leadership and operates by the guiding principle "How you get results is more important than the results themselves."*

# Chapter 40

# Serve the People

## CHERYL BACHELDER

*I met Cheryl Bachelder at a conference sponsored by the Servant Leadership Institute at Datron World Communications. I'm always looking for good news stories of top managers who put common sense into practice and make a major difference in their company. Cheryl certainly did that during her tenure as CEO of Popeyes Louisiana Kitchen. What a wonderful example of how servant leadership can turn an organization around. —KB*

IN 2007, POPEYES was a struggling brand and company. The restaurants were declining in sales and profitability. The franchisees—the owners who had invested in the facilities and the people—were not happy. They had committed their money and life to Popeyes, and they wanted to know what the franchisor—the corporation—was going to do about it.

When I accepted the role of Popeyes CEO in November 2007, I knew it was a difficult time. Even so, this comment from a veteran franchisee caught me by surprise: "Don't expect us to trust you any time soon. We've been abused children. And it will take a long time to get the past behind us."

In short, the franchise owners had not been served well. That would have to change.

I have worked in franchising, observing the relationship dynamics between franchisors and franchisees, since 1995. The business model is set up as a symbiotic partnership. The franchisor provides the brand, the menu, the marketing message, the operating systems, and often the food and packaging supplies. The franchisee builds the restaurants, hires and trains the people, and operates the restaurant by the policy guidebook. Both parties must do their job, and do it well, or the results falter.

Given the nature of the business, I am always surprised by the animosity and outright battle mindsets that so often characterize the franchisor-franchisee relationship. As one of my leaders liked to say: "There has never been a brand with positive sales and profit growth that is at war with its franchise owners."

It was this very predicament that my Popeyes leadership team decided to address as our strategy for turning around business performance. Simply put, we decided to serve the franchisees well. We began calling them our number-one customer. More important, we began treating them that way—as servant leaders.

Our principle was simple. If we served the franchise owners well, and they experienced sales and profit growth, they would be excited about the future—and would build more Popeyes restaurants. When they built more restaurants, our shareholders and other stakeholders would also be well served. Serve the people well. And the rest will take care of itself.

So where did we begin the turnaround—and what drove the positive outcome?

Our first decision was to spend a lot of time with our owners, looking at the business and working collaboratively to make the results better. We chose to focus on the core strategies of a successful chain restaurant: build a distinctive and relevant brand, run great restaurants, and make money for the owners. Those strategies were important to the turnaround. But I would tell you that our principles for *how* we did business with our franchise owners were the more important factor. We landed on six servant leadership principles that would guide our actions.

## Principles for Serving the People

### We Are Passionate about What We Do

To state the obvious, small business owners like Popeyes franchisees are passionate by design. They are risk takers. They put big money down on the brand idea—and with that comes their passion for getting it right. At Popeyes, the greatest passion is for the superior food. Popeyes people want only the best quality and innovation in the restaurants.

Our first principle was to respect the passion of our owners. They had made the investment of their money and their lives in Popeyes. We would treat that as a sacred trust. We would respect and admire their passion for the business. Passion would be the fuel of our business plan.

### *We Listen Carefully . . .*

If you've ever had an argument with someone you care about, you have experienced what happens when you don't listen well to another person. You miss their point. You overlook their real concern. You lack vital information. And the argument escalates. The same is true in the franchising business.

Our first road trip in the fall of 2007 was called a *listening tour*. We went to seven cities and listened carefully to our franchise owners, our restaurant managers, and our Popeyes guests. We asked them what was wrong and what their ideas were for fixing the problems. We asked clarifying questions and we didn't try to sell them anything. In doing so, we heard all the issues we needed to address going forward. We demonstrated respect for our people. And when we got back home, we had the beginnings of an action plan.

Listening carefully to our franchise owners, and learning from them, became an essential principle of our success.

### *. . . and Learn Continuously*

The retail food business is dynamic and fast paced. There are many competitors chasing share of market. As a result, your business can be performing brilliantly and one day later an aggressive competitor can change the trend with one new menu innovation, one new service approach, or one new value offering.

In the fall of 2008, we were ready to launch our big marketing plan to turn around sales at Popeyes. We had alignment with our owners, we had set aside a big budget for advertising, and we were going to take the market by storm. Little did we know that America's banks were on the verge of collapse and the economy was at the beginning of the biggest recession of our lifetime. We were about to learn some lessons.

We did not experience a sales turnaround in those next few months, but we learned continuously. We stayed in close dialog with our franchise leaders. We analyzed the results quickly. And we made agile decisions to change to plans that would be effective in this new world order. Our willingness to learn and act on that learning resulted in the beginning of a remarkable turnaround in early 2009 and we continued to hold this principle dear.

## We Are Fact-Based and Planful

Popeyes was a thirty-five-year-old company in 2007. That would lead you to believe that we had long established planning processes and performance metrics to help us manage the business. Wrong.

Our business plan looked forward about ninety days. We had one dataset: how much money our franchisees were sending us in fees and royalties. We did not have a detailed annual plan or a five-year strategic plan. We did not have a pipeline of new products, promotions, and restaurant locations. We did not collect any data on important things like guest satisfaction, speed of service, or restaurant operating profits.

Remember our first principle—passion? Well, passion that goes ungoverned by any facts and plans is just raw, unbridled emotion. And that was the nature of our conversations with franchisees in the early days. Until we had facts and plans, we would be at the mercy of whomever yelled the loudest.

One of our operators said, "You move what you measure." And we began to measure just about everything that moved. First on the list were guest transactions, guest satisfaction, speed of service, and restaurant operating profit. Second on the list were the returns to our owners on new restaurant investments.

Two things happened. Our franchise owners started improving key measures of the business. And when we met to plan the future, we had facts in front of us to guide our decisions. We could argue passionately—but our emotions were bound by the reality of information. Facts and plans made our success sustainable.

## We Coach and Develop Our People

Sometimes the most important decision you can make is to acknowledge your weakness. At Popeyes, we had virtually no people capability—coaching and development of our talent was not a principle of our culture. We openly stated this weakness to ourselves, our team, and our owners. Then we began a journey of making coaching and development important in our culture.

We established the business competencies and the cultural principles needed for success, and then focused on coaching and developing our people toward those capabilities. Even though we were not the best coaches, our people saw our efforts as a sign that they were valued—and they began to grow.

The benefit to our franchises? They were being served now by people growing in their capability because their leaders were investing time and attention in coaching. Our talent grew by leaps and bounds—and our franchisees noticed the difference.

### We Are Personally Accountable

A relationship without accountability is destined for dissatisfaction and dysfunction. As I mentioned earlier, in our business model, each of us had roles and responsibilities we had to do for the business to prosper. The franchisor had to provide a compelling brand and an effective operating system. The franchise owner had to provide top quality people, food, and guest experiences. When we all did our piece of the puzzle, we could expect positive outcomes. When one of us dropped the ball, we had to accept personal responsibility to correct our actions quickly.

Our culture became one of "no excuses, no blame." We accepted our role and responsibility to make things right. And worked to avoid victim behavior. Productivity soared when accountability was high.

### We Value Humility

The last principle we chose may have been the most important to the turnaround of Popeyes. It was the principle that underscored the Popeyes purpose statement: *Inspire servant leaders to achieve superior results.* It was both our belief and our work experience that when we served our franchise owners well, the business prospered—and over time, our own career goals and needs were met as well.

Being humble on a daily basis is difficult. It's also difficult to teach humility to leaders who have viewed it as a leadership weakness in the past. But getting ourselves out of the way was essential to serving our franchise owners well.

Our definition of humility was one I've heard attributed to Rick Warren, Ken Blanchard, and others: "Humility is not thinking less of yourself, it is thinking of yourself less."

At Popeyes, we were ordinary people who struggled to not be self-centered in our daily actions. We believed—and we had experienced—that when we acted out of self-interest, the relationship with our owners was damaged and our business outcomes suffered. Alternatively, when we put their interests above our own, the relationship *and* business outcomes flourished.

## The Results

During the period from 2007 to 2016, Popeyes became a prosperous enterprise with restaurant sales, profits, and unit growth rates that were the envy of its competitors. Franchise owners were served well, with 95 percent rating their satisfaction with the Popeyes system at good or very good. And 90 percent said they would recommend Popeyes to another franchisee. The decision to serve the franchisees also benefited other stakeholders, including the shareholders. The stock price moved from $11 per share in 2007 to $64 per share at the end of 2016, which I believe to be a direct result of our leadership approach. When the company was sold by the board of directors in March 2017, the buyer paid a $15 premium—a share price of $79.

They always say hindsight is 20/20. And that is certainly true in the Popeyes story.

When this story began, we didn't know it would be servant leadership that drove success. We didn't have a plaque in the office that stated our purpose and principles. What we did have was a team of leaders who were willing to focus their passion and ambition on the success of the people and the enterprise before their own interests. And as Jim Collins predicted in his book *Good to Great*, the results were phenomenal. Collins states great leaders "are a paradoxical mix of personal humility and professional will. They are ambitious, to be sure, but ambitious first and foremost for the company, not themselves."[1]

*Cheryl A. Bachelder (www.cherylbachelder.com) served as CEO of Popeyes Louisiana Kitchen, Inc., from 2007 to 2017. She has more than thirty-five years of leadership experience at companies like Yum! Brands, Domino's Pizza, RJR Nabisco, Gillette, and Procter & Gamble. In 2012 she was recognized as Leader of the Year by the Women's Foodservice Forum and also received the Silver Plate from the International Food Manufacturer's Association. She is author of the bestselling book* Dare to Serve: How to Drive Superior Results by Serving Others.

## Note

1. Jim Collins, *Good to Great: Why Some Companies Make the Leap and Others Don't* (New York: HarperBusiness, 2001).

# Chapter 41

# Waste Connections

## *A Servant Leadership Success Story*

### Rico Maranto

*I met Ron Mittelstaedt, CEO and founder of Waste Connections,
a number of years ago when I spoke to his CEO roundtable. Ron and
I discovered we were kindred spirits in leadership philosophy.
As a result, I got to do some work with Ron and his key managers
as they progressed on their servant leadership journey. This essay,
written by Rico Maranto, guardian of the culture and servant
leadership evangelist for Waste Connections (I love that title), will
show you how the influence of the top manager can make servant
leadership come alive and create great human satisfaction and
results. —KB*

WASTE CONNECTIONS WAS founded in 1997 when founder and CEO Ron
Mittelstaedt acquired a few solid waste companies in the Northwest. Within
a few years, Waste Connections had become the fourth-largest solid waste
company in the United States and a formidable player in the industry, significantly outperforming its competitors in the stock market.

## The Problem

Despite its apparent success, Waste Connections was losing good employees.
Out of a staff of 3,000, between 1,200 and 1,400 employees were leaving the
organization each year—a turnover rate of more than 40 percent. What's
more, 80 percent of those losses were voluntary. People were *choosing* to leave
the company.

Mittelstaedt knew the company would not remain successful if it had to replace and retrain 40 percent of its staff every year. He was particularly concerned about the number of employees who were resigning—and he knew he needed to find a way to keep them.

To help management understand the reason for the high turnover, for a period of two years each person who left the company was asked to fill out an exit survey. More than two thousand survey respondents spelled out the problem: their leaders had failed them. Forty-five percent of those surveyed said they could not have a candid conversation with their manager. An equal number said they were not doing the work they had been hired to do.

Waste Connections' executive leaders needed the managers to take a hard look at themselves. The managers needed to recognize they were the ones their people couldn't talk to. They were the ones who hired people and gave them false expectations. If they wanted to increase employee retention, the leaders had to fix themselves.

Looking back, Mittelstaedt says, "We realized people expected more from the employee/employer relationship than simple management of day-to-day tasks. People needed to feel included, familial, cared for, and empowered. They wanted to know their voice mattered—that they were more than a number. We had to make a wholesale change. It was a matter of survival. The direction we were heading was not sustainable."

## The Solution

During his search for a solution to this operational crisis, Mittelstaedt heard about a concept called servant leadership. He learned that it turns the traditional leadership pyramid upside down, placing leaders at the bottom so that they can serve the employees at the top. He learned it requires humility instead of ego. The servant leader's role is to help others succeed—to serve, not be served. The servant leader seeks to understand what a win looks like for each employee and how to serve each person to help them get that win.

Mittelstaedt considered the premise that employees do not leave companies; they leave managers. He was told servant leadership could make better leaders, create a better place to work, and increase employee retention. But it seemed like soft leadership—so different from the traditional command and control, autocratic style prevalent in the waste management industry. What if employees took advantage of a servant leader's selflessness? Could a company really achieve outstanding results if leaders simply cared about their people? Would servant leadership work?

Mittelstaedt was convinced it would. He introduced the concept to Waste Connections senior leaders, saying, "We have a typical top-down leadership pyramid. It may have worked for us at first, but it's not working now. Times have changed. People have changed. Therefore, we must change. Let's turn this mindset upside down!"

In support of the initiative was Waste Connections CFO, Worthing Jackman, who stated at the time, "I'll have a higher degree of confidence in our ability to hit financial projections and commitments made by our managers if servant leadership gets embedded in our culture. We'll actually be running the business, rather than the business running us."

## The Implementation

Mittelstaedt introduced servant leadership at the 2005 annual managers' meeting. He discussed the employee turnover problem, explained the long-term impact of high turnover on the organization, shared the results of the employee exit surveys, and set the expectation of change. He then defined servant leadership and invited all of the managers to become servant leaders.

Ken Blanchard was the keynote speaker at that meeting. Ken explained how servant leadership was not soft leadership—yes, it was about relationships, but it was also about results—*both* results *and* relationships.

Waste Connections is a decentralized organization. Field leaders are expected to be true entrepreneurs and are empowered to run their sites as if they own them. They are held accountable for results (safety, turnover, financial, etc.), but not for their management methods. Because of the decentralized structure at Waste Connections, corporate leaders rarely tell field leaders what to do or how to do it.

In the spirit of decentralization, Mittelstaedt said to the managers, "We hope you will become servant leaders. We won't make you do it, but we believe you'll get better results if you do. And you will be judged by your performance."

## Changing the Culture

Mittelstaedt knew servant leadership would be a monumental change in the organization's culture. "It was like pushing a snowball uphill for two years," he says. "There were a lot of dissenters because the concept was so foreign. People thought it wouldn't work. They wanted to keep doing things the way we had always done them."

President Steve Bouck says, "The managers were skeptical. They would say, 'We're running a lot of trucks and we've got a lot of work to do. If I tell an employee what to do, they'd just better do it.' Helping managers adopt servant leadership required consistent, persistent communication and alignment of incentives."

COO Darrell Chambliss adds, "Implementing servant leadership is hard. It requires continuous reinforcement. We still constantly talk about it and spend resources on it. Unless an organization is committed to doing that, servant leadership will become a dusty book on the shelf."

Waste Connections did a number of things to change the culture and help managers embrace servant leadership. These were a few of the key initiatives:

- *Introduce a vision, purpose, and values.* "The introduction of our values and our vision of self-directed, empowered employees was a critical piece that helped shape the framework of our culture and leadership style," says Bouck.
- *Conduct servant leadership training.* Initially, Mittelstaedt and senior leaders taught full-day servant leadership seminars for all managers. District manager training evolved from teaching how to manage a waste business to teaching how to be a servant leader—and from technical skills to soft skills.

  After a period of time, Mittelstaedt hired a director of leadership development who developed and began teaching a series of seven servant leadership courses. The new director attended every meeting possible to discuss servant leadership, sent out weekly servant leadership emails to all managers, and talked about servant leadership at every opportunity.

  Mittelstaedt says, "That took servant leadership to a whole new level. It gave servant leadership an identity in the company."
- *Distribute a servant leader newsletter.* Managers who adopted servant leadership began to have successes. To inspire others, a newsletter was created as a medium to share success stories.
- *Distribute a servant leadership survey.* In 2007, a survey was distributed to all employees. The survey asked each employee to rate their supervisor on various servant leadership characteristics. The following year, a percentage of each manager's bonus—for some, as much as 25 percent—was determined by survey results.

- *Create a Servant Leader Playbook.* At the 2007 annual managers' meeting, Mittelstaedt announced that servant leadership is a lifestyle, not a program. To illustrate, he gave a diet analogy. He said, "There are thousands of diets out there. If you stick to one, you'll lose weight. Many people lose weight but then gain it back and say, 'I was on a diet but now I'm not.' The people who keep the weight off start with a diet and it becomes a lifestyle. Healthy living becomes part of their DNA—who they are. We will give you the servant leadership diet. You need to decide if it will become your lifestyle."

  The "diet" Mittelstaedt suggested became known as the *Servant Leader Playbook.* The playbook translated the idea of servant leadership into actions any manager could take to become a better servant leader. This helped servant leadership gain even more traction in the company. Some of the plays in the playbook included:

  - manage by walking around
  - post the company's vision, purpose, and values in your department
  - meet with your team and discuss accountability for vision, purpose, and values
  - reinforce the values (walk the talk)
  - catch people doing something right
  - allow time in every meeting for employees to give their manager a to-do list to hold the manager accountable
  - coach every day.

- *Create servant leadership awards.* Each year, Waste Connections had recognized managers with awards like Manager of the Year or Most Improved EBITDA (earnings before interest, tax, depreciation, and amortization). But now the company wanted to recognize not only *what* the best managers did, but *how* they did what they did. So a Servant Leader of the Year award was created, recognizing the manager who best embodied servant leadership. It is the premier award—the "best picture" of the company's Oscars.

- *Get self-serving leaders off the bus.* By 2008, servant leadership had gained momentum. About 90 percent of managers had adopted servant leadership and were achieving significant results. At that year's annual managers' meeting, Mittelstaedt made an announcement: servant leadership was no longer optional. It was the expected method of leadership throughout the company.

One of the company's division vice presidents (DVPs) had been recognized two consecutive years at the annual managers' meeting and seemed to build good relationships with his employees. He achieved impressive results and spoke like a servant leader when talking with senior leadership. Everyone thought he was a good servant leader—everyone but his employees. In their servant leader surveys, they described a very different manager—one who was egotistical and hypocritical.

When the DVP's character came to light, Mittelstaedt and other executives had to make a crucial decision: *Do we keep a manager who gets great results but is not a servant leader?*

Mittelstaedt noted the manager had done very well managing the senior leaders' perception of him. "But," he said, "servant leadership isn't about worrying up; it's about worrying down. It's not about what your boss thinks of you; it's about what your people think of their boss." Then he stated flatly: "If we have a cancer in our culture, we have to cut it out."

They fired the DVP. Soon afterward, between fifteen and twenty other managers were either shared with the competition or demoted to an individual contributor position. This sent a clear message to everyone that servant leadership was not an option.

Sue Netherton, vice president of people training and development, explains, "We have to be willing to let people go who are not servant leaders, even if they get good results. Keeping them would be a reflection on our leadership—and would compromise our servant leadership culture."

- *Hire for character.* Waste Connections also needed to elevate the employee candidate pool, so they changed their hiring practices. In the past, they had hired applicants with the desired competencies—skill and experience. They learned to hire less for competency and more for character—because, as Mittelstaedt would say, "You can't train character." Before they considered a candidate's skill and experience, the recruiters asked questions to learn if a candidate's personal values aligned with company values.

## The Results

By the end of 2010, overall turnover had dropped from 40 percent to 17 percent. And of that, only 56 percent was voluntary, down from 80 percent.

Waste Connections' stock was outpacing all of their competitors as well as the S&P, and safety incident rates had dropped 40 percent.

Netherton describes the introduction of servant leadership to Waste Connections as "a defining moment that ultimately led to the success of the organization."

"Servant leadership made Waste Connections a place where employees *wanted* to be instead of where they *had* to be," says Bouck. "It was a better place to work, in a tough industry."

Mittelstaedt says, "People hear we have a better company and a great culture, and it attracts better employees. We now find and keep the kind of employees we want to have."

"Servant leadership defined the expectation of how we wanted the company run by those who run the company," Chambliss says. "It taught supervisors it was okay to have friendly relationships with their employees. It taught us to communicate from the receiver's point of view, not just the boss's. It made us better members of our own families and better members of our communities."

Mittelstaedt sums up the impact of servant leadership: "The whole idea of servant leadership is that it has a positive ripple effect. The way our leaders treat their employees becomes the employees' vision of leadership. The employees then go out and coach little league teams, serve in their church or community, lead in their families, and leave an indelible servant leadership thumbprint. Their influence improves their families and communities and continues to ripple outward as others lead the way they have been led."

## Waste Connections Update

In 2016, Waste Connections stock continued to outperform its competitors and the S&P. Safety incident rates were the lowest in the industry. Overall turnover continued to be low and voluntary turnover was lower than it had ever been.

In the summer of 2016, Waste Connections merged with a similar but slightly larger company in terms of employees. The two companies were in the same industry, used similar equipment, and had similar safety standards—but were achieving very different results. The other firm's voluntary termination rate was 80 percent higher than that of Waste Connections, and their incident rate was four times higher. They had had thirty-one employee/third-party fatalities over the previous four years while Waste Connections had none. They were essentially in the same place Waste Connections had been ten years earlier.

If the companies were so similar, why such different results? A servant leader culture.

Dean DiValerio, an assistant regional vice president who joined Waste Connections in the merger, says, "As I look back at various waste companies I've worked for, I realize we all used the same trucks and got our employees from the same candidate pool. The true differentiator that has made Waste Connections so successful is servant leadership. It separates them from everyone else in the industry."

After the merger, Waste Connections immediately introduced the incoming managers to servant leadership. More than forty classes were held for more than a thousand managers. The excitement about servant leadership was palpable.

Within nine months, their employee turnover had dropped 14 percentage points, their safety incidents had dropped more than 66 percent, and Waste Connections' stock price had increased from $66 to $86 per share. Servant leadership gets results!

Mittelstaedt explains, "Servant leadership has become our DNA—the core of our company. It's how we do things."

As Waste Connections moves into the future, servant leadership will continue to be how they do what they do: foster real relationships as they achieve unparalleled results.

*A learning and development professional with more than twenty-five years of experience, Rico Maranto's passion is helping others embrace servant leadership so that they can become better servant leaders in their homes, communities, and workplaces. He holds an MS in organization leadership and HR management from Regis University.*

# Chapter 42

# Don't Mark My Paper, Help Me Get an A

## GARRY RIDGE

*Garry Ridge and I got to know each other shortly after he had become president at WD-40 Company, when he was a student in the masters in leadership program my wife, Margie, and I cofounded at University of San Diego. Garry is one of those people who, when he has a powerful learning, begins to implement it the next day. His journey to make WD-40 Company a great servant leadership company motivated me to write a book with him entitled* Helping People Win at Work. *After all, one of the key aspects of servant leadership is to help people win—accomplish their goals. Garry's story is well worth replicating in your company. —KB*

AT THE AGE of forty, I decided it was time to expand my learning. Although I had long ago earned a diploma from Sydney Technical College and was serving as CEO of WD-40 Company, I wanted to confirm what I thought I knew and learn what I didn't. So I enrolled in the Master of Science in Executive Leadership degree program at the University of San Diego, a joint venture between the university and The Ken Blanchard Companies. That's where I met Ken and heard him talk about his philosophy, as a college professor, of giving his students the final exam at the beginning of the semester—and then throughout the course teaching them the answers—so when they got to the final exam they each would get an A.

Ken feels that life is about helping people get As—not force-fitting them into a normal distribution curve. Yet, in most organizations, managers are expected to rate a few people high, a few people low, and the rest as average performers. Even when a company doesn't have a normal distribution curve evaluation system, managers are afraid to rate all their people high because then *they* would be rated low. They would be accused of being easy—or soft—managers. As a result, the normal distribution curve is alive and well throughout the world. Ken's philosophy resonated with my own personal values. That's when I became excited about implementing his final exam philosophy into our performance review system at WD-40 Company.

## Changing the Culture

To make a significant change in something as important as an organization's performance review system, you first have to focus on the culture. Culture refers to the assumptions, beliefs, values, customs, and behaviors of the organization's employees, supervisors, and leaders. According to Edgar Schein and others, culture is "the way we do things around here." Impacting the WD-40 Company culture I inherited was not a quick fix. It required several steps before I could revamp our performance review system.

First, we needed to create a learning environment. What keeps people in organizations from wanting to learn? They look at mistakes as career-damaging events rather than opportunities to learn. Therefore, they cover up mistakes in the hope that no one finds out. What I needed to do was to help people realize that mistakes were inevitable but not necessarily fatal. To do that, I had to redefine the concept of mistakes. I needed to teach people not to be afraid to fail. As a result, we determined that at WD-40, when things go wrong, we don't call them *mistakes*; we call them *learning moments*.

The second thing I tackled was clarifying the company's vision and values. A vision gives you a sense of direction, and values give you a compass to keep you on course. Having a clear vision and values is just as important as having a learning culture.

Our WD-40 vision is clear: we're in the memories business. Our products solve problems in 176 countries. In essence, we are in the quality-of-life business. By solving everyday problems in an almost magical way, we make people's lives better and, in the process, create positive, lasting memories for our customers.

Once the vision is set, values are needed as principles that guide our behavior while we're scaling the mountain we have set out to climb. Values need to be simple yet strong, and they need to be clearly communicated as the only acceptable behavior. The rank-ordered values that guide our behavior at WD-40 Company are:

1. Doing the right thing
2. Creating positive, lasting memories in all our relationships
3. Making it better than it is today
4. Succeeding as a tribe while excelling as individuals
5. Owning it and passionately acting on it
6. Sustaining the WD-40 economy

It's interesting to note that our last value is "Sustaining the WD-40 economy." I've seen a number of companies that never mention financial well-being as a value. When you don't do that, everyone knows that the values are a joke. Why? Because when finances aren't going well, a lot of energy gets focused in that direction.

Ranking our financial value last among our other values tells people it's important—it's one of our core values—but we will do nothing to make money that compromises any of the other values. Stating the value as "Sustaining the WD-40 economy" is broader than valuing profits. If people saw the word "profit," they would think all we care about is making money. When we talk about a thriving economy, it implies the well-being of all involved, not just top management.

The final cultural change I needed to make to set up our "Don't Mark My Paper, Help Me Get an A" philosophy was to ask our people to think of us not as a *team* but rather as a *tribe*. Using tribal terminology gave me a vehicle to talk about a wide range of organizational attributes that were important to WD-40 Company, rather than just the attributes I'd be limited to if I were to use the word "team." A team is about winning and getting stuff done in a positive way. While that's important, a tribe is a much richer concept. A tribe is a place you belong; a team is something you play on once in a while.

The tribal concept set the tone for the open communication we needed in our company. It also helped establish a partnership philosophy that is necessary to implement the "Don't Mark My Paper, Help Me Get an A" concept.

## A New Performance Management System

There are three aspects of our "Don't Mark My Paper, Help Me Get an A" performance review system: *planning*, *execution*, and *review and learning*.

## Planning

When it comes to planning, once a year every tribe leader has a conversation with each of his or her direct reports to establish the tribe members' final exam that consists of three to five short-term SMART goals. SMART is a widely used acronym for what a well-defined goal looks like:

- S stands for *specific*—the goal is observable and measureable.
- M stands for *motivational*—the goal is something that the tribe member is excited about and willing to pursue.
- A stands for *attainable*—the goal is moderately difficult but achievable for the person.
- R stands for *relevant*—the goal directly contributes to the company's bottom line or supports the efforts of those who do.
- T stands for *trackable*—the goal can be tracked over time so the individual can be praised or redirected, depending on their progress on the goal, in a timely manner.

One of the things I've learned over the years is that all good performance starts with clear goals—that sets up the *leadership* aspect of servant leadership. When establishing a final exam with someone, it's important to be certain that the person knows exactly what he or she is being asked to do. That's what establishing SMART goals does. It makes sure that people are being evaluated on observable, measurable goals, not on fuzzy, subjective expectations.

The rules at WD-40 Company are simple: if people attain their observable, measurable goals at the end of the fiscal year, they will get an A—as long as they're in good shape with living the company's values. This means that a high performer who continually violates our values might be facing a career crisis.

## Execution

Once people are clear on their final exam and the observable, measurable goals that the exam consists of, we move on to execution—the *servant* aspect of servant leadership. At this stage, people must begin to perform on their agreed-upon goals. This is where day-to-day coaching comes into play. This is a major emphasis in the "Don't Mark My Paper, Help Me Get an A" philosophy. This means that tribe leaders have to keep up their end of the partnership on a day-to-day basis, helping and coaching their tribe members to get an A on each of their goals. To help that process, WD-40 Company uses Ken Blanchard's Situational Leadership® II model, which helps tribe leaders determine the amount of direction and support they need to give tribe members on each goal. While the leadership aspect of servant leadership—in our case, clear goals—gets things going, the real action is with the servant aspect of servant leadership—helping people achieve their goals. This sets up the third part of our performance review system: review and learning.

## Review and Learning

Continually planning and executing without the value of review and learning could blindside you with what we call a typhoon—a destructive event. That's when somebody makes a mistake that hurts both the organization and that person's reputation. Since we don't want that to happen, it is important to take time to pause, review progress, and look for any learning—whether or not a mistake has been made.

At WD-40 Company the review and learning process is a continuous conversation throughout the year. Why do we say review and learning is an ongoing process? Because we don't want to save up feedback until somebody fails. Periodically, you want to be able to give people feedback that either is positive or redirects their efforts.

As part of that process, four times a year all tribe leaders have a conversation with each of their tribe members, which we call *informal/formal discussions*. The first item of business is to review the agreed-upon final exam. Is it still relevant? Rather than filing goals that are established at the beginning of the year and then pulling them out at the end for the annual performance review, at WD-40 Company we think that goal setting is an ongoing process. In fact, if circumstances change, tribe members can renegotiate their goals even at the beginning of the fourth quarter.

After reviewing the final exam each quarter, the tribe leader and tribe member begin to look at the tribe member's performance. In most organizations, at the end of the year every manager has to complete an evaluation for each direct report. We do that differently. At each quarterly meeting, performance is evaluated—but rather than the tribe leader doing the initial evaluation, the tribe member does it. Each tribe member gives themselves an A, B, C, or L on each of his or her agreed-upon goals. An L means that the tribe member is in a learning mode on that goal and isn't ready for evaluation yet. The job of the tribe leader is to agree or disagree with the tribe member's evaluation, and to do what needs to be done to help that person move each goal toward an A.

This evaluation process is repeated at the end of every quarter as well as at the end of the year during the final annual review. It is important to reiterate that tribe leaders fill out a performance evaluation only on themselves. They do not fill out evaluation forms on the tribe members who report to them.

Does everyone get an A? Not necessarily. Sometimes people are in the wrong job. If a person is a values-driven tribe member, we may look for another position for them within WD-40 Company. If the person is not a values-driven tribe member and we think termination is necessary, we kindly say to them, "Let's share you with a competitor." WD-40 Company is not for everyone.

## Servant Leadership with an Edge

To help everyone in WD-40 Company share our "Don't Mark My Paper, Help Me Get an A" philosophy and integrate it into the new culture we had created, I initiated a new leadership model dubbed "Servant Leadership with an Edge." We describe this model as a circular, continuous process beginning with our vision and values, then moving to planning and execution, followed by review and learning, and finally cycling back to vision.

This total process is about creating and enabling leaders to partner for success with their people. First we define with tribe members what an A embodies, and then we create a culture where people can achieve an A.

Does this work? You'd better believe it. In the tough economic years of 2010 to 2012, we had the best financial results in the history of our company. In our 2016 annual Employee Opinion Survey, the following were the five questions with the highest percentage of people indicating an affirmative answer:

1. I feel my opinions and values are a good fit with the WD-40 Company culture (99.1%)
2. I am clear on the company's goals (98.4%)
3. I love to tell people that I work for WD-40 Company (98.4%)
4. I know what results are expected of me (97.9%)
5. I understand how my job contributes to achieving WD-40 Company's goals (97.9%)

To me, helping people get an A is servant leadership in action. It's the only way to get both great results and human satisfaction.

*A native of Australia, Garry Ridge is president and CEO of WD-40 Company, where he has worked since 1987. He received his Masters of Science in Executive Leadership (MSEL) degree in 2001 from the University of San Diego, where he is now an adjunct professor for the MSEL program. In 2009, Garry and Ken Blanchard coauthored the book* Helping People Win at Work: A Business Philosophy Called 'Don't Mark My Paper, Help Me Get an A.' *Garry is a popular speaker on the topic of humanizing the performance review process.*

# Final Comments

## *The Power of Love,*
## *Not the Love of Power*

### KEN BLANCHARD AND
### RENEE BROADWELL

IN THE FIRST chapter of this book, Ken mentioned that when he talks to companies about servant leadership they often think he's talking about the inmates running the prison or trying to please everyone. It takes them a while to realize that servant leadership is the only way to get great relationships and results.

After reading this book, we hope you understand that reality. If you do, we hope you not only implement it where you're planted but also spread the word to everyone who will listen. All the great companies Ken has worked with or observed realize that profit really is the applause they get for creating a motivating environment for their people so they will take good care of their customers.

Ken got a letter from a New Zealander a few years ago that summed up this philosophy. He said, "Ken, you're in the business of teaching people the power of love rather than the love of power."

As Ken said earlier, the world is in desperate need of a different leadership role model. We have seen the negative impact of self-serving leaders in every sector of society around the world. We need servant leadership disciples—and we nominate you. Go forth and spread the word. And remember: your job is to teach people the power of love rather than the love of power. After all, servant leadership is love in action. Peace to you, and God bless.

# Acknowledgments

This book has been one of the most interesting and challenging projects either of us has ever taken on: pulling together the thoughts and writings of more than forty subject-matter experts to present to the world a coherent picture of what servant leadership looks like.

First and foremost, we are grateful to all of our contributors—each one a servant leader who gives the gift of their unique perspective. We hope our readers will pass along the message of servant leadership to others in their homes, workplaces, and communities, and together we can make a positive difference in thousands of lives.

We thank our friends at Berrett-Koehler Publishers—Steve Piersanti, Jeevan Sivasubramaniam, David Marshall, and the rest of the BK team. You are always a joy to work with!

We also thank our colleagues at The Ken Blanchard Companies—Martha Lawrence, Richard Andrews, Debbie Castro, and Margery Allen—for being there for us.

Ken is grateful to his wife, Margie, for loving him for more than fifty-five years—and to their daughter Debbie and son Scott, Scott's wife Madeleine, and Margie's brother, Tom, for their support and leadership of our company.

Renee is grateful to Grant for being an ambassador of unconditional love, and to Trevor, Justine, and Jocelyn for inspiring her every day and making her a proud and happy mama.

# Index

Abrams, Creighton, 122
accountability: of human beings, 58, 75, 105–6, 119, 126, 208–9, 235; principle of, 229
action: against culture of shame, 73; compassion by, 92–94; contribution from, 31–32; credibility through, 111; leadership in, 245; mindset and, 83
addiction, 104, 106
affirmation: from employees, 244–45; as a habit, 77–80
African American community in 1960s, 153–54
AIWATT, 66, 69
ambition and leadership, 179, 230
Anderson, Jerry, 79
apprentice, 150, 165–66
Arbinger Institute, 82–84
Army: commander's intent within, 126; contributions of servant leadership to, 127; operation of, 122; service in, 122–27; succession planning within, 125; trusted relationships in, 126–27; values of, 123–24
artist, 112–13
asking: where someone is, 102; to help, 213–14
assessment: improvement through, 97; of position in hierarchy, 59; of signs of shame culture, 72; of trustworthiness, 30
authenticity, 27–28, 111, 113
avoidance, 88–89

awareness: as a characteristic of a servant leader, 16

behavior: of caring, 86; through disengagement, 74; and misfortune, 67; presence and, 54; and shame culture, 72; through structure, 66; and trust, 28–29, 32
Benioff, Mark, 47
bias, natural, 36
Blackaby, Henry, 168–70
blame, 67, 74–75
Blanchard, James W., 205
Blanchard, Ken, 34, 39, 110, 201, 202, 206, 219, 221, 229, 239–40
Blanchard, Margie, 201–202, 239, 249
Blanchard, Scott, 140
Body Shop, 111–12
Bouck, Steve, 234, 237
Brengle, Samuel, 180
Buntin, Nancy, 207
business: and Conscious Capitalism, 19–20, 23; of Disney, 8; of Jesus, 148; profitability of, 43; pruning process of, 209–10; service and, 47–48, 206–7

cabinet issues, 118–21
calling, servant leadership as, 25, 51, 131
caring: behavioral extensions of, 86; characteristics of caring support, 46; compassion and, 91–94
carpentry model, for leadership, 149–50

**251**

# About the Editors

## Ken Blanchard

Ken Blanchard, one of the most influential leadership experts in the world, is the coauthor of the iconic bestseller *The One Minute Manager* and more than sixty other books that have combined sales of more than twenty-one million copies in forty-two languages. In 2005 he was inducted into Amazon's Hall of Fame as one of the top twenty-five bestselling authors of all time.

Ken is the cofounder and chief spiritual officer of The Ken Blanchard Companies, an international training and consulting firm that he and his wife, Margie, began in 1979 in San Diego, California. In addition to being a renowned speaker and consultant, Ken is also cofounder of Lead Like Jesus, a global ministry committed to helping people become servant leaders.

Born in New Jersey and raised in New Rochelle, New York, Ken received a master's degree from Colgate University and a bachelor's and PhD from Cornell University.

Find out more about Ken and his books at www.kenblanchardbooks.com, and follow him on Twitter: @kenblanchard and on Facebook at www.facebook.com/KenBlanchardFanPage.

## Renee Broadwell

Renee Broadwell has been an editor with The Ken Blanchard Companies for more than ten years, working directly with Ken as lead editor on several book projects including *Lead with LUV, Legendary Service, Fit at Last, Collaboration Begins with You, Lead Like Jesus Revisited*, and *The Simple Truths of Service*. She also serves as editor on articles, blogs, other social media, and special projects, partnering with various Blanchard departments including communications, marketing, and the executive suite.

Renee previously held positions with Alaska Airlines, Nordstrom, Inc., and The Art Institute of California-San Diego. She and her husband Grant live in Escondido, California, and their grown children live nearby.

# Services Available

## The Ken Blanchard Companies

The Ken Blanchard Companies is committed to helping leaders and organizations perform at a higher level. Ken, his company, and Blanchard International—a global network of world-class consultants, trainers, and coaches—have been helping organizations improve workplace productivity, employee satisfaction, and customer loyalty around the world for decades.

If you would like information on the services, programs, and products offered by Blanchard International, please contact us.

The Ken Blanchard Companies
World Headquarters
125 State Place
Escondido, California 92029
United States
Phone: +1-760-489-5005
Email: International@kenblanchard.com
Website: www.kenblanchard.com

## Lead Like Jesus

CEO or teacher, pastor or parent, shopkeeper or student—if you want to know more about the Lead Like Jesus organization, go to www.leadlikejesus.com or follow LLJ on Twitter: @leadlikejesus, or on Facebook at www.facebook .com/Lead-Like-Jesus-137597419629033.

# Join Us Online

**Visit the Ken Blanchard Books website: www.kenblanchardbooks.com**

Learn about Ken and his books. Read his blog. Meet his coauthors. Browse his library.

**Follow Ken's Twitter Updates @kenblanchard**

Receive timely messages and thoughts from Ken. Find out about books he's reading, events he's attending, and what's on his mind.

**Join the Ken Blanchard Fan Page on Facebook: www.facebook.com/ KenBlanchardFanPage**

Be part of our inner circle and follow Ken's Fan Page on Facebook. Meet other fans of Ken and his books. Access videos and photos and get invited to special events.

**Join Conversations with Ken Blanchard at www.howwelead.org**

Blanchard's blog was created to inspire positive change. It is a public service site devoted to leadership topics that connect us all. This site is nonpartisan, secular, and does not solicit or accept donations. It is a social network where you will meet people who care deeply about responsible leadership. And it's a place where Ken Blanchard would like to hear your opinion.

**Visit Blanchard on YouTube at www.youtube.com/user/KenBlanchardCos**

Watch thought leaders from The Ken Blanchard Companies in action. Subscribe to Blanchard's channel and you'll receive updates as new videos are posted.

# Berrett–Koehler
# Publishers

**Berrett-Koehler** is an independent publisher dedicated to an ambitious mission: *Connecting people and ideas to create a world that works for all.*

We believe that the solutions to the world's problems will come from all of us, working at all levels: in our organizations, in our society, and in our own lives. Our BK Business books help people make their organizations more humane, democratic, diverse, and effective (we don't think there's any contradiction there). Our BK Currents books offer pathways to creating a more just, equitable, and sustainable society. Our BK Life books help people create positive change in their lives and align their personal practices with their aspirations for a better world.

All of our books are designed to bring people seeking positive change together around the ideas that empower them to see and shape the world in a new way.

And we strive to practice what we preach. At the core of our approach is Stewardship, a deep sense of responsibility to administer the company for the benefit of all of our stakeholder groups including authors, customers, employees, investors, service providers, and the communities and environment around us. Everything we do is built around this and our other key values of quality, partnership, inclusion, and sustainability.

This is why we are both a B-Corporation and a California Benefit Corporation—a certification and a for-profit legal status that require us to adhere to the highest standards for corporate, social, and environmental performance.

We are grateful to our readers, authors, and other friends of the company who consider themselves to be part of the BK Community. We hope that you, too, will join us in our mission.

**A BK Business Book**

We hope you enjoy this BK Business book. BK Business books pioneer new leadership and management practices and socially responsible approaches to business. They are designed to provide you with groundbreaking and practical tools to transform your work and organizations while upholding the triple bottom line of people, planet, and profits. High-five!

To find out more, visit **www.bkconnection.com**.

## Berrett–Koehler
## Publishers

Connecting people and ideas
to create a world that works for all

Dear Reader,

Thank you for picking up this book and joining our worldwide community
of Berrett-Koehler readers. We share ideas that bring positive change into
people's lives, organizations, and society.

**To welcome you, we'd like to offer you a free e-book.** You can pick from
among twelve of our bestselling books by entering the promotional code
**BKP92E** here: http://www.bkconnection.com/welcome.

When you claim your free e-book, we'll also send you a copy of our e-news-
letter, the *BK Communiqué*. Although you're free to unsubscribe, there are
many benefits to sticking around. In every issue of our newsletter you'll find

- A free e-book
- Tips from famous authors
- Discounts on spotlight titles
- Hilarious insider publishing news
- A chance to win a prize for answering a riddle

Best of all, our readers tell us, "Your newsletter is the only one I actually
read." So claim your gift today, and please stay in touch!

Sincerely,

Charlotte Ashlock
Steward of the BK Website

Questions? Comments? Contact me at bkcommunity@bkpub.com.

**Certified**

**Corporation**
bcorporation.net